BABE RUTH

LAUNCHING THE LEGEND

JIM REISLER

McGraw·Hill

New York Chicago San Francisco Lisbon London Madrid Mexico City
Milan New Delhi San Juan Seoul Singapore Sydney Toronto

Library of Congress Cataloging-in-Publication Data

Reisler, Jim, 1958–
    Babe Ruth : launching the legend / by Jim Reisler.
       p.   cm.
    ISBN 0-07-143244-2
       1. Ruth, Babe, 1895–1948.   2. New York Yankees (Baseball team).
   3. Baseball—United States—History.   I. Title.

  GV865.R8R45   2004
  796.357'092—dc22   2003018013

1 2 3 4 5 6 7 8 9 0 AGM/AGM 3 2 1 0 9 8 7 6 5 4

ISBN 0-07-143244-2

Interior design by Nick Panos

McGraw-Hill books are available at special quantity discounts to use as premiums and sales promotions, or for use in corporate training programs. For more information, please write to the Director of Special Sales, Professional Publishing, McGraw-Hill, Two Penn Plaza, New York, NY 10121-2298. Or contact your local bookstore.

This book is printed on acid-free paper.

For Tobie and Julia

"I could have hit .600, but I'm paid to hit homers."
—BABE RUTH

Contents

Acknowledgments

How we roll our eyes when baseball managers spin clichés about the virtues of the "team"—even the utility infielder who hit .211 and has no range.

But writing a book *is* a team effort, and there are several people whose considerable talents and time made it happen. Frank Scatoni and Greg Dinkin of Venture Literary were early believers, gave the story shape and form, and became true mentors. The National Baseball Hall of Fame crew of Tim Wiles, Gabe Schechter, and Bill Burdick patiently answered my many questions and offered expert counsel on research and photos. Matthew Carnicelli, Katherine Hinkebein, and Mandy Huber of McGraw-Hill filled enough gaps in the text to help this wonderful, long-ago saga of Babe Ruth's first year in New York spring to life. To all go my enduring thanks and a bottle of watered-down Polo Grounds orange soda on me.

Thank you as well to Jim and Michael Gardner, David Walk, Gregg Bangs, and Mary Kounitz who endured my many ramblings about the life and times of Babe Ruth and the 1920 Yankees, and never seemed bored. But my biggest thank-you of all is reserved for my wife, Tobie, and daughter, Julia; they're the real all-stars of this venture and of my life. To them go two bottles each of orange soda—and my love.

Introduction

"Who is this Baby Ruth?" George Bernard Shaw asked. "And what does she do?"

For starters, this son of a Baltimore saloonkeeper did things on a baseball diamond that will never be matched. But getting to the true legend of Ruth requires deeper examination. Never a poster child, this pear-shaped, moon-faced man-child defied description—eating, drinking, whoring, belching, overspending, wearing silly hats and silk underwear, and generally attacking life with the gusto of someone just sprung from jail—and in 1920, he became the biggest phenomenon of the era.

In the fast-moving Jazz Age, Ruth lived life in overdrive—succeeding on the ballfield while talking louder, staying up later than the others, and even eating more, too, commonly stuffing himself with a midnight snack of a half-dozen hot dogs washed down by as many sodas. The quintessential Babe Ruth story? For a man whose appetites burned the candle at both ends—he was as much at home in the ballpark as the orphanage, the society cotillion, or the cathouse—there are many. Suffice to say it was a bit of this and a dash of that for a man who tipped a Detroit hotel chambermaid $500 when she found a watch fob Ruth had lost, once lost $35,000 at a Havana racetrack, and could still go out on a ballfield and perform to an unmatched standard.

The mists of time obscure the essence of this baseball phenomenon. Most baseball fans can recite key Ruthian accomplishments—the Babe's early pitching success with the Boston Red Sox, followed by his headline-grabbing sale to New York and the 60 home runs in 1927, the 714 lifetime home runs, and the four world championships that his bat helped the Yankees win. Blame many factors, starting with Ruth's notoriously poor memory and propensity to forget facts and names, which often obscured the real story. Thinking he was pitching to Leslie Mann in the 1918 World Series, Ruth plunked Max Flack instead. Turning down a dinner invitation from Mary Pickford and Douglas Fairbanks Jr., then the biggest names in movies, Ruth was asked who was throwing the party. "Oh, a couple of actors I met in Hollywood," he said. For the Babe, who couldn't remember a name to save his life, most teammates and people under 40 were "Kid," while anyone older was "Doc" or "Mom."

Blame Hollywood as well, which has turned out a couple of clunkers about Ruth, both of which were riddled with errors and absurdities. Most notable was the 1948 film *The Babe Ruth Story*, in which a decidedly un-Ruthian-looking William Bendix, as the Babe, hears the pleas of a freckle-faced boy to save his sick dog, Pee Wee, and preposterously prolongs a pitching slump by tipping off the batters by sticking out his tongue when throwing the curve. Fueling the fiction was the 1992 film *The Babe*, where a blubbery, bleary-eyed John Goodman may have captured the boisterous side of Ruth, but looked grossly overweight and wholly incapable of hitting a barn door, let alone a Walter Johnson fastball. Ruth *was* obese in his later playing days, but for most of his career he was 6'2" and 215 pounds of solid muscle and possessed of the kind of baseball skills you might see once in a generation.

How unfortunate that such nonsense colors generations of perceptions about Babe Ruth. Hardly the buffoonish braggart, he was surprisingly complex. Virtually uneducated, he was hardly dumb. The product of a bleak childhood, as an adult he was blessed with an insatiable gusto for life, a profound love for children, and once he settled down, a genuine sense of family. Yes, Babe Ruth really did perform to excess on and off the field—but he also visited sick kids in orphanages, never met a camera he didn't like, and proved insatiably charismatic to just about everyone. "The Babe's affable warmth and humanity, his magnetic presence, encouraged the boisterousness in others," wrote James Mote in *Everything Baseball*, "especially the men who wanted to shake his hand, the kids who wanted his autograph, and the adoring women who wanted the pleasure of his company."

Baseball had certainly never seen anything like him on or off the field. The game's biggest star before Ruth was Ty Cobb, brilliant but possessed of demons that made him nasty, vicious, and prone to periodic displays of violence. Or perhaps it was Shoeless Joe Jackson, a great batsman but quiet and sensitive to the teasing about his Southern roots and inability to read or write. "Hey Jackson," a spectator once yelled as Shoeless Joe slid into third with a triple. "Can you spell *cat*?" "Hey Mister," answered the glaring Jackson, "Can you spell *shit*?" Ruth would have laughed; everyone would have laughed, with the hecklers silenced and drawn to his side. Indeed, with every home run the Babe hit that glorious year of 1920, he became bigger and bigger news. By midsummer, he was the Madonna of his day, followed in the streets, covered by the emerging tabloid press for his personal life in addition to baseball, and enjoying every minute of it. He even changed the language; by then, every player hitting the long ball was "Babe Ruthing" it, while particularly long home runs were, well, "Ruthian."

Babe Ruth had something else going for him in 1920: timing. America that year was a society on the cusp—tired of bad news and anxious to move on and catch its breath after the devastation of World War I, then known as the "Great War," which had ended less than two years before. When the war started, back in 1914, President Woodrow Wilson was desperate to keep the United States out of what was seen as a largely European conflict. Wilson was reelected in 1916 on the slogan, "He kept us out of the war." But in his second term, Wilson could no longer maintain neutrality, and the United States joined the Allies in the struggle against the German-led Central Powers.

Once young Americans started coming back from Europe in body bags, Wilson oversaw an alarming assault on civil liberties. Opponents of the war were jailed, including Eugene Debs, the Socialist candidate who had run against Wilson for president. Brahms and Beethoven were banned, German shopkeepers were harassed, and newsreels showed children throwing away German books. And if that wasn't enough, others were falling victim to a deadly, fast-moving flu epidemic that killed millions and left others afraid to step outside.

Also on the minds of Americans in 1920 was how to deal with Prohibition, the Eighteenth Amendment to the Constitution, which went into effect with the New Year and made illegal the manufacture, sale, and transport of all alcoholic beverages. You'd have thought Americans would welcome a drink at that time, but somehow, sympathy for the temperance movement had overridden an overwhelming antipathy in New York toward this strange new law. But New Yorkers soon got around the law by opening some 32,000 speakeasies within a few years, twice the number of the legal saloons in the city before Prohibition.

So what in the world does any of this have to do with Babe Ruth and the Yankees? Plenty. America in 1920 wanted desperately to move on, to drink, dance the Charleston, and sit back with a good book, like the just-published *This Side of Paradise*, which articulated what its author, a 23-year-old adman named F. Scott Fitzgerald, called the new morality of "flaming youth." And America wanted nothing more than to dabble in the stock market, watch baseball, and forget the recent past. So here was Babe Ruth, ready to help them enjoy the present.

So if Ruth came to personify the fast-moving Jazz Age, 1920 was the year he struck it big, really big, on America's biggest stage: New York. He had become a phenomenon in 1919 by hitting a record 29 home runs, but his 1920 season made him a megastar who transcended baseball, and arguably *saved* it. Ruth hit 54 home runs that year—25 more than the year before, more than every major-league team save one, and 35 home runs more than George Sisler, second in the American League home run race with 19.

Ruth's home runs unleashed a new way to play the game—with power, which others quickly copied. And they did more than launch the Yankee dynasty; they helped the New Yorkers become the first team in major-league history to draw more than 1 million spectators at home, and generated a level of unparalleled excitement at a time baseball sorely needed it. As the world sadly discovered in late summer of 1920, members of Joe Jackson's Chicago White Sox had been enticed by warring groups of double-crossing gamblers as they were polished off with ease—too much ease—by the Cincinnati Reds in the previous year's World Series. Their deliberate loss, later known as the Black Sox scandal, threw baseball from the sports section to the front page and shook it to its core. Yes, baseball badly needed the charisma and bat of Babe Ruth in 1920.

If real life were a Hollywood script, 1920 would be the year that Ruth—inspired to hit home runs for sick children, never striking out, helping dogs, and never uttering so much as a single belch—would have helped the Yankees to their first American League pennant and World Series title. That it didn't happen that way makes for an even better story: Ruth still performed at a level never seen before or since that season. In doing so, he became baseball's savior and helped launch the great Yankee teams of legend that three years later would win their first of 26 World Series titles.

In doing so, Ruth helped generate a level of excitement in baseball that has arguably never been matched. The Babe was *the* story in 1920, regardless of the Black Sox, the late-season pennant charge by the Cleveland Indians, or anything else for that matter. "I swing big, with everything I got," Ruth once said. "I hit big or I miss big. I like to live as big as I can." It's no irony that on the morning of September 25, 1920, America woke to news that members of the White Sox had told a Cook County grand jury about the World Series fix—an extraordinary tale, but one that was obscured by another baseball event of the previous day: the Babe's 50th and 51st home runs of the season.

Ruth pounded his 50th off the Senators' Jose Acosta in the first game of a doubleheader at the Polo Grounds, the ball striking the roof of the right-field grandstand and bounding back onto the field. The shot, which sent the 25,000 spectators into hysteria, "gave the slugger a whoop and a hurrah he will never forget," the *New York Times* reported. "It was one of those events in sport, which will furnish chatter for years to come. Baseball has never before developed a figure of such tremendously picturesque proportions as this home-run king of the Yankees." The superlatives more than balanced the big sports headlines picked up by the Black Sox.

So Barry Bonds hit 73 home runs in 2001, 13 beyond Ruth's record of 60, and 19 more than Ruth's 54 in 1920. Perhaps the biggest story after the feat itself was how little excitement his race for the record generated, particularly as Bonds played through September and into early October. Not only was Bonds, with a reputation for surliness, competing against the record set only three years before by the popular Mark McGwire, as well as Babe Ruth's ghost, he was doing so in a sports world jammed with ESPN highlights, sports talk radio, college football, stock car racing, hockey, golf, and basketball. Contrast that to 1920, when the sports world was far less cluttered and baseball was king—and news of the Babe's every move dominated.

"Ruth was made for New York," his biographer Robert Creamer wrote. "It has been said that where youth sees discovery, age sees coincidence, and perhaps the retrospect of years makes Ruth's arrival in Manhattan . . . seem only a fortuitous juxtaposition of man and place in time."

That was Babe Ruth in 1920, a year when it was a magical and important time to be a baseball fan in America's biggest city. Ruth, who lived life the way he played—big, loud, and in a constant swirl of commotion, which mirrored the times—had arrived at the ideal moment. Not even heavyweight champ Jack Dempsey and his thundering knockouts measured up. Here is how it happened.

"I Can't Turn That Down"

Babe Ruth Becomes a Yankee

The day that would change the course of baseball history wasn't launched by a thundering home run, a bases-clearing triple, or even a bunt to advance the runners. Kicking things off was a bloop single of sorts—actually, a telephone call.

Answering the telephone at his Riverside Drive home on the Upper West Side in New York City that Sunday morning in December 1919 was one Ed Barrow, manager of the Boston Red Sox, who was about to step into the shower. On the other end was Harry H. Frazee, Broadway impresario turned Red Sox owner, with instructions for Barrow to meet him that evening in the bar of the Hotel Knickerbocker. Frazee had something important to discuss.

That night at the bar, Frazee wasted little time getting to the point. "Simon," Frazee told Barrow, who was nicknamed "Simon Legree" for his hard-nosed ways and the strict discipline he demanded from players, "I'm going to sell Ruth to the Yankees. My shows on Broadway aren't going so good. [Yankee owners] Ruppert and Huston will give me over $100,000 for Ruth and they've also agreed to lend me $350,000. I can't turn that down."

It was an astounding decision. Babe Ruth was the Red Sox's best player, and in 1919 he had put together a season for the ages—an unheard-of 29 home runs and a hefty .322 batting average in only 130 games, more than justifying Barrow's decision the season before to turn Ruth, one of the game's best pitchers, into an everyday player.

Barrow was stunned. "You think you're getting a lot of money for Ruth, but you're not," he told Frazee.

But Frazee's mind was set, and on December 26 the deal with the Yankees was consummated. Ten days later, on January 5, 1920, the deal was announced, and the headlines in the next day's newspapers blared the news that Ruth was the new Yankee right fielder. The final sale price was $125,000, the highest amount ever paid for a ballplayer, and more than double the previous record of $57,500 paid by Cleveland to the Red Sox for Tris Speaker in 1916. The acquisition not only strengthened the New Yorkers in their weakest department, hitting, but according to Yankee pitcher Bob Shawkey virtually assured the pennant—something the Yankees hadn't been able to win in all of their frustrating, underperforming 16-year history. "Ruth was such a sensation last season that he supplanted the great Ty Cobb as baseball's greatest attraction," gushed the *New York Times*, "and in obtaining the services of Ruth for next season the New York club made a ten-strike." The *Daily News* agreed: "Col. Jacob Ruppert and Colonel T. L. Huston can use Ruth very well. . . . [They] will feature him as a box office attraction, of course, and if his record is as good this season as it was last the investment was well worthwhile."

On and on the New York papers went about the havoc that the left-handed-swinging Ruth could wreak in the relatively short 256-foot right field of the Yankees' home park, the Polo Grounds. On and on they went about the truly wondrous season the 25-year-old Baltimore native had enjoyed in 1919. Just as wondrous was the strange arc of Ruth's career—he had started as a pitcher and developed into the lefty mainstay of the Red Sox's 1916 and 1918 World Series championship teams, before his 11 home runs in 1918 gave a hint of the power hitter than lurked within.

The Yankees had pulled off the sports steal of the century. Its genesis was in the friendship of Frazee with Yankee co-owner Tillinghast L'Hommedieu Huston, mercifully known as "Cap," a reference to his one-time military rank. The two men shared not just many a barstool, but also an office on West 42nd Street in midtown Manhattan. Cynics have even suggested that Barrow himself may have played a role in the deal, since less than a year later he would join the Yankees as general manager, and judging by the Boston-to–New York player pipeline that seemed to emerge whenever Frazee wanted to fund a new show.

The most common version of the story is that in October 1919, after the Yankees had finished a respectable third in the American League race, Huston's fellow co-owner, Jacob Ruppert, asked Yankee manager Miller Huggins what the team needed to produce a champion. The diminutive, blunt-talking, acid-tongued Huggins, who never backed down from anything, didn't this time either: "Get Ruth from Boston," he said, explaining that Frazee was in desperate need of cash to pay for his Broadway shows.

Huggins's idea wasn't as preposterous as it seemed. On his mind was recent history, namely a Yankees–Red Sox dispute from the year before that caused considerable turmoil and put Frazee in a dealing kind of mind. In the second inning of a July 13, 1919, game against the White Sox, Boston pitching ace Carl Mays stormed off the field in anger over his teammates' sloppy fielding, which Mays figured had caused him to lose several tight games. Mays not only left the mound, he jumped the team, taking off on a prolonged Pennsylvania fishing trip and vowing to never again play for the Red Sox.

While Red Sox management figured out how to respond, several teams, including the Yankees, made offers for Mays. American League president Ban Johnson warned Boston not to make a deal until Mays rejoined the team, but Frazee went ahead and sold Mays anyway—to the Yankees for $75,000 and two pitchers, Bob McGraw and Allen Russell. Johnson hit the ceiling and suspended Mays, and ordered the Yankees not to use him. But Yankee owner Jacob Ruppert got a court order restraining the league president from interfering, and pitched Mays anyway, eroding Johnson's authority and standing. The squabbling intensified—growing so acrimonious that Frazee, Ruppert, Huston, and White Sox owner Charles Comiskey strongly considered leaving the American League to join the Nationals. Early in 1920, Ruppert got Mays reinstated, with damages, and he joined the Yankees for good.

In fact, Mays was only one of several Red Sox who became Yankees over the next decade. In constant need of cash to fund his shows, Frazee discovered a quick solution to financial problems: sell his players to the Yankees. Swapped for cash from Boston to New York in 1918 and 1919 were pitchers Ernie Shore and Dutch Leonard and outfielder Duffy Lewis. In the 1920s, other Boston players, such as Waite Hoyt, Herb Pennock, and Everett Scott, would be shipped to New York and become big Yankee contributors.

So when Huggins journeyed up to Boston to see Frazee about Ruth, "it was like dispatching someone to a supermarket with a bundle of cash," as Ruth biographer Kal Wagenheim wrote. Set the price at $125,000, Huggins suggested to Ruppert, and Frazee would "begin talking." Ruppert was floored. "Who ever heard of a ballplayer being worth $125,000 in cash?" he wondered aloud. But Huggins was emphatic: line Ruth up and with that short right-field porch at the Polo Grounds he'll hit 35 home runs, maybe more.

Not quite 40 years old, H. Harrison Frazee was a young man with an itch to make it big—quickly. He had come to baseball in roundabout fashion, working in his native Peoria as a bellhop before moving to Chicago to run the Cort Theater. Landing in New York, he moved into a plush Park Avenue apartment and set his sights on Broadway—buying the Longacre Theater, producing his own shows, and even promoting heavyweight prizefights.

His 1916 purchase of the Red Sox at the age of 36 from Joe Lannin made the fast-talking, moon-faced Frazee big-league baseball's youngest owner—giving him another way to be in the midst of things. To meet the steep $675,000 Red Sox price tag, Frazee and his two partners—Hugh Ward and G. M. Anderson, both of whom ignored baseball—agreed to pay half in cash and the rest in the form of notes, which put Frazee in an immediate financial bind.

To raise the rest of the money, Frazee turned to Broadway, where he needed to produce hits. One was the 1916 smash comedy *Nothing but the Truth*, and a year or so later came another success, *Leave It to Jane*, with words and music by Guy Bolton and P. G. Wodehouse. For a while anyway, the strategy worked, as the money poured in and Frazee brought good players and championships to Boston. Led by Hall of Famers like Tris Speaker and Harry Hooper in the field and Ruth and Carl Mays on the mound, the Sox took two World Series titles in his first three years of ownership.

In those days, Frazee spent freely, wheeled and dealed, and was rewarded accordingly. Regarded warily at first by Boston's hard-core fans and writers, he won praise from both when, after the 1916 World Series triumph, he offered the Senators $60,000 for pitcher Walter Johnson, although even for that price Washington owner Clark Griffith wasn't about to unload his franchise player. Trading Speaker after the 1916 season to the Indians would prove a mistake, as Tris raised his batting average in 1917 by 64 points to .386 to take the A.L. batting title. But even that move was softened when, with several players on military duty in Europe, Frazee swiftly brought to Boston frontline stars such as Stuffy McInnis, Amos Strunk, Wally Schang, and Bullet Joe Bush, who all became crucial parts of Boston's Series winners in 1918.

Frazee endeared himself to Bostonians in other ways too. When the rest of baseball's National Commission received the "play or fight" order of 1918, it was Frazee who led a drive to postpone the order from July to September to get in as much of a regular, 154-game schedule as possible. Along the way, he urged his American League owner comrades to raise money for the war effort with proceeds donated to the Red Cross. Frazee even tried more than once during the 1918 season to organize a real "World" Series—that is, to take it to Europe as entertainment for American troops. But the idea stalled.

So just why Frazee needed cash in 1919—and large infusions of it quickly—is still, more than 80 years later, a bit of a mystery. The common explanation is that he needed to finance his new play, *No No Nanette*, but that play did not open until 1924 at a Frazee-owned theater in Chicago, and only reached Broadway in 1925. The play hit the jackpot, bringing some stability to Frazee's fortunes—but that was two years after he had sold the Red Sox and left the chronic financial uncertainty of baseball life.

A more likely explanation is that in late 1919, Frazee was still heavily in debt to previous Red Sox owner Joe Lannin. On buying the team in 1916, Frazee had paid Lannin $262,000, but less than a month after Ruth arrived in New York, Lannin's attorneys went to court, asserting that Frazee owed Lannin $125,000—ironically, the same amount Frazee had received for Ruth—which had been due the previous November. Frazee countered by stating he owed only $60,000, which he said he would pay "anytime Lannin is willing to concede . . . the amount that is due." The case appeared to be headed for the courts, but the two settled their differences away from public scrutiny.

Even so, Harry Frazee would go to his grave known to the world as the man who sold Babe Ruth to the Yankees.

Stepping off the train in Los Angeles on a barnstorming tour following the 1919 season, Babe Ruth professed his interest in the movies. But when reporters questioned him about it, he demanded an immediate payment of $10,000 before he would even set foot on a set, a statement that did not endear him to the local Hollywood crowd. And if that wasn't enough, the

Babe even took a swipe at the weather, proclaiming it wasn't quite the kind he liked. Not a good start.

Things didn't improve at the ballpark. In Los Angeles, Ruth was booed after striking out twice, doubling, and hitting no home runs. By the time he and the other barnstormers reached Oakland on November 10, rumors were rampant that Ruth was ready to leave baseball for a boxing career, of all things, fueled by the persistent story that the Babe was about to sign up for a title fight against heavyweight champ Jack Dempsey, whom he had met in Hollywood.

If Harry Frazee had clearly mastered the art of spin control, Babe Ruth in late 1919 was a man in dire need of a lesson in how not to offend. Before Ruth even became a Yankee, he had decided after the 1919 season to hold out for more money from the Red Sox. The holdout coincided with Ruth's November arrival in Los Angeles, which attracted enormous local interest. Stepping from the train, the Babe proclaimed himself ready for some rest and relaxation by combining golf with barnstorming baseball against Pacific Coast League teams as a member of White Sox third baseman Buck Weaver's all-star team.

Thanks to his major-league record 29 home runs in 1919, the Babe was the biggest story in baseball; in less than two years as a full-time batter he had shattered the big-league home run record. His star just rising, Ruth was already displaying an interest in being in the movies.

Meanwhile, the Boston papers continued to hurl unflattering publicity at Ruth, painting him as an overpaid ingrate. The stories, no doubt fueled by Frazee, focused on Ruth's gigantic earnings from the year before, including one report stating that the Babe's income in 1919 was substantially greater than his $10,000 salary—in itself among baseball's highest. In addition to straight salary, according to the *Herald*, Ruth received a $5,000 gift from Frazee in September at Babe Ruth Day at Fenway, another $2,500 for playing in two exhibition games in October, and $10,000 as a member of Weaver's all-stars.

In Oakland, Ruth only fueled the fires, telling the *Sporting News* that "a player is worth just as much as he can get," and used Ty Cobb as an example of someone who "has been paid all that he is worth." That, in turn, riled the surly Cobb, who promptly labeled Ruth a "contract violator" for holding out. Ruth then challenged the cantankerous Detroit star to a fight, saying he'd "lick [him] on sight" if given the chance. "I wouldn't say anything against Cobb if he held out for $100,000, [so] why should he say anything about me?" Ruth said. "He ought to be tickled to see any player get as much as he can. I'll settle the question when I meet Cobb."

On it went, with media on both coasts lapping it up and the *Sporting News* in late November reporting that the Babe's holdout was "more serious . . . than is generally believed in the East." From the way Frazee and others were making it sound, Babe Ruth was more trouble than he was worth.

"I still can't believe what I saw," an aged Harry Hooper said, looking back at the phenomenon of Babe Ruth. "A 19-year-old kid, crude and poorly educated, only lightly brushed by the social veneer we call civilization, gradually transformed into the idol of American youth, and the symbol of baseball the world over. [He was] a man loved by more people and with an intensity of feeling that perhaps has never been equaled before or since."

Suffice it to say that the Babe Ruth sold to the Yankees in early 1920 was closer in spirit to the coarse 19-year-old than the superstar later worshiped by a nation. Only six years removed from the dismal Baltimore orphanage that served as his childhood home, Ruth was a pop psychologist's dream—a young man of 25 who was very intent on making up for lost time. "When they let him out," a teammate once said, "it was like turning a wild animal out of a cage."

For the young Babe Ruth, life was all about satisfying an insatiable appetite—devouring vast quantities of food and drink, having sex as much as possible, and driving faster, staying up later, and hitting a baseball farther than anyone else. Lord, how he could hit a baseball, swinging so hard that when he connected, someone said, "it was like two billiard balls, like a sound of solid things crashing together."

Given what Ruth accomplished as a Yankee, it's hard to fathom how good he'd become in Boston. Here's how good:

- Signed in 1914 out of St. Mary's School by Jack Dunn of the International League's Baltimore Orioles, Ruth made an outstanding impression in spring training that year. Playing in an intra-squad game in Fayetteville, North Carolina, on March 7, Ruth smacked a ball, as Roger Pippen of the Baltimore *News-American* put it, "that will live in the memory of all who saw it. . . . The ball carried so far to right field that he walked around the bases."

- Four months later, Ruth was in the big leagues as a Red Sox pitcher. The next year, 1915, he went 18–8 with a 2.44 ERA, and served notice of things to come by belting four home runs, his first coming on May 6 off Jack Warhop of the Yankees at the Polo Grounds. Four home runs may not seem like a lot, but in 1915 the rest of the Red Sox hit ten; A.L. leader Braggo Roth hit seven. Ruth's slugging prowess was already apparent.
- By 1916, Ruth was the best left-hander on baseball's best team, going 23–12 with a 1.75 ERA and nine shutouts. That fall in the World Series against Brooklyn, Ruth gave up a run in the first inning, drove in the tying run himself, and then held the Robins scoreless for 13 innings until his team scored the winning run in the 14th.
- In 1917, Ruth's record was 24–13 with a 2.01 ERA, nine shutouts, and 35 complete games.
- In 1918, he tied the A's Tilly Walker for the home run title with 11, batted .300, and pitched the Red Sox to two wins against the Cubs in the World Series while setting a record for postseason consecutive scoreless innings that lasted for 43 years. Remarkably, he pitched his final game against the Cubs with a badly bruised knuckle on the middle finger of his pitching hand—the very finger a pitcher needs for control.

Ed Barrow recognized that for all Ruth's prodigious talents on the mound, the Babe could be of more value with his bat. On April 4, 1919, in a spring training game at the old fairgrounds in Tampa against John McGraw's Giants, Ruth cracked what Barrow called many years later "the longest home run in history." Batting in the second inning against "Columbia George" Smith, so named for the university he had attended—rare was the big leaguer who attended college in those days—Ruth sent a pitch high over the right-center-field wall, far above right fielder Ross Youngs's head, clear out of the fairgrounds and into a neighboring hospital yard. After the game, as Youngs stood where the ball fell, a group of writers watched as somebody dug up a surveyor's tape and measured the distance to home plate—579 feet.

Ruth had become a slugger—continuing to hit moon shots and acquiring all the quirks, mannerisms, and swagger of a home run hitter. He always used the same dark ash wood bat, carrying it on and off the field himself and not letting anyone, even the clubhouse boy, so much as touch it. Like Shoeless Joe Jackson, the marvelous White Sox hitter whose swing Ruth said he emulated, Ruth would coat his bats with tobacco juice and lovingly pat them before lugging one up to home plate and bashing another long hit.

One day, when Harry Hooper asked Ruth to lend him the bat once he was finished with it, Ruth replied, "I will like hell. I'll keep this baby as long as I live." But a few weeks later the bat cracked, and after the game Ruth tried to repair it using a hammer, tiny nails, and tape. A few days later, when he was called out on a third strike, Ruth became so indignant that he slammed the bat like an axe on home plate, cracking it beyond repair.

Ruth turned and walked back toward the dugout, his eyes still "blazing" with anger, Hooper would say years later. In the dugout after a few minutes of silence, Hooper again brought up the bat.

"Babe, how about that bat?" he asked.

"Take the son of a bitch," Ruth said. "I don't want to see it as long as I live!"

Hooper took the bat, held onto it, and with a noble sense of history, donated it decades later to the National Baseball Hall of Fame in Cooperstown.

If you think that Ruth's sale generated excitement in New York, double it and you have an idea of how the news hit Boston that frosty Monday in early January 1920. For the city's loyal baseball fans, news of the sale struck with the force of a New England nor'easter.

The city's relationship to its Red Sox was deep, intense, occasionally complicated, and very much subject to the state of the American League pennant race. A charter A.L. member in 1901 and winners of the first World Series in 1903, the Red Sox—known as the Americans until 1916—attracted a large and passionate fan base, whose core were a particularly rabid gang of supporters called the Royal Rooters. The Rooters had evolved from the Winter League as a group of Boston businessmen who would leave their offices to rush out to the Sox's home park, the Huntington Grounds, after work, remove their ties and hats, and play baseball till dark. And leading the Rooters in revelry was a Boston saloonkeeper right from central casting with a name to match—Michael T. "'Nuf Said" McGreevy. Not that 'Nuf Said exactly ran a shot-and-beer joint; he was an important political figure himself, and ran the main meeting place for Boston's key government and sports figures. McGreevy became the final arbiter of all debates, and people turned to him for his opinion. Once he ruled, that was that. 'Nuf said.

The Red Sox typically drew twice the crowds that their poor crosstown cousins the Braves drew, even in 1914, when the team dubbed the "Miracle Braves" inexplicably took the pennant and swept the heavily favored Philadelphia A's in the World Series. Although the years 1917 and 1918 were hard on attendance at all big-league parks, in 1919 the Sox drew reasonably good crowds, with 417,000 spectators traveling to Fenway Park, not as many as they had earlier in the decade, but more than Washington and St. Louis. Clearly, Boston loved its Red Sox.

By 1920, Boston had 11 daily newspapers, most of which devoted sizable space and resources to keep its citizens abreast of baseball doings. In a world where baseball on the radio was still two years away, television was a generation away, and thankfully there was no such thing as yet called sports talk radio, newspapers generated the most accurate gauge of a community's feelings.

As in New York, those feelings generated a swift and passionate response to the sale of Babe Ruth. Whereas the Ruth deal is today recognized as the most lopsided sports transaction in history—the one that Red Sox fans cite as the start of a curse against their team, the Curse of the Bambino, the reason they have not won a World Series since—the initial reaction was curiously mixed.

To one side were the naysayers, the ones who asked, "What in the world could Harry Frazee be thinking?" At the Suffolk Athletic Club, just north of Boston, men "groaned, hissed, and booed" on hearing news of the deal. An editorial in the January 6 *Boston Post* summed up the collective thoughts of many: "Cy Young and Tris Speaker went their ways, much to the disgust of the faithful, but the club did not suffer materially. But Ruth is different. He is of a class of ballplayers who flash across the firmament once in a great while. . . . During the past 20 years there have been three great superstars—Wagner, Cobb, and Ruth. Wagner stayed with Pittsburgh. . . . Cobb will never play except for Detroit. Money could not buy these two men. But Boston with Ruth is another story."

In the *Boston Evening American*, Nick Flatley wrote that the Red Sox had "lost the greatest drawing card the game has ever known, and the esteem of many of thousands of supporters." Calling Ruth "a bird [who] hops into the picture once in a lifetime," Flatley predicted the quick demise of a Ruth-less Red Sox and the prompt elevation of the Yankees into pennant contention.

In the *Herald*, cartoonist Franklin Collier penned a cartoon showing "for sale" signs on the Boston Public Library, the Boston Common, and Paul Revere's statue. *Herald* columnist Bob Dunbar wrote that Red Sox fans were "astonished and staggered" at the news, adding that "the departing of Ruth . . . is regretted by all."

But not *all*, at least not then. The *Boston Evening Transcript* got solidly behind Frazee, writing that there was "remarkable unanimity of opinion that the Red Sox made a good deal in disposing of the home run hitter."

"Nearly everyone agrees that Ruth is too big to stay in Boston," the *Evening Transcript* concluded, obviously not speaking to members of the Suffolk Athletic Club. "Red Sox players doubtless will be pleased with the disposal of the incorrigible slugger."

In the *Globe*, James O'Leary stood solidly behind Frazee, stating, "It is hard to see how [he] could have turned down New York's offer for [Ruth], and it looks as if he had made a good bargain." O'Leary continued his rant in the January 15 edition of the *Sporting News* by summarizing what he called Frazee's "many convincing points" in selling Ruth. "When it began to look as if Ruth regarded himself as bigger than the Boston club, bigger than the game itself, Frazee made up his mind that there would have to be a change, in order to avoid more serious trouble in the future."

Matching the mixed response were baseball people themselves. Supporting Ruth were two of his former Red Sox managers, Bill Carrigan and Jack Barry. Carrigan said Ruth was nowhere "near the hard proposition to handle that he was made out to be," forgetting perhaps that he had ordered Ruth to room next door to him on road trips and that he had even designated infielder Heinie Wagner as Ruth's chaperone. Barry called Ruth "the most willing member of my team," stating that any problems with him stemmed from the ballplayer wanting to pitch too much.

But backing the move was retired Boston Braves hero Hugh Duffy, who claimed that "no matter how great a star [Ruth] is, he hurts a team if he does not fit in with his fellow players." In hindsight, Duffy may have been siding with Boston ownership with an eye to his future; indeed, Frazee would hire him to manage the Red Sox in 1921.

How curious that so many of Frazee's defenders focused on Ruth's behavior. He was bigger than the team and "incorrigible," they wrote. Suffice to say that Frazee's defenders were the victims of an old-fashioned game of spin control launched by the Red Sox owner himself.

With the January 5 announcement of the deal, Frazee shrewdly orchestrated a blunt, one-man public relations campaign, which he kicked off by proclaiming that Ruth's wayward ways had left him no alternative but to get rid of the star slugger. Frazee did so by explaining his reasons in a 1,500-word statement that was printed in the *Post*.

"Twice within the past two seasons, Babe has jumped the club and revolted," Frazee wrote. "He refused to obey the orders of the manager and he finally became so arrogant that discipline in his case was ruined. . . . He had no regard for the feelings of anyone but himself. He was a bad influence upon other and still younger players."

His comments came as Ruth demanded that his three-year contract for $10,000 a year be doubled to $20,000 a year in 1920. Reportedly, Ruth was basing his demand on the way that Carl Mays had walked out and put into motion the events that got him traded to the Yankees, where he received a substantial salary increase. If Mays, the surly submarine pitcher, could do it, the Babe figured he could too, reasoned the *Herald*. Citing a source "close to Ruth," the paper wrote that the Babe "based this astounding action on the belief that he is doing himself an injustice not to better himself in any way possible."

Frazee had a real advantage in the war of words: logistics. Ruth was on the West Coast on a prolonged golfing and barnstorming vacation, giving the Red Sox owner the opportunity to fire the opening salvo in what became weeks of venomous, back-and-forth accusations. In the days after the announcement, Frazee grew increasingly defensive, revealing how wounded he was personally by Ruth's way of life. "Out there on the West Coast, I could have prevented him from playing a single game as his contract signed by him gives me that right. But I allowed him to play unmolested. Then he sends me back his contract in an envelope without a scrap of writing for explanation. This is just a sample of how Ruth respects his written word and his obligations."

Even the Babe's conditioning became an issue. "Ruth is taking on weight tremendously," Frazee said. "He doesn't know how to keep himself in shape. . . . He has floating cartilage in his knee . . . that may make him a cripple at any time and put him out of baseball."

Harry Frazee had mastered the essentials of Pubic Relations 101. Nowhere was there mention of his severe cash-flow problems, which had triggered the big transaction. He had essentially thrown the focus away from himself and spread the notion that Ruth's behavior had left him little choice beyond unloading the star. He had done away with Ruth while the star vacationed. But it was Ruth who would have the last laugh.

TWO

"I Still Can't Believe
What I Saw"

Legend in the Making

The escalating war of words with Harry Frazee had made Babe Ruth suspicious that the Red Sox would soon try to deal him. Those feelings were confirmed just after New Year's Day as he stepped off the golf course of Griffith Park in Los Angeles.

Waiting for him was a nattily dressed but gaunt, diminutive man. "I'm Miller Huggins of the Yankees, Babe," he said. "I'd like to talk to you."

The Yankee manager of three years needed no introduction. Ruth knew him and followed his suggestion that the two find a quiet place to talk. Just getting to that point had taken some doing—immediately after Huston and Frazee had come to a tentative agreement to make a deal on Ruth, the Yankee owners had assigned Huggins the delicate task of informing Ruth that he'd been sold. So Huggins boarded a train for the West Coast shortly after New Year's and searched Los Angeles for three days before finally finding the slugger.

The two chitchatted for a few minutes before Huggins got down to business. "Babe, how would you like to play for the Yankees?"

"Have I been traded?"

"Well, the deal hasn't been made yet," Huggins said. "I'd like to find out a few things. I want to know if you'll behave yourself if you come to New York."

"I'm happy with the Red Sox," Ruth countered, a tad flustered. "I like Boston. But if Frazee sends me to the Yankees, I'll play as hard for them as I did for him."

"Babe, you've been a pretty wild boy in Boston. In New York, you'll have to behave. You'll have to be strictly business."

Ruth bristled. "I already told you I'll play the best I can. Let's get down to business. How much are you going to pay me?"

When Huggins brought up the two years remaining on Ruth's $10,000 a year contract, Ruth bristled some more, saying, "I want a lot more dough than that."

"All right," Huggins said. "If you promise to behave yourself, Colonel Ruppert will give you a new contract."

He mentioned $15,000 a year, then $17,500. Ruth balked, saying he wouldn't play for a penny less than $20,000, a figure he'd mentioned that fall to Frazee. He also wanted a slice of the sale price the Red Sox would be getting for him. Huggins waved him off, saying he'd have to first talk it over with the Yankees. But two days, several telegrams, and some haggling later, Ruth signed the contract and became a Yankee.

The Yankees were still taking no chances, and the language in the contract was a barometer of their concern. It stated that the deal would be off if Ruth failed to report to New York by July 1 and that Frazee would return the cash and the notes, thought to be worth more than $400,000. A further clause stated that if the Yankees "deem it necessary to increase the salary in order to retain the services of said player," they would pay an increase up to $15,000, but that the Red Sox would have to foot anything beyond that amount. Still another clause stated that if Ruth demanded a bonus for playing with New York, the Yankees would pay the first $10,000—equal to his 1919 salary with the Red Sox—with Boston forking over anything above that up to $15,000.

In reality, Ruth would continue to play for the $10,000 stipulated by his old contract, but would also receive a $1,000 signing bonus and $20,000 more over the next two seasons, to be paid in $2,500 sums regularly through each year. The percentage of the sale price was not included.

Frazee said he'd use proceeds from the sale of Ruth to bring in other talented players to bring the pennant back to Fenway Park. Big names were thrown about, and the owner said he was on the cusp of deals with Detroit, St. Louis, and particularly the White Sox, who were said to be interested in unloading Happy Felsch.

Precedent was on the side of the Boston owner, for the Red Sox had lost Cy Young after the 1908 season, and Speaker in 1916, and managed to remain winners. But the fact was Harry Frazee was finding it a lot harder to bring in new talent than unload players he didn't want. Still, he promised. "So who would it be?" wondered the Royal Rooters.

Then, on March 27, 1920, Bostonians got the answer they were waiting for: there were no new players of note. With the Red Sox at spring training and the new season just weeks away, word from New York came that Frazee had purchased the Harris Theater on Broadway for a reported price of $500,000, throwing him into debt and ending any hope Sox fans had for good, new players.

That July, Frazee redecorated the Harris and renamed it "The Frazee." By then, the Red Sox were a shell of a team, well on the way to a generation in the second division, with their cash-starved owner having discovered a surefire way to raise fast money: sell ballplayers to the Yankees. No wonder the wags on Broadway had a new nickname for the Sox: "New York's best farm club." The Curse of the Bambino, the bane to this day of Red Sox Nation, was fully under way.

Frazee's loyalties had become glaringly apparent. "Pennants and world championships were great fun, but the principal stars in Frazee's eyes were those of the Broadway variety," wrote Donald Honig in his book *Baseball America*. "Even as Ruth was making the Fenway turnstiles spin like dervishes, Frazee was producing a string of musicals that were hitting the New York stages like so many wet cabbages dropped from the roof of the Flatiron Building."

Just how deeply in debt Frazee had fallen became apparent that spring when an enterprising reporter in Chicago stumbled onto a transcript from Boston's Suffolk County Courthouse stating that the Red Sox, as part of the Ruth deal, had mortgaged Fenway Park for $300,000 to one Jacob Ruppert. That not only meant Ruth belonged to the Yankee owner but the Sox's home park, Fenway Park, did too.

Miller Huggins had been eyeing Ruth as the missing link to making his promising Yankee ballclub a real contender in 1920. Those looking for evidence that baseball had quite suddenly found a slugger of truly prodigious talent needed only to go back to early April 1919, when he had connected for the nearly 600-foot home run, giving the world a taste of what was to come.

No wonder reporters stalked the defending champs and their celebrated new slugger, as big crowds stormed ballparks all the way north to see Ruth for themselves.

The Babe followed the big home run in Tampa with two more hits the next day, and seven runs batted in over the two games. Sportswriters grew giddy and wondered in print just how many home runs he'd hit in the regular season. Could he break the American League record of 16, set back in 1902 by Ralph "Socks" Seybold? "Easy," said the Boston writers. "No problem," agreed the New York writers, who seemed just as excited about Ruth's slugging prospects for 1919.

Decidedly not impressed was Giants manager John McGraw, the "Little Napoleon" and the master of dead-ball baseball, which called for a bunt here, a stolen base there, and a hit-and-run or two in working for the single run. McGraw played what was called "inside baseball" to perfection, and abhorred the home run as a black mark on the purity of the game, something that could wreck with one swing the ebb and flow of a game. "If he plays every day," McGraw said of Ruth while in Tampa to play the Red Sox, "the bum will hit into a hundred double plays."

But Ruth was up to the challenge. Every time he got another hit off a Giants pitcher, he'd look at the Giants' bench and bellow, "How's that for a double-play ball, Mac?" McGraw just seethed, and the two men endured a testy relationship for the rest of their days.

Ruth made the 1919 Red Sox exciting. In Winston-Salem, city fathers declared a half-holiday so people could head to the ballpark and see them play. In Charleston, Ruth swung at a pitch with such force that he spun around and wrenched an ankle. Despite being carried off the field, which drew headlines warning of a serious injury, Ruth was on the field the next day—a pattern that he would follow through his career, promptly returning after a seemingly bad injury.

On April 15, against Randolph-Macon College, Ruth hit the longest home run ever seen in Richmond. Three days later in Baltimore against his old Oriole teammates, he put on a stupendous display of hitting, walloping four home runs and walking twice in six at-bats. In the season opener on May 1 at Fenway Park against the Yankees, Ruth wasn't on the mound but in left field. Two days later, he pitched a complete-game seven-hitter as the Red Sox came from behind to beat the New Yorkers 3–2.

For a time anyway, Ruth would be a left fielder *and* a pitcher. Calling the Babe into his office, manager Ed Barrow was curious what the young slugger thought about this experimental dual role in which he'd play the outfield three days and still pitch every four days. After all, he reminded

Ruth, "pitching and outfielding call for top-notch physical condition"—a hint to his young outfielder that a little less carousing might be in order.

"Eddie, I can keep right on pitching and doing things every day," Ruth said. "If you think that the club will be the gainer by my hurling and fly-chasing, that's OK with me. I want to do the things that will help you and Harry Frazee."

Ruth's gosh-golly answer was no fluke. Despite his night-crawling and uncouth ways, he could really talk like that, especially to older men he related to as mentors. Although he referred to the gruff, no-nonsense Barrow as "Eddie," something no one else on the Red Sox would dare to do, Ruth respected this wily, bushy-browed bear of a man who was much like Brother Matthias back at the St. Mary's School in Baltimore where he'd grown up.

No wonder Edward Grant Barrow was nicknamed "Simon Legree." At 50, Barrow was more than twice Ruth's age and carried a 250-pound frame, which he used to maintain a commanding clubhouse presence. Named Red Sox skipper in 1918, Barrow won the World Series in his first year. Winning was no fluke given his long career in baseball, which combined a nose for talent with a publicist's flair and a restless case of ambition.

Born in a covered wagon traveling along the Nebraska prairie as his father, a Civil War veteran, moved his family west, Barrow was the agrarian equivalent of a military brat. Raised primarily in Ohio and Iowa, he turned a rambling life as a young man into an eclectic array of professions: boxing, working as a city editor in Iowa, and running a Toronto hotel. Eventually, he found baseball—but on the business side, running concessions with ballpark hot-dog king Harry Stevens.

Barrow's early baseball days were a smattering of this and a dab of that, all of which contributed to his sound grasp of the game from the business office to the playing field. For many years, he wandered about the wilds of the low minor leagues—managing Wheeling, West Virginia, of the Interstate League and Paterson, New Jersey, of the Atlantic League, where he discovered the great Honus Wagner, before switching to the front office and running the Atlantic League from 1897 to 1899.

By 1903, Barrow had reached the big leagues as manager of the Tigers, but left after one year in a dispute with the general manager. Over the next several years, he moved on to manage Indianapolis, Toronto, and Montreal, before running another league—the International League—in 1911. Back in the big leagues for good in 1918 to replace Jack Barry as Red Sox manager, Barrow inherited both a collection of elite veterans and a talented young left-handed pitcher with a wild streak named Ruth.

The two first met in January 1918, when Ruth, along with first baseman Stuffy McInnis, went to the Red Sox office and signed their contracts for the coming season—Ruth's called for $7,500 with the promise he would earn $10,000 the following season if he did well. McInnis also signed that day with little hardship, and Barrow, pleased that he had inked two of his best players, gave Red Sox secretary Larry Graver $5 and told him to take the ballplayers out for a celebratory lunch. Now $5 was more than enough to cover a big meal for three in those days, but not when one of the participants was Babe Ruth. Later that afternoon, when Graver returned and demanded another $2.85 from Barrow, the manager wondered why. "Have you ever seen that big guy eat?" Graver said. "He had a whole custard pie for dessert!"

So he did. All of four years removed from St. Mary's, Babe Ruth was a young man still sampling a lot of life for the first time. How best to describe him in those days? Where do you start? Ruth's propensity to flaunt authority during his first years in the big leagues gave rise to a widespread opinion that he was mentally deficient, even retarded. But he wasn't. "You have to remember, he had grown up in that Catholic reformatory," said Red Sox teammate Ernie Shore. "When they let him out, it was like turning a wild animal out of a cage. He wanted to go every place and see everything and do everything."

Traveling south for the first time to spring training in 1914, Ruth had left Maryland, traveled on a train, and stayed in a hotel—all for the first time. At spring training with the Orioles, Ruth, smitten with the technology, rode up and down continuously in the hotel elevator—he had never been on one of those either. When Ruth spotted a bicycle, he'd borrow it and go for a ride, hardly thinking it peculiar. And he loved waking early to head to the train station to watch the trains roar by. Sold by Dunn and the financially strapped Orioles to the Red Sox in July 1914, he roomed with Shore and irritated him to no end by using his toothbrush, his razor, and even his soap.

In the dining hall, Ruth was usually first in line and achieved legendary eating status before he was ever a home run hitter. "Lord, could he eat," recalled teammate Harry Hooper. For breakfast, he'd start with pancakes slathered in syrup, and slap on helping after helping of bacon, ham, and eggs, washed down with gallons of coffee and juice. Lunch and dinner would be similar displays of gluttony, and Ruth would wolf down slabs of beef, half a dozen hot dogs, and endless bottles of soda—he wasn't yet the drinker he'd be in later years. "I've seen him at midnight, propped up in bed, order six club sandwiches, a platter of pigs' knuckles, and a pitcher of beer," Ty Cobb said. "He'd down all that while smoking a big black cigar. Next day, if he hit a homer, he'd trot around the bases complaining about gas pains and a bellyache."

Neither Shore nor the other Red Sox players knew what to make of their young teammate. While most of his teammates were mildly educated at best and not exactly models of civility themselves, compared to them Ruth was brash, vulgar, loud, and completely uninhibited. He thought nothing of wearing the same underwear for days on end. He belched and farted louder than a tractor—facts he liked to share with anyone within earshot. He drove fast too, and piled up speeding tickets. On the road, he'd hit the dining car of the train and think nothing of polishing off dinner with a double order of thick beefsteaks.

"He was a very simple man, in some ways a primitive man," said long-time Yankee writer Frank Graham. "He had little education, and little need for what he had." Introduced before a game to a man suffering from a cold, Ruth reached into the pocket of his uniform and pulled out an oversized onion. "Here, gnaw on this," he said. "Raw onions are cold-killers." Asked about political unrest in China, he replied, "The hell with it." Asked what he was reading, Ruth said he had given it up. "Reading isn't good for a ballplayer," he said. "Not good for his eyes. If my eyes went bad even a little bit I couldn't hit home runs."

Even Ruth's voice was a little too loud and sonorous—a deep baritone with a trace of the Southern drawl. Baseball, for instance, came out more as "base-bowl." Much of what he said was crude, and Ruth enjoyed intentionally sprinkling his conversation with vulgarities. "Piss pass the butter," he would say to a teammate with an impish smile. Once when relaxing with several teammates and their wives at spring training, Ruth excused himself, saying, "I've got to take a piss." Taken aside by a teammate who followed him to the men's room, he was told that wasn't advisable in mixed company. Back they headed to the gathering, where Ruth coughed up his apology: "I'm sorry I said *piss*."

Ruth proved particularly appealing to two groups of people—women and children. There are many stories, some apocryphal, about Ruth's insatiable appetite for sex. Suffice it to say he craved sex and bedded down scores of women, from an entire St. Louis whorehouse, all in a single night—true—to women in every American League port of call, many of them willing to visit Ruth's hotel room, often two and three at a time. A psychologist might say that as with most things Ruth did, he was making up for all the time he lost in the orphanage. And it didn't matter if a roommate was there or not—Ruth just entertained with the self-absorbed drive of someone satisfying an itch. Indeed, his sex drive abated only slightly in later years, even after he was married for the second time, to Claire, and she was traveling with the team; to meet his needs, the Babe just borrowed keys from his teammates and used their rooms.

It's hard to believe then that for virtually his entire big-league career, Ruth was married—first to the former Helen Woodford, a waitress he met in 1914 at Landers Coffee Shop in Boston. The 19-year-old Babe met the 16-year-old Helen, a Manchester, New Hampshire, native, within his first six weeks in Boston, and was immediately smitten. One morning, when she was waiting on Ruth at the coffee shop, Ruth said to her, "How about you and me getting married, hon?" So they did, on October 18, 1914, in Ellicot City, Maryland.

One can only imagine how Helen endured her husband's constant philandering, most often pursued on road trips. Even so, they seemed to enjoy one another's company and could often be seen bowling or skating, which became particular passions of Ruth's. Helen would hang in there, moving with the Babe to New York City in 1920 and adopting a little girl in 1921, but the couple soon separated.

Never, ever suffering from the same sort of strain was Ruth's genuine lifelong fondness for children. Essentially a big kid himself, he never tired from their attention, and visited orphanages and hospitals wherever he went, often without a shred of attention or publicity. When in 1918 a fire nearly destroyed St. Mary's, Ruth took to raising funds for his old school, often hosting the school band in various American League ballparks.

Early in his career, Ruth's teammates rode him hard, not letting him near the batting cage and sawing his bats in half. Most big leaguers in those days had a nickname, some of them cruel. Giants pitcher Luther Taylor, who was deaf, was called "Dummy," a reference to the "deaf and dumb" expression of the era. Other nicknames were kinder, like Boston third baseman Everett "Deacon" Smith's and left fielder (and earlier star pitcher) "Smokey" Joe Wood's. Looking at Ruth's tanned, powerful physique and moon-shaped face with particularly thick lips—he was also hairy and loud—his teammates christened him "the Big Baboon." While his teammates enjoyed the nickname, Ruth hated it, and more than once he challenged a teammate to a fight over it, for which there were understandably no takers.

For a time he was called "Tarzan" with some good-natured affection by his teammates—that is until Ruth found out that the name was for the "king of the apes." Ruth complained, and his teammates stopped. To opposing bench jockeys, Ruth was a baboon, an "ape," a "monkey," and worse, a "nigger," which helped give rise to enduring rumors that Ruth had African American blood, and led in part to a considerable lifelong following among African Americans, many of whom sat and cheered for him in segregated sections of Griffith Stadium in Washington and Sportsman's Park in St. Louis.

For his own part, Ruth had a devil of a time remembering names—but had no trouble giving teammates nicknames of his own making, most based on physical characteristics, among them Horse Nose, Rubber Belly, and Chicken Neck. And in most cases with people he didn't know, men were "Doc" or "Kid," older men were "Pop," and older women "Mom." In his autobiography, Ruth writes of his first wife as Helen Woodring, not Woodford, and he often called Claire, his second wife, "Clara."

Not that anyone cared very much. "Don't tell me about Ruth: I've seen what he did to people," said teammate Waite Hoyt, reminiscing as an old man. "I've seen them—fans—driving miles in open wagons through the prairies of Oklahoma to see him in exhibition games as we headed north in spring. I've seen them: kids, men, women, worshipers all, hoping to get his famous name on a torn, dirty piece of paper, or hoping to get a grunt of recognition when they said, 'Hiya, Babe.' He never let them down; not once."

Mercifully, the Frazee-Ruth feud died down. But after Ruth left the West Coast in late February and stopped off in Boston to discuss receiving a share of the proceeds of the sale to the Yankees, Frazee refused to see him. But the Babe was a Yankee now—so he headed to the team headquarters on 42nd Street in Midtown Manhattan to see his new employers.

Striding into his meeting with Yankee owners Ruppert and Huston, along with Huggins, Ruth cracked a wide smile on his deeply tanned face and pulled out a bunch of his nickel Babe Ruth brand cigars—big sellers in New England—offering them to one and all.

Ruppert took one and puffed away. Huston, still recovering from his previous night's escapades, took one too, but paced the office, distracted as he took up Huggins's mantra and warned his new charge to behave: Huggins's word was "law" he warned, to which Ruth, dragging on one of his cigars himself and squinting through the smoke, listened for a spell before finally blurting out, "Look at ya! Too fat and too old to have any fun!" Glancing at Ruppert, the Babe added, "That goes for him too!" Even Huggins got the irreverent Ruthian treatment: "As for that shrimp," the Babe thundered, pointing a thumb at the Yankee manager, "he's half dead right now!"

And so ended Ruth's first trip to the Yankee offices. Ruth's attitude left the Yankee owners grinning—sort of—but convinced them to take a large insurance policy out on their new ballplayer and, looking ahead to spring training, assign an old ballplayer turned coach and a fellow Baltimore native named Joe Kelley to keep an eye on him. But Huston's telephone rang late one night with a collect call from Baltimore as the Yanks began heading south for spring training in Florida. "Uh-oh," thought Huston to himself, "Ruth must have fled from Kelley's sight!" Not quite. On the line was Ruth, with a plea of his own: "Colonel, it's that old guy Kelley. I can't get him on the train. He met some pals here and don't wanna leave."

The Yankees' destination that spring was the thriving northeastern Florida port town of Jacksonville, where they were to set up shop at the Hotel Burbridge. Advertising itself as "the Winter Playground of America," Jacksonville was a town of 52,000, Florida's largest, and anxious to become a destination for northern snowbirds. A devastating fire had leveled most of its downtown back in 1901, but Jacksonville by 1920 was recovering— and doing surprisingly well, thanks to its deep harbor, a thriving port, and a 144-acre municipal dock and terminal. Throw in a booming shipbuild- ing industry, lumberyards, cigar factories, and coffee and spice mills—all served by five major rail lines—and Jacksonville was a surprisingly sophisticated town. It had two daily newspapers, and five countries—Belgium, Britain, Cuba, Mexico, and Norway—actually had consulates in Jacksonville, a nod to its shipping business. Old photos of the city center, except for the palm trees and people in panama hats, resemble the hustle and bustle of other major U.S. cities of the era.

With an eye to the northern tourist trade, Jacksonville was early in declaring itself open to big-league ballclubs. Big-league baseball had arrived in town way back in March 1888, when a New York Giants pitcher named Cannonball beat the Washington Nationals in an exhibition game at the Great Sub-Tropical Exposition at Waterworks Park, north of downtown. Although there were actually two New Yorkers in the lineup that day named Cannonball, Titcomb and Crane, history does not record which one was the pitcher of record.

In 1905, Cincinnati became the first big-league club to hold its spring training in Jacksonville. The Boston Braves followed in 1906, and the Giants, this time under John McGraw, stopped in for a few games in 1911 on their way to Cuba. Then came Connie Mack—he had been a part of that first game back in 1888—and his Philadelphia A's in 1916 and 1917, followed by the Pirates in 1918, and the Yanks in 1919. Joining the New Yorkers in 1920 in Jacksonville were the Brooklyn Dodgers, now managed by Wilbert Robinson.

Home for the Yankees that spring was Southside Park, across the St. John's River from downtown, which the teams reached by ferryboat. The park, with bleachers for 4,800, was the creation of a Jacksonville whiskey magnate named Randolph Rose, who put his ballpark near Dixieland Amusement Park, with its 30 acres and river frontage, 1,600-seat theater, toboggan, merry-go-round, and electric fountain. Opened in 1907, Dixieland was "the Coney Island for the South," according to the Jacksonville *Times-Union*, and became the entertainment hub of Jacksonville. The area also featured the aptly named Ostrich Farm—where tourists could watch ostrich races, ride in ostrich-drawn carts, and even saddle up on one of the big birds.

Jacksonville businessmen were smart: Start by throwing open their beaches and golf courses to the visiting contingent of ballplayers and team officials, they figured. Be sure to make it attractive to visiting newspapermen—the big boys from the big papers in the big cities up north—and chances are their fair city would receive glowing reviews up north, making it a destination for impressionable northern snowbirds anxious for warm weather R and R. After all, spring training was for most, as it is today, a time to focus on the frivolous, to put the long winter behind while emphasizing a welcome change to a warmer, more pleasant climate.

That was particularly so for newspapermen—those few, fortunate souls chosen to tag along southward to report on how the teams were getting along in preparation for the coming season. Baseball coverage in the early 1920s was hardly as it is today, with the gulf between wealthy ballplayers and middle-class baseball reporters wider than the Hudson River. Not so then: instead of stories on salary arbitration, complete with every kind of conceivable angle and statistic, and game summaries full of quotes from managers and players alike, old-time baseball coverage was more like public relations, which left it collegial, chatty, seldom challenging, and rarely unpleasant.

Part of the reason was the time itself, post–World War I, when baseball seemed like the perfect antidote to a public weary of bad news. Westbrook Pegler, then a young sportswriter in New York, called the 1920s "The Era of Wonderful Nonsense," and the description was apt. "The lads took a turn at slugging the old orange," wrote Damon Runyon of the *New York American* from the Yankee camp in Jacksonville. "It was very exciting. It was almost as exciting as watching the grass grow. The second day of training is always like that. So is the third. And the fourth. And the fifth."

Top writers like Runyon, Ring Lardner, Heywood Broun, and Arthur "Bugs" Baer could get away with that. Hard drinkers and hard livers, they personified baseball coverage of the era, with their interest more in turning a phrase and trying to outwit one another than accurately reporting what had happened. Who cared that their quotes were a tad embellished, that they rarely quoted anyone but Ping Bodie of the Yankees, or failed to report a critical injury? They were exceptional writers who could fall back on their own humor, and didn't have to try terribly hard to track down news.

The teams themselves basked in the prerequisite two-month dose of upbeat publicity, timed to get the folks back home pumped up for opening day. There was a ritual to spring coverage in the papers, starting in early February with brief articles about which players had signed for the coming season, and who had yet to return their contracts. Then would come a big day when teams departed Penn Station for the trip south, followed by weeks of stories about veterans who looked sharp and hot prospects who might stick.

Game summaries came without the context or detail of today, although the coverage of 1920 was certainly more comprehensive than in the early dead-ball days when readers seldom received more than a two-paragraph summation and a box score of a game. Baseball reporting by 1920 had evolved into a slightly more detailed accounting of what had happened on the field, with perhaps a note or two on the weather, the attendance, and in the case of Opening Day, what celebrities showed up and who threw out the first ball. With only a few exceptions this style endured until the mid-1950s, when Dick Young of the New York *Daily News* broke the mold and ventured regularly into clubhouses for player quotes and more detailed analyses.

The formula fit the times. Top byliners like Lardner, Runyon, and Grantland Rice did well, pulling in as much as $35,000 a year if they had a syndicated column. With radio and television still years away, young sassy magazines like the *Saturday Evening Post, Vanity Fair,* and *Cosmopolitan* (the *New Yorker* was still five years from its launch) fed a war-weary public a steady dose of articles on the social scene, fashion, crime, movie stars, and sports. Fueling the trend was an explosion of newsprint, aided in large part by the birth of the tabloids, which featured big photos, eye-catching headlines, and short, snappy copy. Setting the standard was the 1919 birth of William Randolph Hearst's *Illustrated Daily News,* soon renamed the *Daily News,* which merged a lot of photos with simple text set off by catchy headlines like "Baby Sleeps As Parents Are Robbed" and "Waitress Battles Alleged Thief Until Police Arrive" to reach a circulation of 750,000 within five years.

Driven by a desperate circulation fight with Joseph Pulitzer's *New York World,* Hearst tapped a new audience that had not previously read a morning paper. "You could read all that has ever been written about the Clock Room in Paris, where the [World War I] peace conference is being held, and get no clear idea of it," the *Daily News* spelled out in its inaugural editorial. "Look at a single picture of the same room, and you know exactly what it is like." In fact, war coverage had produced much of the technology that made the picture press possible; although a synchronized scanning device that sent pictures over the electric wires had been around for more than a half-century, it was only in the early 1920s that a commercially feasible photo transmission was developed. Critics blasted tabloid journalism as "picture-writing" and "gutter journalism," but Hearst had the last laugh: within four years of the birth of the *News*, tabloids popped up in Washington, Baltimore, Los Angeles, and San Francisco; in 1924, Hearst started yet another tabloid, the *Mirror*, which by 1925 when combined with the *News* reached a daily circulation of nearly 1.15 million.

By 1920, Manhattan alone had 11 major dailies, all of which recognized Ruth as baseball's best player about to hit the country's biggest stage. Ruth was quotable, engaging, interesting, and appealing to men and women, adults and children, Joe Sixpack and the society matron. Purposely left out by writers were the naughty bits, like Ruth's coarse language, much of it related to sex and body parts. "I can knock the penis off any ball that ever was pitched," Ruth would boast to anyone within earshot. No wonder he was seldom quoted accurately. In his memoirs, Fred Lieb recalled sitting on the train playing cards with other writers on a barnstorming trip when Ruth suddenly burst down the aisle, pursued by an irate dark-haired woman carrying a knife pointed at the Babe's back. Ruth wasn't hurt, and the woman, the wife of a Louisiana state senator, calmed down, but the writers chose to keep on playing cards and ignore the incident. "I still wonder why we newspapermen acted as we did," Lieb wrote. "There were 11 of us sitting there and no one said a word. We just went on typing, reading magazines, and playing cards."

The most likely explanation? That's just the way it was in those days. And why hurt the Babe? He oozed charisma, was generally approachable and friendly, and was incurably newsworthy. By season's end, he'd be more than just the best baseball player in the land—he'd be the most publicized athlete of all time. "Here was the champion slugger of all time," wrote Ruth biographer Kal Wagenheim, "in all his uncouth splendor, walking onstage precisely at the outset of America's most flamboyant decade."

For the group of 13 New York writers set to follow the Yankees south for spring training—more than triple the usual contingent—Ruth meant good copy. No wonder all eyes were on the lookout for the Babe on February 28 at Penn Station as the team got ready to climb aboard the 6:20 P.M. Florida Flier bound for Jacksonville. But where was he? Ping Bodie showed up in good time, as did George Mogridge, Herb Thormahlen, and a large contingent of Yankee fans to wish them a good trip.

Bodie, Mogridge, and Thormahlen were all early arrivals and, as the *Times* duly reported, "did not attract any unusual attention." But by 6 P.M. the Babe had still not arrived, disappointing many in the crowd. Then, at 6:10 P.M., with only 10 minutes to spare, Ruth appeared, clad in a big leather coat and pushing his way down the staircase and through the mob toward the train. The crowd cheered and flashbulbs popped. Ruth gave his golf bags to the red cap porter, who became "the envy of all his brother red caps," the *Times* hypothesized. He posed briefly with the other Yankee ballplayers, grinned toward the crowd, and ducked into the train, ready for the long, 26-hour trip south.

With the Babe in tow, the newspapermen had their story, and the Florida Flier pushed off toward New Jersey. Joining the train in Philadelphia were Bob Shawkey and Del Pratt. Joe Kelley, Chick Fewster, and Harry Biemiller hopped aboard in Baltimore. Others like Carl Mays, first baseman Wally Pipp, Muddy Ruel, Bob Meusel, Ernie Shore, Aaron Ward, and shortstop Roger Peckinpaugh got to Jacksonville on their own. Conspicuously absent was manager Huggins, in bed with a bad cold, but due to leave New York as soon as he felt fit.

The reporters were a colorful bunch. From the *Daily News* came Marshall Hunt to cover the Babe as a full-time beat. Hunt became Ruth's most persistent "ghost," which, starting that April, led to a real coup—a regular Monday feature "by" Ruth but actually written by Hunt about the season. From the *Herald-Tribune* came the veteran Dan Daniel, who in the days when many writers were still paid by the word could cover an event to such lengths, mentioning everyone who attended and what they had for lunch, that his paper soon put him on a straight salary.

Providing more sober analysis was another veteran, William J. Macbeth, whose paper, the *Tribune*, also carried the work of Grantland Rice. Covering the entire New York baseball scene from back in New York for the *Sporting News*—not just the Yankees, but the Brooklyn Dodgers, also set up that spring in Jacksonville, and the Giants in San Antonio, Texas—was Joe Vila. Vila was a hard-drinking, Harvard-educated veteran who still wrote for the *Sun* and who, back in 1903, had played a key role in the formation of the Yankees—introducing A.L. president Ban Johnson to the team's original owners.

Vila was the most seasoned writer of the bunch. He worked hard, and back in December had used his many sources to become among the first in print to acknowledge the disturbing and persistent rumors that the Chicago White Sox seemed mysteriously flat in the 1919 World Series against the Cincinnati Reds and may have lost in eight games on purpose. "Personally, I don't believe for a moment that anything was wrong in the World's Series," he wrote in the December 25 *Sporting News*. "But the fact remains that . . . the fans have a right to demand a public investigation of the so-called indictment."

Vila remained an ardent American League booster, particularly of the Yankees, and often attributed the snakebitten team's 16-year run of mysterious failures and inability to win a pennant to "hoodoo." And it was Vila who always seemed to tap into his contacts to stay a step ahead of his competition when it came to the scoop on trades, and who recognized from the get-go the enormity of Ruth's landing in New York.

Too bad Vila didn't make it to Florida with the rest of the reporters, who included Sam Crane of the *Evening Journal*, Week Dickinson of the *Morning Telegraph*, Sid Mercer of the *Globe*, George Daley of the *World*, and the great Damon Runyon of the *American*. Vila was missing all the fun. After their dispatches from Penn Station, the bulk of the writers covering the Yankees didn't hop on the players' train, but instead boarded another headed for Captain Huston's estate near Brunswick, Georgia, for a diversionary day of hunting and carousing. For Huston, such generosity assured not just good feelings all around, but upbeat newspaper coverage as well.

The suddenness of Ruth's arrival as a slugger was particularly hard to fathom given that it was all of one year before that he'd become an everyday player—spending every three days early in the 1919 season as an outfielder and the fourth as a pitcher. The combination turned the 1919 Red Sox into prohibitive favorites to repeat as A.L. champions—and they rolled on Opening Day, blanking the Yankees 10–0 at the Polo Grounds behind Carl Mays. Batting fourth, Ruth had two hits including a home run. After the rest of the series in New York was rained out, Boston moved on to Washington, D.C., where the Sox won two more games, with Ruth belting two triples and a double and scoring five runs.

Ruth was hot, but Barrow was concerned about his young star. Both in New York and Washington, Ruth was carousing and staying out till all hours; he hadn't been home since leaving for spring training, nor had he seen Helen for weeks. It hardly mattered that Barrow had appointed a guardian for Ruth, Red Sox coach Dan Howley, who accepted his role with the claim, "I'll take care of that guy if I have to put a ring through his nose." But there wasn't much Howley could do, and Barrow was determined to rein in his nocturnal star.

On April 28, Boston took its second straight game from Washington. That night, Barrow sat in the lobby of the Raleigh Hotel waiting for Ruth to return, before finally giving up at 4 A.M. and going to bed.

The next afternoon, Ruth went hitless and the Red Sox lost. That night, an angry Barrow resumed his lobby sitting, hoping to confront Ruth. Growing more incensed at Ruth's flagrant flaunting of the rules but needing some sleep, Barrow found the night porter, and, giving him a hefty tip, asked if he might let him know when Ruth came in. "Wake me up," Barrow told him. "I don't care what time it is. Wake me up and tell me."

The knock on Barrow's door came in the gray of dawn, at 6 A.M. "That fellow just came in," the porter said.

Barrow muttered his thanks, put on his robe, and shuffled off to Ruth and Howley's room. In the crack under the door he could see a light was on, and hearing voices, he knocked. The voices stopped, and a second or so later, the light clicked off. Getting angrier by the moment, Barrow turned the knob, opened the unlocked door, and walked in.

Ruth was in bed and awake, with the covers up to his chin. Under the covers, he held a lighted pipe. Meantime, Howley's bed was empty; the man who had pledged to keep an eye on Ruth was hiding in the bathroom, out of the line of Barrow's angry fire.

"You always smoke a pipe this time of night?" Barrow growled.

"Sure," said Ruth. "It's very relaxing."

Barrow headed toward the bed, tore off the covers, and found Ruth completely dressed right down to his shoes and socks.

"You're a fine citizen, Babe," Barrow said. "I must say, you're a fine citizen."

Barrow turned away and headed back toward the door, saying as he left the room, "I'll see you at the ballpark."

Ruth had been caught red-handed. Normally discreet about his midnight ramblings, he'd been found out and embarrassed. As the morning wore on, so did his resentment, and by the time Ruth reached the ballpark that afternoon he was bursting for a fight. In the locker room, Barrow closed the door and lectured his Red Sox about the importance of playing by the rules, glaring at Ruth as he went on about curfews and regulations.

Their eyes met, and Ruth exploded. "If you ever come into my room like that again, you ————, I'll knock your goddamn head off." Ruth's exact epithet for Barrow is lost to history, but assured it wasn't something you'd hear at a garden party.

Nobody moved. The room was silent. The next to speak was Barrow, shaking with anger. "You fellows finish dressing and get out of here, all except Ruth," he bellowed at the team. But Ruth joined his teammates and scooted out the door and was soon shagging fly balls in the outfield during batting practice.

Heading back to the dugout shortly before game time, Ruth jogged over to where Barrow was sitting and making out the lineup card, and asked meekly if he was playing.

"Go in and take your uniform off," Barrow said, never looking up from the lineup card. "You're suspended."

So that evening, aboard the train headed back to Boston, the buzzer rang at Barrow's door. It was Ruth, shame-faced, guilty, and contrite. "Will you speak to me, manager?" he asked.

So they spoke for quite some time that night. Ruth told Barrow of his hardscrabble childhood and pleaded to be reinstated to the team. "My heart went out to this big, overgrown boy, and I understood him better," Barrow said. "Most of all, he didn't want to be suspended. That was the greatest punishment I could give him, because he loved to play baseball."

Barrow lifted the suspension, and the two men came to an understanding. From that point on whenever the Red Sox were traveling, Ruth would leave a note in Barrow's hotel mailbox stating what time he had come back to the hotel. He kept his word, and for the rest of the season Barrow got notes from Ruth, each one beginning with "Dear Eddie."

"I don't know whether he ever lied to me or not," Barrow said. "I took his word. And besides, who could complain about a few wild nights, when there were all those home runs in the afternoon?"

THREE

"I'll Show You Some Hitting of the Old Apple"

The 1920 Yanks Take Shape

Perched before a mob of reporters as his ballplayers took batting practice at Southside Park in Jacksonville, Miller Huggins was gushing as the Yankees prepared to open the spring training season on March 13 against Brooklyn.

"There's one thing about our outfield we haven't had, and that's fortification," he said, referring to his thin 1919 outfield contingent. "I have been in a position that if one outfielder flopped on me, I was gone. . . . But no such thing can happen this year. Not with such men as Lewis, Bodie, Vick, Ruth, and Gleich."

Huggins was being kind in mentioning second-stringers like Sammy Vick and Frank Gleich. As spring training opened, all eyes were on Ruth and all things Ruth—what he did in practices, what he said in between, his clothes, and what he had for lunch. Never before had there been such a relentless focus on a single ballplayer; that it involved a New Yorker brought in three times as many reporters, creating in Yankee spring training America's first mix of sports and celebrity journalism.

The hoopla had kicked off a few weeks before. "Managers McGraw, Huggins and Robinson will take big squads South with a view of discovering new material," the *Times* wrote in late February of the looming journeys to spring training for the Giants, Yankees, and Dodgers. "Unless some surprisingly talented young players are unearthed during the training period, it looks as if the lineup[s] would be much the same as last season with the exception of the Yankees, who have added the home run slugger [Ruth] to their roster."

Not exactly. Huggins actually had several other decisions on his hands regarding new and largely unproven personnel. Critical to the Yanks' success in 1920 would be a replacement at third base for Home Run Baker, who had earned his memorable moniker in 1911 when, as a member of the Philadelphia A's "$100,000 Infield," he led the American League in home runs with nine, hitting two more that fall to lead his team to a six-game World Series victory over the Giants.

The 34-year-old Marylander was a slugger of the dead-ball era—never hitting more than 12 home runs in a season—but was a lifetime .300 hitter, drove in runs in bunches, and was a hot glove too. Following a prolonged salary dispute with Connie Mack, Baker was sold before the 1916 season for $37,500 to New York, where he put together four productive seasons. However, Baker had decided to sit out the 1920 season after his wife, Ottalee, passed away in early February, telling Huggins that he'd be reluctant to leave his two children at home given the demands of baseball travels.

For the Yankees, the good news was that there were several promising youngsters who might fit in at third. One candidate, 23-year-old Aaron Ward, had gotten a look in 27 games in 1919, playing each of the infield positions but batting a paltry .206. Another possibility was Bob Meusel, also 23 and heralded as a Yankee star of the future, but the strapping Californian with a rifle arm and long-ball power was considered more of an outfielder.

The odds-on favorite for third was Baltimorian Wilson "Chick" Fewster. The old man of the potential trio of replacements at age 24, Fewster had broken in with Richmond in 1915, gone to Baltimore in 1916, then Worcester, before joining the Yankees for short spells in 1917 and 1918. Fewster was Huggins's kind of player—versatile with good range in the infield, and a hustler, with a tendency to crowd the plate and dare pitchers to throw the ball tight. All were attributes that the Yankee manager himself was noted for as a player a decade or so before.

Fewster had joined the service in 1918, which limited his playing time through 1919, making 1920 his window of opportunity. He even resembled Huggins—nearly five inches taller, but slight and wiry, which looked wholly out of place amidst the big Yankee sluggers. "Chick has everything," raved Huggins. "I have never seen a greater prospect."

Other decisions required delicate handling. Ruth's desire to play center field left Huggins with the question of where to put the incumbent Yankee center fielder Ping Bodie. Another Californian, the 32-year-old Bodie had joined the New Yorkers in 1918 after four seasons with the White Sox and another with the A's at the insistence of Huggins, who admired his heads-up, aggressive play. No question that the Yankee skipper wanted to keep Bodie, a popular player with power, a memorable name, a knack for self-promotion, and a legendary appetite, having once defeated an ostrich named Percy in a spring training eating contest.

His name was actually Francis Stephano Pezzolo. A native of the North Beach section of San Francisco, he took the name "Bodie" from the California town where his father had once been a gold miner. The "Ping" came from the sound his 52-ounce bat made when it crashed into the "dead" baseball of his era (a time when most bats weighed 36 to 40 ounces), which it did resoundingly in 1910 when Bodie joined the San Francisco Seals of the Pacific Coast League and slugged a league record 30 home runs.

Bodie's power drew headlines and the attention of the White Sox, who brought him to the majors in 1911. But after opening the season on the bench, Bodie stalked into the front office and demanded that owner Charles Comiskey "put me in the lineup, and I'll show you some hitting of the old apple."

Traded in 1918 from the A's to the Yanks for first baseman George Burns, Bodie kept his word, hitting .256 that season and .278 the next. But he lumbered on the basepaths, which his many newspaper friends took pleasure in reporting. Said Bugs Baer of the *American* of an attempted steal by Bodie: "Ping has larceny in his heart, but his feet were honest."

In an age when ballplayers were seldom quoted in print, Ping was a columnist's dream, making him the Yogi Berra of his day. "You should have heard me crash the old apple," he would say in describing his home runs, or "I whaled the onion." Other favorites: "I rammycackled the old persimmon." "I really hemstitched the spheroid." When playing with the A's, Bodie said, "I and the Liberty Bell are the only attractions in Philadelphia."

Bodie provided much of the material and inspiration for Ring Lardner in creating his famous fictional series *You Know Me Al*, about the adventures of a hayseed who makes it big in baseball. Paired with Babe Ruth, he provided one of the game's greatest quotes when asked what it was like rooming with the new slugger.

"How should I know?" said Bodie. "I room with his suitcase."

When writer Fred Lieb and his wife, Mary Ann, found they were rooming next door to Bodie and Ruth, they tried to change rooms because the noise of the elevator was keeping them awake at night. But when the hotel clerk explained to Mrs. Lieb that the elevator was nowhere near their room, she listened harder the following night and realized the sound was snoring. "She thought it was a duet," the Babe explained in his autobiography, "but I set her straight by telling her that Bodie could snore an opera."

Bodie was also notable as the second major leaguer of Italian ancestry, after Ed Abbaticchio, for three years a Pirate back in Honus Wagner's day and better known as "Abbey" in the box scores. Bodie inspired a number of West Coast Italians who followed him to the big leagues, like the three DiMaggio brothers, Tony Lazzeri, and Frank Crosetti. But one person wasn't impressed: Bodie's father, the onetime gold miner: "He said I should have carried the name 'Pezzolo' to fame," Ping explained.

Fortunately for the Yankees, the pitching staff was considerably stronger from a year ago with the addition of Carl Mays, who had joined the team in midsummer 1919 after walking out on the Red Sox and gone 9–3. Big things were expected of the cranky right-hander, who was coming to camp in fine condition after weeks of hunting in the Ozarks. He'd be joining a veteran staff that was mostly set—right-handers Bob Shawkey, 20–11 in 1919, and the veteran Jack Quinn (15–14), along with a couple of lefties, Jersey City native Hank Thormahlen (13–10) and George Mogridge (10–7).

Fighting for a job as well would be right-hander Ernie Shore, a former Red Sox starter and onetime Ruth teammate. Shore had won 18 games in 1915, 15 the next year, and 13 after that, combining lots of innings pitched with exquisite control. And it is Shore who is forever joined in history with Ruth as a participant in one of baseball's quirkiest, most memorable games: On June 23, 1917, when Ruth got tossed for punching home plate umpire Brick Owens after walking the game's opening batter on four pitches, Shore was summoned for emergency duty despite pitching only two days before. The batter who had walked, Ray Morgan, was caught stealing for the first out. The lanky Shore then retired the next 26 Washington batters, with nobody reaching base, for baseball's most unusual no-hitter.

But then things went sour for Ernie Shore. He missed all of the 1918 season while in the military, and that December he joined the Yankees in a multiplayer deal that also brought Duffy Lewis to New York in return for outfielder Frank Gilhooley, catcher Roxy Walters, pitchers Ray Caldwell and Slim Love, and $15,000. In New York, Shore never got on track, winning only five games, losing eight, and compiling a 4.17 ERA. Was it the layoff? No one could say, although writers in those days described workhorse pitchers who suddenly lost their effectiveness as having a "tired arm." A contemporary analysis suggests Shore may have permanently hurt his arm through overwork, having from 1915 through 1917 averaged a hefty 233 innings a year. But now Shore was headed to Jacksonville, hoping to regain his form.

As with many top sluggers, Ruth clubbed home runs in bunches. On July 5, 1919, against the A's, Ruth had hit two home runs in a single game—the first time he had done so in an official big-league game—helping him match the league-leading 11 homers he had hit the year before. On July 18, he hit two more in a single game against the Cleveland Naps, the last one a grand slam in the bottom of the ninth of game two of a doubleheader to give the Red Sox a dramatic 8–7 come-from-behind win. Afterward, Fritz Coumbe, the pitcher who gave up the grand slam, broke down and cried. The next day, Naps manager Leo Fohl was fired and replaced by Ruth's old Boston teammate Tris Speaker.

Ruth in 1919 was drilling home runs at a dizzying clip. On July 29, he hit his ninth of the month and 16th of the season, tying Socks Seybold's American League record. And although Ruth was still pitching during that period—in part to help out in a pinch after Carl Mays left the team—he wasn't throwing as well as in previous years, which was understandable given his focus on the bat. He started three games in July, losing two—more than enough to convince manager Ed Barrow that Ruth's future belonged at bat as a full-time outfielder. The Red Sox wasted little time, and on July 31 brought in 19-year-old Waite Hoyt to assume Ruth's pitching role. Hoyt didn't disappoint, winning his debut 2–1 in 12 innings and assuming Ruth's rotation spot.

To reporters breathlessly covering his every at-bat, Ruth was "the Clouting Hercules," "the Boston Battering Ram," and "the Uncrowned King of Fenway Park." Statistics detailing his record pace crowded the sports pages, giving a push to baseball's mania for numbers. Ruth had become a phenomenon; crowds filled the parks to see him play, his mail at Fenway Park filled up baskets, and even Hollywood called to see if he'd be interested in making a film. But for two weeks, Ruth's bat went cold, and he didn't hit home run number 17 until August 14 off the White Sox's Erskine Mayer, a blast that took care of Seybold's A.L. record, clearing the right-field wall at Comiskey Park and landing in a soccer field.

And just like that, the Babe's home run stroke was back. The next target was the modern or post-1900 major-league record of 24, set in 1915 by Gavvy Cravath of the Phillies, and after that the pre-1900 record of 25 set by Buck Freeman of Washington in 1899. But then someone rooting around in old files—remember this was long before anyone much cared for statistics—unearthed the curious case of one Edward Nagle "Ned" Williamson, who had hit 27 home runs for the National League Chicago White Stockings back in 1884.

Just how Ned Williamson clubbed all those home runs was a fluke. The White Stockings' home that year was Lake Front Park, which had the shortest outfield distances in major-league history—180 feet to left field and 196 feet to right. Of Williamson's 27 home runs, 25 were at home. For the record, the White Stockings the year before had hit 13 home runs, 2 by Williamson. But in 1884, in tiny Lake Front Park, they hit 142, with Williamson's teammates Fred Pfeffer hitting 25, Abner Dalrymple 22, and Cap Anson 21. The previous season, the four of them had hit a total of 5 homers. In Williamson's next best season for home runs, he hit 9.

Fluke or no fluke, the record stood, and Ruth soldiered on. On August 17, he hit number 19 in St. Louis for his third home run in four games. Number 20 came August 23 in Detroit off Hooks Dauss, and it was a glorious shot—his fourth grand slam of the season, an American League mark that would stand for 40 years.

Ruth hit three more home runs in the series against Ty Cobb's Tigers—he had a knack for tattooing Detroit pitchers—and in doing so, marked a true changing of the guard in the evolution from the dead-ball to the lively ball era. Not only did the series draw huge crowds to Detroit's Navin Field, but Ruth's prodigious drives scored runs in a hurry, and seemed to be a whole lot more efficient than the "scientific" game, as personified by Cobb. "No wonder Harry Frazee's wearing that smile that won't come off in signing Babe Ruth to a three-year contract," wrote Arthur Duffey in the *Boston Post*. "Guess any other big-league magnate would feel the same way about it if they had such a star delivering as the Babe has been this season."

Everything Ruth did, home run or not, got people talking. Distances didn't seem to matter, because Ruth's drives cleared the fences with ease and deposited baseballs in alleys, front yards, and neighboring fields blocks from the ballpark. When he struck out, he did so with such force—such aplomb—that the fans were entertained. Even Ruth's other base hits were hit harder and sometimes even higher than anyone had seen; back home in Boston against Philadelphia, he hit a triple, as one put it, "that for altitude had anything ever seen at Fenway Park beaten by a city block." Nor did it seem to matter to anyone but Barrow that the Red Sox, despite the early season optimism, were headed nowhere—Boston would finish the year in sixth place, five games under .500—because all anyone wanted to talk about was Babe Ruth and his pursuit of the record books.

That Ruth hit for such unimaginable power and still drew occasional pitching duties built his mystique. Then, as now, only a few pitchers were considered adequate batsmen. But here was a pitcher hitting the tar off the ball. It was remarkable. At Fenway on September 1, in a Labor Day doubleheader against the Senators, Ruth pitched the first game—a complete-game 2–1 win, in which he tripled to drive in the first run and scored the second. Playing the outfield in game two, he homered to right field—number 24—as the Sox won, 4–1. When the game ended, fans stormed the field and carried Ruth off shoulder-high to the dugout steps.

"If ever a monarch received the adoring adulation of his subjects," the *Post* wrote the next day, "then Boston's mighty swatter, the champion slugger of all time, gave such an exhibition yesterday, and nearly 30,000 fans, . . . lured by the reputation of Boston's home run king, paid tribute to our Babe."

Our Babe. Ruth's relationship with Red Sox fans had become a virtual lovefest in 1919, despite the team's mediocre performance. Later that week, he tied Freeman's mark with number 25 and barely missed another when his drive hit the wall just below the top of the right-field fence. Number 26 came a few days later at the Polo Grounds. Said Freeman, somewhat soberly, after Ruth tied and then broke his ancient record: "I must congratulate him on his great work. Look at his wrists and you will find that they are tremendous. A man that hits as hard as he does must have abnormal development of the wrist and forearm."

With only Williamson's mark of 27 ahead, Ruth went dry again, which only heightened the drama and became a pattern of sorts for his career. For

11 days, the baseball world waited for another home run, during which Ruth hit a lot of singles before busting out. On September 20—the day the Red Sox decided to honor Ruth at Fenway—he tied Williamson's mark with a booming shot to left off the White Sox's Claud "Lefty" Williams. The shot not only won the game, but also awed those who were there; that a left-handed hitter could send such a booming home run off a left-handed pitcher was remarkable, particularly off someone as talented as Williams. Said White Sox third baseman Buck Weaver: "That was the most unbelievable poke I ever saw."

After Ruth was sold to the Yankees at the end of that year, the truth about a tale connected to Babe Ruth Day at Fenway became a heated issue, the resentment still smoldering. Ruth accused Frazee of not even paying for his wife's ticket to the game, and the supposed oversight was widely publicized. But for the moment, it was a glorious day, with 31,000 fans, 5,000 of whom stood behind ropes in the deepest outfield, jamming the park to honor their young hero. In between games of the day's doubleheader, Ruth sauntered to home plate and received $600 worth of U.S. Treasury certificates, spiked golf shoes, a fountain pen, and cuff links. The Red Sox presented Helen Ruth with a traveling bag, and each of the Babe's teammates with a box of cigars. For good measure, in game two Ruth doubled and scored the winning run in a 5–4 Boston win.

Three days later at the Polo Grounds, Ruth homered for number 28, breaking Williamson's record. In Washington, D.C., the following weekend, he hit his 29th and final home run of the extraordinary season. That last shot, struck off Rip Jordan, was patented Ruth, clearing the 45-foot right-field wall by 20 feet. It was also Ruth's first home run of the season in Washington, D.C., giving him the distinction of homering in every American League ballpark that year, a feat that no one had ever accomplished. How inconceivable it seemed at the time that it was Ruth's last home run as a member of the Red Sox.

Only 24 years old, Babe Ruth had become the king of baseball, its biggest draw and most popular player. He had accounted for all of 49 home runs in his brief career; yet he was being heralded as the game's greatest slugger ever with a future that seemed limitless. About the only long-distance record Ruth hadn't broken was Roger Connor's big-league lifetime home run title of 136, but that was only a matter of time. (Ruth passed Connor just two years later, in 1921.)

All those home runs left others in the dust. Ruth's 29 in 1919 were miles beyond the next slugger, Frank "Home Run" Baker of the Yanks, who hit 10. Gavvy Cravath took the N.L. title with 12. Ruth also finished atop the major leagues in RBIs with 114, runs with 103, total bases, along with slugging and home run percentage. He hit .322, stole seven bases, and drew 101 walks—stupendous numbers, the likes of which nobody had ever before seen in baseball. He even went 9–5 in his last year as a pitcher, with a 2.97 ERA.

"Ruth stands alone," an admirer wrote. Indeed, after just five big-league seasons, he had done more to change the game in one season than Ty Cobb or anyone else for that matter, could ever do. But bigger changes were just ahead.

By sending Damon Runyon to Jacksonville with the Yankees and Bugs Baer to San Antonio with the Giants, the *American* was making a fierce bid for the hearts and minds of baseball-hungry readers back in New York. Runyon would be "scanning the daily doings of Babe Ruth and his teammates . . . so cleverly . . . that every line in his tale would be a gem," the newspaper boasted. The hype wasn't far off, for by 1920 Runyon was among journalism's most creative talents, and well on his way to developing his distinctive style as the chronicler of Broadway and creator of memorable characters like "Nathan Detroit," "Sky Masterson," and "Harry the Horse."

A Kansas native raised in Colorado, Runyon arrived in New York in 1911 at the age of 29—focusing not just on baseball but Broadway, or more accurately, the characters around Broadway. His forte was incorporating into his writing the characters he met along the way—the ballplayers, actors, racetrack bookies, chorus girls, promoters, and assorted wise guys, hoods, and hangers-on—and making their antics the focus of his short stories and plays.

Take Runyon's story "Baseball Hattie": "It comes on springtime, and the little birdies are singing in the trees in Central Park, and the grass is green all around and about, and I am at the Polo Grounds on the opening day of the baseball season, when who do I behold but Baseball Hattie?" the story started.

It turns out that Hattie, a groupie or "Baseball Annie" of sorts, fell for and married a hot left-handed prospect named Haystack Duggeler. Haystack got off to a grand start with the Giants, but fell in with a bad crowd led by a gambler named Armand Fibleman. Then came his discovery of the racetrack, and big debts are soon owed to Armand. After that, the plot grows real complicated, real fast. It's a story resplendent with baseball, betting, racetracks, and all the familiar Runyon flourishes.

From the get-go, Runyon showed a flair for describing baseball with irreverence, but finding his way to the quirky and unusual. In 1911 alone, Runyon made a hero of a rundown alcoholic Giants pitcher named "Bugs" Raymond, who had one too many encounters with the bottle and would be dead a year later. He focused on the erratic behavior of one Charles "Victory" Faust, a Kansas simpleton who showed up in St. Louis proclaiming that a fortune-teller had told him he would pitch the Giants to the pennant. Faust couldn't pitch a lick, but manager John McGraw took a liking to him because he kept the team loose and the Giants won whenever he was around. Runyon wrote about Faust as though he were a prophet, attributing lengthy quotes to him about baseball, New York, and the meaning of life. Faust hit vaudeville before disappearing and dying just four years later in a Washington mental institution; meantime, Runyon's reputation was cemented.

Runyon became a media star. From his chair in the Polo Grounds' press box behind home plate, Runyon looked around the stands and wrote about the latest fashions. He quoted the poetry of old Colorado friends who stopped by the ballpark, quoted the gamblers on the trains headed to the park, and developed a long list of enduring pet themes, from cold weather to Pittsburgh cab drivers who drove too fast and Christy Mathewson's skill at pitching and checkers. The style was effective, and Runyon was rewarded by *American* publisher William Randolph Hearst, who habitually interrupted the reporter's trips to the Polo Grounds by sending him on other assignments like the 1914 round-the-world tour of the Giants and White Sox, an interview in Mexico with Pancho Villa, and political conventions. In 1917, Runyon went to France and wrote dispatches from the war front. Everything and anything was prey to his keen observations, remarkable versatility, and humor. Runyon's coverage of a notorious incident in 1912 when Ty Cobb jumped into the stands at Hilltop Park in New York to beat up a heckler is a case in point:

> In the fourth inning, when the Tigers were at bat, [Cobb] hopped the low barrier between the seats and the field, and began shaking

right and lefts out of his system full upon the upturned face of A. Fan. Some confusion resulted. "Silk" O'Loughlin and Westervelt, the umpires, hastened to the scene, remarking to one another upon what a busy place the Hill has become. All the ball players flocked to the spot in large quantities—the Detroit delegation being especially energetic in flocking. Those of the spectators who held ringside seats moved closer . . . a canvass of the audience gives the popular decision to Cobb by a plurality of 354.

On the sports page, Runyon wrote interchangeably about baseball, horse racing, and boxing, with football a distant fourth. He covered most big prizefights, rarely missed a Kentucky Derby, and enjoyed hating golf. He took to baseball, in part, because most games started in midafternoon and rarely stretched beyond two hours, giving him plenty of time to file his copy and then head out on the town, where he typically stayed up all night before heading around dawn to his Upper West Side apartment, where he'd bang out more copy about what he found along Broadway. He also worked fast, banging out whole columns in minutes, all of which left more time for him to sit back and absorb the color.

Baseball was Runyon's entrée to a host of memorable characters like McGraw, a member of New York's Lambs Club, a haunt of actors, which in turn afforded Runyon entrée to the Broadway crowd. And baseball became one of the vehicles Runyon used to develop the characters in his memorable short stories, in which men were always "guys," women were "dolls," and money "potatoes." Even the names of his short stories were classics: "Blue Plate Special" and "A Slight Case of Murder."

Runyon's joint was Lindy's, the well-known Midtown Manhattan restaurant he immortalized as "Mindy's." It was there that many of the actors, wise guys, gamblers, sharks, and assorted night owls met only to find themselves later worked into a short story. An alcoholic gone sober, Runyon would occupy a seat at Lindy's for hours, consuming up to 60 cups of coffee a night as he hosted a steady stream of characters for his short stories and newspaper columns, establishing himself as the spiritual forerunner to Jimmy Breslin. Said one regular, after reading a Runyon piece: "It ain't hard to spot the guys in the stories."

For a time, Runyon tried joining those he wrote about—owning racehorses that rarely won and promoting boxers. He even dressed the part, usually appearing in pinstriped suits and fancying himself as the dude. He especially liked shoes, and traveled with such an enormous quantity of footwear that he required a whole extra trunk.

Setting up with the Yankees in Jacksonville from his room at the Hotel Burbridge, Runyon went to work on what he did best—spinning a phrase and being irreverent, and occasionally even touching on baseball—while continuing to churn out his column, "The Mornin's Mornin'," with tales of who went where as if he had never left Broadway.

The Jacksonville weather in early March was windy, wet, and raw, offering Runyon his first theme, not exactly what the locals had in mind for coverage back north: "There is no doubt the weather they are now enjoying hereabouts at the current typewriting is unusual for Jacksonville, but that fellow hasn't been around yet to mention that this is the first time in twenty years they had had such weather," he wrote March 8. "You know that fellow. Every town has him. Possibly the reason he hasn't been around to speak to the Yanks so far is because he has had a tip they are laying for him with murderous intent."

The wind and poor field conditions at Southside Park meant more leisure time for golf and fishing, endeavors for which Runyon reserved particular venom. "Not all the Yanks played golf today," he wrote of a Sunday excursion of ballplayers trying to enjoy themselves on a rare sunny day. "Some did worse. Some went fishing. Of these, the less said the better. A Sunday fisherman is hopeless. It begins with week-day fishing, and gradually the little brain cells become a tangle of bait and sinkers. A man's willpower is destroyed and Sunday fishing follows. The family of a Sunday fisherman is entitled to the sincere sympathy of the entire community. . . . The names of the Sunday fishermen are withheld. Enough scandal is being printed in the papers as it is."

When Miller Huggins, recovered from his cold, arrived in camp March 3, the press contingent had their first legitimate story. "M. Huggins' first official motion was to flatwheel himself twice around the busting behemoth [Ruth], admiring the graceful proportions of Babe from the belt down, which was as far as M. [c]ould see without getting a crimp in his neck," Runyon wrote in exaggerated tones of a scene that probably never happened. "Then, he sent the Babe up to belt a few for him."

Those first days of spring training were delicious fodder for Runyon. With memories still fresh of Ping Bodie's legendary eating contest against Percy the Ostrich, a similar contest was cooked up—but this time, only with humans. Among the contestants were a trio of hefty eaters—Ruth, Vick, and writer Irvin Shrewsbury Cobb, "the famous eating-author" and noted war correspondent, in town for a lecture. The venue: the Burbridge dining room.

"It was decided that Mr. Cobb should start from scratch with Ruth, and that they shall spot their competitors one Virginia ham each, and a double porterhouse," Runyon reported. "George Mogridge, who is managing Ruth, insisted on a rule that Mr. Cobb shall not be permitted to tell any stories during the encounter [so that Ruth doesn't have] to stop and laugh. Mr. Cobb's ability to laugh and eat at the same time is well known. He can emit a raucous guffaw and chamber a Dill pickle simultaneously."

Runyon reported the preparations as if he was covering a Madison Square Garden boxing match. "Sam Vick is really not in condition as yet, and his admirers are sorely disappointed," he wrote. "He warmed up last night on a side of bacon, a few dozen oysters and other odds and ends in the way of chops and hot cakes and ice cream, but he showed little form."

The same went for Ping Bodie, "the mighty eater of other days," which the ballplayer fully admitted. "If it was . . . spaghetti, I'd show them something, but after I get through one of these hotel menus, my appetite is dead for half an hour," Ping said. "Maybe it's the climate."

Preparations for what Runyon called the "great All-American table stakes" grew elaborate. There were shifting odds, and the betting seemed to draw in everyone from the ballplayers and writers to Yankee officials, and even the waiters at the Dodgers' training camp up the road at the Hotel Seminole. That no report exists of how it all turned out doesn't really matter; it was all in fun, and helped round the folks back in New York into a baseball frame of mind.

Like the other beat writers, Runyon focused on Ruth, who he called everything from "the Billion-Dollar fish" to "the diamond studded ball buster," "the busting behemoth," "the Home Run King," or, in later years, simply "Mr. Ruth," since everyone knew who he meant. "If we seem to speak of Babe more than somewhat, we trust the reader will bear with us," he wrote. "All our life we have been poor, and Babe cost so much money that even to talk about it gives us a wealthy feeling."

If his dispatches weren't exactly accurate, who cared? Runyon reported of one Ruthian batting practice shot—a "two-miler"—that the ball landed into the lap of a small boy who stuck it in his pocket and ran home. That drive, Runyon said, broke Babe's bat. "And it broke Yankee business manager Harry Sparrow's heart as well," he wrote. "Harry pays for both balls and bats." Even the long shots that didn't require the tape measure drew comment. "There was no excessive Babe Ruthing during the afternoon," Runyon wrote one day early in camp. "Nothing was knocked over the fence except a few foolish fouls. The distinguished young man who cost the Colonels [Ruppert and Huston] so much that they have sympathetic pains whenever they think about it stepped to the plate a couple of times in batting practice and loosened the covers on a couple of pills, but his efforts were not unduly thrilling."

For a writer with Runyon's gifts, Ruth provided great copy away from the park, too, especially when there wasn't much to write about in the early days of camp. Readers of the *American* were dutifully informed as the Babe headed off one Sunday morning in early March to the golf course dressed "in a rash of white flannel pants," even as the weather continued cold and rainy.

He said he had put on his white flannel pants because he had been informed that Florida is conducive to white flannel pants at this time of the year, and he'd be dog dried if he was going to be shunned out of wearing his white flannel pants.

"Trousers," interrupted Bob Shawkey, with a pained look. "Trousers, my dear fellow."

"Mine's pants," said Babe, firmly. "When it gets to such a thing as the weather can tell me what kind of pants I got to wear, I'm going to quit."

While golfing, Ruth ran into Rube Marquard, the onetime Giants mainstay now pitching with Brooklyn. "Folks gathered close to the noble grouping," Runyon wrote of the encounter, "and inclined attentive ears to hear what burning words as might fall from the mouths of these parties."

" 'Lo, Rube," said the Babe.

" 'Lo, Babe," said Rube.

"The much-anticipated meeting ended in a second. The illustrious Babe hauled off and socked a golf ball three miles, or more, to hear the witnesses tell, and moved off it, while Richard DeMarkee DeMarquard faded into the obscurity of his absurdly low price of many, many years ago." The reference was to the once-exorbitant $11,000 that Marquard had cost the Giants a dozen years back.

When Runyon couldn't think of anything else to write about, he returned to the cold and the wind, which continued its March onslaught. "Pieces of the cold spell which is pounding up and down in the West flew off and hit Jax today, and most of the Yanks hung around the hotel lobby all day, dripping intermittent and clammy conversation as an icicle drips perspiration."

You get the impression that Runyon didn't care much for ballplayers and seldom ventured from his room in search of a story idea, unless he happened to spot Babe Ruth's white flannel pants, catch wind of something while in the bar, or show up to watch practice. "Did you ever sit looking into the faces of a lot of dull, unresponsive typewriter keys for a quarter of an hour on a cold Friday in Florida?" he asked readers. "It's very monotonous. But the alternative in this case is going down to the lobby of the Burbridge, and gazing at the maps of the baseball players. So here we are at the old Underwood."

Miller Huggins hardly looked like the man to lead this swaggering assortment of baseball talent. Only 5'6½" and packing all of 140 pounds onto a gaunt frame, he was a bantamweight among heavyweights, a man whose slight stature and brooding nature hid a sharp, cerebral mind and iron will that backed down to no one and could stand the pressures of managing in New York.

Born 41 years earlier in Cincinnati, he had grown up in the rough-and-tumble Fourth Ward and learned to defend himself early. Huggins showed promise as a rangy shortstop and baseball captain at Walnut Hills High School, but due to the stringent objections of his father didn't dare think of making a career of baseball. Huggins's father James was an English immigrant who considered baseball players somewhere between prisoners and vaudevillians on the social scale, which in those randy days wasn't far off. To please his father, Miller Huggins in 1898 enrolled at the University of Cincinnati to study law—combining his studies with playing semipro ball under a pseudonym. An 1898 box score of an Interstate League game in Ohio between Mansfield and Dayton lists one "Proctor" playing third base, with one at-bat for Mansfield. It was Huggins's first professional game, complete with a sly reference to the Cincinnati soap company so his dad wouldn't know.

Somehow, Huggins combined his law school studies with baseball. He kept playing with Mansfield and during the summers toured with New York's independent Fleischman Catskill Mountain team, owned by Julius Fleischman, the former mayor of Cincinnati and part owner of the Reds.

In 1902, Huggins graduated from law school and was admitted to the Ohio bar. By then, James Huggins, acknowledging that his son was more interested in Texas leaguers than torts and encouraged by the game's growing respectability among the middle class, was resigned to Miller's interest in a baseball career. At least Huggins tried law—spending six months in a law office—but it bored him. "I gave up the law for baseball," he said, "because it's more than a game, for the real ball player employs his brains as much as the shrewdest businessman."

In 1903, Huggins signed his first professional contract, with St. Paul of the American Association, and never regretted it. A year later, he was the regular second baseman for his hometown Reds. In time, he developed into a sure-handed fielder, a steady hitter, and a good bunter with speed on the base paths. His style fit the dead-ball era—scratching for a run here and there with "inside" baseball, in which bunting the runner over and stealing second was as valued as the home run.

The diminutive player's success surprised everyone, including himself. Should baseball not work out, Huggins reasoned, he could always go into the roller skating business, which had fascinated him ever since as a boy he'd become captivated by the sport. Huggins even spent several winters working at a Cincinnati rink, where he'd become a part owner and director. Traveling from town to town during baseball season, he would inspect every roller skating rink he could find, imagining its income and the architectural improvements he would make as owner. Huggins once said he regretted never making it to Europe because he missed a chance to see how they ran their roller skating rinks.

References to Huggins's small size never stopped. Later called "the Mighty Mite" and "the Little Pilot," his playing-day nicknames were more along the lines of "the Rabbit" and "Little Mr. Everywhere." Although many of the monikers were placed by friendly writers, the names became fodder for bench jockeys. Even umpires acted up, as happened when ump Bill Guthrie called Huggins "the batboy" while tossing him from a game.

Huggins developed a thick skin and pretended not to listen. On the field, he drove himself, watching, learning, and preparing better than anyone else—hallmarks of a budding manager. "A man must have an exhaustive knowledge of baseball . . . not only a knowledge of the play, but a knowledge of the history of the game, the men who played it long ago and the men who are playing it now," Huggins once said. Inhibited by his size from reaching curveballs on the outside corner of the plate, he spent a winter swinging at a ball suspended by twine from his basement ceiling. Huggins became a switch-hitter by teaching himself to bat left-handed, and away from the ballpark developed a regimen of eating, drinking, and even chopping wood left-handed. It worked, and the record books list Huggins as a lifetime switch-hitter.

In Cincinnati, Huggins played for a succession of middle-of-the-pack teams, but took the opportunity to learn under the wings of a couple of wily former outfielders turned managers: Joe Kelley of the late, great Oriole teams of the 1890s and Ned Hanlon. Traded to the lowly St. Louis Cardinals in 1910, Huggins took over at second base, and by 1913 had replaced Roger Bresnahan as the last-place team's player-manager. A year later, the Cardinals were a third-place team, with their first finish above .500 in 13 years. In 1915 the Cardinals slipped to sixth, and in 1916 again placed last, but in 1917, helped by the batting gifts of the sensational young infielder Rogers Hornsby, rebounded again to third.

Off the field, Huggins was a loner. Never married, he had a few close friends and developed a series of pronounced eccentricities—Huggins was scared of taxis, for instance. He was closest to his sister, Myrtle, who served as his long-term housekeeper. As a manager, Huggins was a man who commanded respect, had the reputation of sticking up for his players with management, and could squeeze every last drop of effort from his teams. "He was a terrific manager," said Yankee Earle Combs. "He made a point of not bawling you out in front of everyone else. If he had something to say to you, he'd take you into his office."

Above all, Huggins valued a player's courage. "The very best characteristic a player can have, the strongest possible foundation for his success, is guts," he told F. C. Lane of *Baseball Magazine*. "I do not know another word which conveys so clearly and concisely those qualities of earnest, courageous, aggressive, good sportsmanship as that short, rather ugly mono-syllable. Let a player of brilliant attainments lack that quality and he will never be more than a disappointment."

With veteran players, Huggins's philosophy was simple: Let them go their own way on and off the field. They knew their business, Huggins reasoned, and if they didn't, he would rather not have them around. Huggins made changes in his lineup, but in the ordinary run of the game let his veterans exercise their own judgment, and only in big games would he give instructions from the bench. It was in most ways a simpler game to manage in the dead-ball era, with few substitutions, platooning still decades away, and no such thing as setup men or closers in the bullpen. Most teams carried four starters and a bullpen of two spot starters. Among the Yankees, the joke was that Huggins had only three signs: one for the hit-and-run, one for a pitchout, and the other reading "Game Postponed on Account of Rain. Doubleheader Tomorrow."

Huggins treated his younger players differently. To them, he was paternalistic, and developed a reputation for recognizing and bringing along talent, particularly smaller, faster players who like himself got by more on drive than talent. With them he would spend hour after hour and year after year, as future charges like Lou Gehrig and Tony Lazzeri would later attest. "There is no doubt that Huggins is one of the smartest managers in baseball," the *Sporting News* wrote. "He has never had a first class club to operate. . . . He has had no $50 gold pieces to hand to pitchers who win games, but he wins his men by his squareness."

It was with the younger players that Huggins shined as a master motivator. "You can't make players do things who can't do them," he said. "The manager of a ballclub is little better than a builder." Above all, he preached confidence, which he called "the mental tonic, which [when] added to physical ability wins so many ball games.

"It is impossible to overestimate the importance of such confidence," Huggins said. On the other hand, "lack of confidence can disorganize a ball club quicker than a series of accidents," he added. "It's the old story: you can't swim so well against the tide as you can with the tide."

In 1917, Huggins retired with a .265 lifetime batting average, 324 steals, and 1,002 walks in 13 big-league seasons—and became a full-time manager. Those third-place finishes had been the highest in Cardinal history, and the *Sporting News* heralded Huggins as "The Little Miracle Worker of the West." But clearly not impressed and angling for a change were Branch Rickey and the new Cardinal ownership, who bought the team in early 1917 and fired Huggins after the season.

So even if Huggins had the last laugh—under Jack Hendricks, St. Louis went right back in the gutter in 1918, finishing dead last—he found himself jobless at season's end, but bursting to stay in baseball. Taking notice were Yankee owners Ruppert and Huston, anxious to start a fire under their team after the mediocrity of consecutive fifth-, fourth-, and sixth-place finishes under Wild Bill Donovan.

With Huston overseas in the service, Ruppert spoke up for the team, deciding the Yankees needed not just new players, but a new manager as well. "I like you, Donovan," he told Wild Bill in his thick German accent at their last meeting, "but we have to make some changes around here."

Huston's choice to guide the team was Wilbert Robinson. The two were close friends, drank together, and hunted during the off-season at Huston's retreat at Dover Hall. In Brooklyn, Robinson was popular with players and fans alike, having guided them to a pennant in 1916 and even overseeing the team nickname change from Dodgers to Robins in his honor (although the team would by 1920 again be called the Dodgers).

But Ruppert didn't take to Robinson. The Yankee co-owner thought the Dodger skipper, at 50, was too old to manage the Yankees, a charge that Robinson found insulting. "No," he told Robinson with his trademark brusqueness, "you will not do." He said as much to Huston in a cable, to which his fellow co-owner fired back with a blistering response—an episode that would lead to a permanent break between the two men.

In stepped American League President Ban Johnson with a plan: sign Huggins, he urged the Yankee owners, and you'd be doing the American League a big favor. A master of baseball's political wars, Johnson was still angry at the National League for luring Branch Rickey across town to the Cardinals from the Browns. Bringing Huggins to the American League, he figured, would be payback. "We'll be taking a good man away from the enemy," he told Ruppert.

While Johnson urged Ruppert to take his advice, Huggins was in New York attending a National League meeting as the representative of the Cardinals. No longer manager, he was still a major stockholder in the team and a popular man in St. Louis with no intention of moving to New York. Thank you, but no, Huggins said—he had no intention to change.

To the rescue came Huggins's friend J. G. Taylor Spink, publisher of the St. Louis–based *Sporting News*. Just meet Ruppert at the brewery, Spink urged Huggins, and you might be inclined to take the position. When Huggins reiterated his intentions, Spink grew exasperated. "If you won't go willingly," he told his friend, "I'll hit you over the head and drag you up there."

Huggins went, and to his surprise, he and Ruppert hit it off. Much as Huston and Robinson were a match, so were Ruppert and Huggins. Both were blunt and spoke their minds. Both were lifelong bachelors who threw themselves into their work, while cultivating an eclectic set of interests away from the office or the ballpark. Ruppert, impressed with Huggins's baseball knowledge and Johnson's enthusiastic endorsement, offered him the position on the spot. Amazing even himself, Huggins quickly accepted.

Huston was mortified. Furious at Ruppert's rejection of Robinson, he was doubly furious that the final decision was made with him still in Europe. The two Yankee owners hurled abuse at one another—a rift that settled into a frosty silence after Huston, recently named colonel, returned to the United States in September 1919. In letters to his many friends on the newspapers, Huston made it clear that Huggins wasn't his choice, and spent a lot of time drifting about the Yankee offices on 42nd Street glowering at the diminitive manager.

Publicly, Huggins bore the pressure and soldiered on. "I never object to criticism," he said, "feeling as I do that when I accept a position in the public eye, I must also expect my share of knocks." Privately, even his steely nerves took a beating. Years later, the taciturn Huggins would finally speak up, saying of the years 1919 to 1923, when Huston finally sold his share in the club, "I wouldn't go [through those years] again for all the money in the world."

Huggins went to work anyway, and did well in 1918, bringing the Yankees in fourth, three games under .500 and 13½ games behind pennant-winning Boston. It was a solid performance considering that 11 Yankees who started the season with the team, among them Shawkey and Pipp, ended up in the armed forces.

Of particular concern to Huggins was the shoddy defense of the Yankee infield, which as baseball historian Leo Trachtenberg put it, "leaked up the middle like a cracked dike." So Huggins sent five Yankees and a wad of the colonels' cash to the St. Louis Browns for the sure-handed, veteran second baseman Del Pratt. The move worked: in 1918, Pratt and the rest of the Yankees committed 64 fewer errors than they had in 1917 and led the A.L. in double plays.

Huggins kept dealing. In December 1918, he dealt for Red Sox mainstay Duffy Lewis to replace Elmer Miller in center field, as part of a blockbuster, multiplayer trade that also brought pitchers Ernie Shore and Dutch Leonard to New York. Lewis, who had spent all of 1918 in the army, was the key—he had been with the Red Sox for close to a decade, and starred in Boston's World Series triumphs of 1912, 1915, and 1916. Playing primarily left field, he was part of a Boston outfield that included Hall of Famers

Tris Speaker and Harry Hooper and was among the finest in big-league history.

Lewis was a lifetime .284 hitter and noted for coming through in the clutch, but he was renowned for his defensive skills, particularly his uncanny ability to catch balls on a slope of grass in left field at Fenway Park named "Duffy's Cliff." The grassy rise, an 8- to 10-foot incline that led up the wall in left field, baffled most outfielders until it was leveled off in 1934. But Lewis, the *Globe* once reported, "could go up and down that incline like a mountain goat."

Lewis mastered the cliff, saying he'd go out to the ballpark in the mornings, stand in left field, and have somebody hit him balls again and again. "I experimented with every angle of approach up the cliff until I learned to play the slope correctly," he once said. "Sometimes it would be tougher coming back down the slope than going up. With runners on base, you had to come down off the cliff throwing."

While Lewis's arm earned him some attention, his bat did as well. "Duffy Lewis is a man who gets about one-tenth the publicity which Babe Ruth does," said Walter Johnson. "But the players all recognize him as one of the greatest hitters in the game. He can hit anything and is doubly dangerous in the pinch."

Dutch Leonard, who had also missed much of 1918 in the army, didn't want to play in New York and ended up with Detroit. Joining the Yanks full time in 1919 after military service was outfielder Sammy Vick, a 23-year-old Mississippian with all of 12 big-league at-bats but a minor-league track record as a heavy hitter. Vick won his job after George Halas, another rookie, suffered an untimely charley horse. Halas, a Chicago native, had speed and had played while in the military with the Great Lakes Naval Station, and before that, the University of Illinois. Halas would play all of 12 games with the Yanks in 1919, hitting .091 before switching full-time to football. It was a good move—he became the Chicago Bears' Hall of Fame coach and owner.

In 1919, Huggins's Yankees got better. The midseason addition of Carl Mays helped; he went 9–3, and, combined with 20 wins from Shawkey, who was back from the navy, and veteran Jack Quinn's 15, the New Yorkers climbed to third, 21 games above .500 and only 7½ games behind the A.L. champion White Sox. So even with Ruth stealing headlines by socking his 29 home runs in Boston and a season shortened to 140 games, the

Yankees made their own buzz in 1919, drawing a whopping 619,164 fans to the Polo Grounds, their most ever by far and, more important, only 90,000 behind the major-league-leading Giants. Not that Huggins ever got credit from either Huston or his newspaper cronies: "The only time Hug got his name in the paper," wrote Frank Graham in his 1943 history of the team, "was when the Yankees lost."

With Miller Huggins wondering aloud about his lineup, Babe Ruth took matters into his own hands—putting a stake in the ground by drifting to center field and planting himself there during practice. It was a subtle move, virtually lost amidst all the daily batting practice balls that Ruth was pasting to distant parts of Southside Park and beyond, and few noticed. But Runyon did: "Maybe they are just letting him stand out there in the sun until they can find a way of grafting him into right field," he wrote. "Fortunately, Ruth doesn't have to chase his own punches or he would be bow-legged in a week."

So the Yankees had their center fielder. Huggins didn't say anything about that for the record. Meanwhile, he kept thinking and nattering, again admitting he was undecided about his Opening-Day lineup, since there were so many first-time Yanks he still needed to evaluate. "Just as likely as not I shall go to a day or two before the opening of the race before deciding on my lineup," Huggins said with an eye toward the opening spring series, set to kick off March 13 against Brooklyn.

By the second week in March, everyone was in camp, including the late arrivals—Bob Meusel and Duffy Lewis, both in from California, and the incumbent shortstop, steady Roger Peckinpaugh, the team captain. With Huggins on the scene, things settled down pretty much to normal, as reporters wired stories detailing the "snappy workouts" and the ongoing Jacksonville cold spell. Meanwhile, Ruth's headline hogging seemed not to bother his teammates in the least. "Rather it has the boys all smoked up over pennant prospects," William Macbeth wrote in the *Tribune*. "The old heads here figure that with Ruth and Mays added the team is surely 20 percent stronger than when it faced the gun a year ago."

Helping to settle things further was the early performance of 23-year-old rookie Bob Meusel. Stepping into the cage on the morning of March 7 under rare sunny skies, Meusel put on a virtual hitting clinic, spraying balls to all parts of the field and doing so with power. Heads turned, including those of the many Jacksonville railbirds—"heads cocked, owl wise and hypercritical," according to the *Times*—who were showing up in ever-increasing numbers to watch practice. Then, Meusel put down his bat and went out to play both the infield and the outfield, where he fielded flawlessly.

Long-legged, with good power from the plate and a rifle right arm, Meusel prompted immediate comparisons with Tiger mainstay and fellow Californian Harry Heilmann. At 6'3" and 190 pounds, Meusel didn't run so much as he loped to the ball, which tended to make his effort appear casual, and used his considerable throwing ability to get the ball where it had to go.

A San Jose native, Meusel grew up mostly in Los Angeles at a time when Californian ballplayers were still a tad bit exotic and made much of in the press. "There is something besides accident which has made California yield more great players in proportion to her population than any other state," John Ward wrote in *Baseball Magazine*. "That something is the unsurpassed climate which permits the playing of baseball games almost all the year round."

Ward was right. "I never played football for I never had time," Meusel told him. "I was too busy playing baseball." So were Meusel's three older brothers, including 27-year-old Emil, a Phillies outfielder known as "Irish" who was three and a half inches shorter than Bob, had a less-powerful arm, and wasn't even Irish (the Meusels were of German heritage).

Bob joined Vernon of the Pacific Coast League in 1917 and spent 1918 in the navy, where he managed to play a lot of baseball and attract attention as a member of a navy team that defeated the Chicago Cubs in spring training. In 1919, Meusel went back to Vernon, where he hit .330 with 14 home runs. Signed by the Yanks that August, Meusel had Huggins almost giddy with excitement in the spring of 1920. "I'll bet he'll be one of the most talked about of hitters in the country this season," the Yankee skipper said. "He is one of those natural hitters with a perfect hitting swing."

If Meusel was looking more like a starter, Huggins had a host of other decisions to make on his lineup. Stories about the possibility of Home Run Baker changing his mind about retirement and returning to baseball—he would stay home at his Maryland farm until 1921—were in and out of the headlines all spring, fueled most prominently by Joe Vila's *Sporting News* reports from New York.

Then there was Frank Gleich, another in the series of youngsters due for a long look, a 26-year-old Columbus, Ohio, native who was up for a cup of coffee in 1919 and anxious to prove himself in 1920. "I don't mind telling you that Gleich to me looks promising, very promising," Huggins told reporters. He wasn't so sure about the infield, he added, "on account of the uncertainty of whether Baker will play. If he doesn't, I may have to use Fewster in the infield, but I'd [like] to use him in the outfield."

Turning to the pitching staff, Ernie Shore was also showing promise, and had people rooting for him. "Shore, who couldn't get the hang of his old Boston delivery last year, appears to have come back in real earnest," Vila wrote in the *Sporting News*. "His arm is as strong as a bundle of steel springs and he is in splendid physical condition. If this great pitcher, when he gets into championship games, masters control and has a few breaks in his favor, he'll surprise a whole lot of persons who passed him up last summer as a good old has-been."

To Vila's mind, the key was getting Shore on track to spell the established staff of Mays, Shawkey, Mogridge, Quinn, and Thormahlen. "Mays and Quinn, who are big, powerful men, can stand plenty of hard work," Vila wrote. "But Shawkey, Mogridge and Thormahlen must be handled with great care, lest they become stale from overexertion, which proved to be the case in 1919."

On March 13, in a listless 3–2 opening loss to the Dodgers at Southside Park, the Yankees managed all of six hits against three Brooklyn pitchers. It was another cold, damp Jacksonville afternoon, which held the crowd to only 600. But none of that mattered: the game marked the actual start of play, which gave the gaggle of writers, who were starting to suffer from a collective case of overanalysis, some real news to report.

And although Ruth went hitless, that hardly mattered either. In the fourth inning, he provided perhaps the game's most dramatic moments, blasting a towering foul ball, "one of the most murderous fouls ever seen," the *Times* wrote, over the right-field fence at the deepest part of the park, and then sending the next pitch nearly as far and also foul. "The [first] wallop convinced the natives that Ruth could hit even though he can't get them safe," the paper gushed.

On tap for the Yankees' spring schedule were 18 games, all but 4 conveniently scheduled in Jacksonville against the surprisingly strong Dodgers. The other 4, against the world champion Cincinnati Reds, would be played in a midmonth, long-weekend dash to Miami and Palm Beach.

Leaving for the series against the Reds, the Yankee players promised to make their only road trip of the spring a memorable one. Two days later in Miami, the Yankees lost 3–2 to the Reds, but won convincingly the next day 9–0, with Shawkey and Quinn combining on a seven-hitter—a nice prologue for a big night on the town.

Baseball etiquette, circa 1920, meant that the hosting Reds were duty-bound to show their guests a good time, which wasn't particularly difficult at the dawn of Prohibition in Miami, a key entry port in the rum-running business. Even Ruth in his autobiography called the trip "one of the wildest excursions ever made by a Big League ball club."

"I suppose [the Reds] felt it their duty to entertain us New Yorkers in proper style," Ruth wrote in his 1948 memoir nearly 30 years later. "And those Yankees who didn't have pals on the Reds found plenty of entertainment when they were on their own."

That went for Huston, his merry band of newspaper reporters, and a few players who chugged off to a party on an island. Returning in the early hours of the morning, one newspaperman who tried to help his colleague board the boat got pulled into Biscayne Bay for his noble efforts. And it took three people to assist Ping Bodie to the train, "but at least Ping didn't fall into the ocean," as Ruth put it.

Somehow, the Yanks managed to rise and shine the next morning for the trip to Palm Beach, where behind a promising 24-year-old recent Texas League graduate named Rip Collins they managed to beat the Reds again, this time 7–3. The venue was a hastily set up field beside the Royal Ponciana Hotel that featured a thick cluster of palm trees in deepest center field and a set of unusual ground rules: with no outfield fences and an inadequate grandstand to hold the crowd of 3,000, most spectators sat or stood on the fringes of the field, prompting the umpires to limit drives smacked into the outfield crowd to a triple. But Cincinnati's Edd Roush was the only one to hit it that far, and when he did, the polite, posh Palm Beach types gave way to allow the Yankee outfielders to chase the ball.

But the Yankees almost wished the crowd hadn't been quite so genial. Chasing a fly ball in fielding practice, Ruth, with no fence to stop him, ran smack dab into one of the palm trees. Knocked cold, he later regained consciousness and doubled in the go-ahead run. Said a deadpan Ruth: "I guess my reflexes were a bit off."

Adding his own footnote to the frivolity in Miami was Damon Runyon. Runyon bought a baby alligator, gave it the grand name Aloysius Dorgan, after his cartoonist friend Ted Dorgan, and housed him temporarily in a wash basin at the Burbridge—proudly reporting any and all news of his young purchase to readers back home. Aloysius was so intelligent, Runyon wrote, "that it is predicted he will grow into a very fine valise, or hand bag, if not a suitcase." Only six months old, he was said to be descended, Runyon added, "from one of the oldest alligator families in Florida."

But young Aloysius probably should have stayed in Florida. Hauled back and forth between the train and hotels as the Yankees barnstormed north some weeks later, Runyon's alligator prodigy developed a frostbitten ear. Twice he fell off a bureau. Retreating to the deep recesses of Colonel Huston's wash basin while on the train, the unfortunate Aloysius suffered a further setback when Huston inadvertently washed his hands, making the water soapy.

The end mercifully came aboard the Pullman in Virginia. "When he opened his eyes on the proud old soil of Virginia," Runyon wrote as his alligator prepared to meet his maker, "it seemed to be snowing exteriorly; and little Aloysius felt that it was no place for him."

His many readers chuckled at the shenanigans of Runyon and young Aloysius Dorgan. But Ruth said he was despondent when the alligator died. No wonder Runyon never again brought up alligators in his column. Given the shenanigans in Miami, no wonder it would be decades before the Yankees returned there for a game.

Back in Jacksonville, Ruth kept chiseling away at building his legend. On March 18, the Yanks lost 3–0 as Carl Mays was batted hard. Ruth again hit the ball long and hard, but wound up with only a single. Then, the next day, the Babe went deep—really deep—pasting a ball 500 feet in a blast that cleared the center-field fence by 20 feet and landed on the heavy, marshy soil 50 feet beyond. Too bad the blow came during batting practice off a young Brown University graduate named Mario De Vitalis, giving the prospect his five minutes of fame in the form of a few lines in the next day's newspapers.

On March 20, the Dodgers took the Yanks, this time 5–1, as Ruth again stole the headlines, but not with his hitting: annoyed by a persistent heckler calling him "a big piece of cheese," according to the family papers of the day, the Babe tore into the left-field stands where the man was sitting. What happened next is lost to history. The effervescent Harry Culley Jr. of the *Times-Union* wrote that Ruth, on realizing his tormentor was only half his size, laughed off the whole episode. But the *Times'* account was probably more accurate: after the man pulled a knife on Ruth, cool-headed Ernie Shore, who had followed the Babe into the stands, got between the two men and urged that everyone simmer down.

Watching the whole episode from his box seat in the grandstand, Huston was exasperated at the behavior of his expensive new star. "That kind of stuff will have to be stopped right away," he said. "If criticism down here gets under Ruth's skin, what will he do in the big-league parks? Star players are always subjected to a certain amount of abuse when they don't deliver every time up, and, if they are sensible, they realize that this is part of the game."

The Dodgers beat the Yankees again, 1–0, on March 23—the Brooklynites' fifth win in a row over their crosstown rivals. Distressingly silent were the Yankee bats, the most prominent belonging to Ruth, who was hitting around .200 and still without a home run. None of it would have meant very much, except that the team's every move was being scrutinized by a pack of newspapermen without a whole lot of solid news to report. They blamed just about everything for the Yankees' slow start, from being out of shape (having only one workout a day) to the lousy weather, Ruth's pressing (probably true), the lingering effects of too much partying in Miami, and the curious case of the missing bats. As the story goes, Ruth's valued collection of bats failed to arrive in Jacksonville for weeks, leaving him so ill at ease using whatever lumber he could find, including an old bat of Frank Baker's, that he once absently stuck it in his mouth and, according to Runyon, "tried to inhale it, as it is about the same size as the cigars Mr. Ruth smokes."

Nobody thought to give the Dodgers any credit, but the fact is the Yankees had run into a trio of wily, veteran pitchers. The Dodger staff featured right-handers Al Mamaux, a 21-game winner back in 1915 and 1916 with the

Pirates, and hard-throwing, 6'3" Jeff Pfeffer, twice a 20-game winner, in 1914 and in 1916. Added to the mix was 30-year-old lefty Rube Marquard, three times a 20-game winner and trying to bounce back from a broken leg in 1919. All mixed a combination of hard stuff with a good curveball, giving the Yankees fits and the Brooklyn fans hope that their beloved Trolley Dodgers could be contenders in 1920.

On March 25, things started off badly for the Yankees and got worse, much worse. In fielding practice, catcher Muddy Ruel fielded a bunt and cut loose with a throw to first base that popped a temporarily distracted Wally Pipp on the jaw, knocking him out. Pipp came to five minutes later, but had suffered a badly swollen jaw and would be gone from the lineup for some time.

Then it was game time, and up stepped the Yanks' first batter, third baseman Chick Fewster. He had worked to a 2–0 count when big Jeff Pfeffer uncorked a fastball that struck Fewster on the temple, the impact sounding "like a coconut shell cracking," the *Times* wrote. Fewster crumpled to the ground, unconscious, and lay for 10 minutes before he could be revived and helped to the clubhouse. It was a devastating injury—a fractured skull and a blood clot that limited Fewster's use of his vocal cords for days. Barely able to speak and facing an uncertain baseball future, Fewster returned two days later to his hometown of Baltimore to begin a long stay at Union Protestant Infirmary. Wheelchair-bound for weeks, Fewster wouldn't return to the Yanks until midseason, and never fulfilled the promise he had displayed early in 1920.

Pfeffer was devastated. He thought that the pitch was in the strike zone, and wondered why Fewster hadn't moved. "I thought perhaps he might have been hypnotized by the ball, and I have heard of such instances," he said. "The batter getting his eyes fixed on the ball seems to be fascinated by it, like a bird before a snake, and can't seem to make up his mind to move until it is too late."

Also dropped from the team was Ping Bodie, who had become expendable with Ruth in the lineup. The quotable outfielder had requested a leave after receiving a telegram asking that he get home immediately to Hoboken for a family emergency. Huggins didn't think the issue was important enough for Bodie to leave, but Ping hopped on the 3:45 P.M.

train for New York anyway, and the manager booted him off the team. "If his personal affairs are more important than business, I don't want him," a seething Huggins told reporters that night back at the Burbridge. "He will never be seen in a New York uniform again."

Despite hitting the "old apple" at a .400 clip, Bodie was never much of a Huggins man anyway. The two had clashed back in 1919 after Huggins had pulled him from a game for missing a fly ball, and hard feelings had remained.

The Yankees were beaten again the next day by the Dodgers, this time 2–0. The Yanks managed only four hits, two from Duffy Lewis, playing his first game since the trip from California. At least the unfortunate Fewster injury cleared up the picture at third, where Meusel, a versatile fielder and about the only Yankee who was hitting, became an immediate fixture. "He is a player I have to get into my club somewhere," Huggins said of the young California slugger. "Meusel is the kind of player who will hit much better later on. He is a long-distance slugger, and by the time we get back North, he will murder [the ball]."

Huggins had both perspective and a solid knowledge of the use of spin control. Recognizing his players were staying out to all hours, he imposed a curfew to get them more focused and demanded they make an appearance in the breakfast room before 9 A.M. each morning. But to reporters, he presented a sunny picture, giving the impression that a few losses were mere bumps in the road. So instead of getting annoyed at the five straight losses to Brooklyn, he said he was happy that his ballclub was facing good pitching, adding it would help them when the big-league season kicked off in April. "There is a tendency to take these things too seriously," he said. "Yet I would rather lose and have the men get good pitching than win because the other team played poor baseball. Batting against these pitchers is giving the Yankees all kinds of practice. By the time we start the season, we will be ready for any kind of pitching—speed, curve-ball pitching, and everything."

Huggins's actions were shrewd, for immediately the Yankees started playing to their ability. Pipp returned to the lineup, and Lewis was working himself into condition, as was the sore-armed incumbent shortstop, Roger Peckinpaugh. Even the skies were brightening, with the temperature hitting a comfortable, dry 80 degrees and allowing the Yanks to have full practice sessions. Said Huston, his mood matching the climate: "There is every reason to believe that we have a strong club."

On March 27, when Pipp cracked a triple off Rube Marquard in the first that drove Sammy Vick home, it marked the first time the Yankees had scored in 24 innings off Dodger pitching. Pipp also scored, which gave Ernie Shore a cushion to pitch four scoreless innings and help the Yanks to a satisfying 3–1 win. Shore's performance, supported by Shawkey, who gave up one run in five innings, underscored what was emerging as the Yanks' overlooked strength: pitching.

The team's roll continued. Monday, March 28, was a glorious day at Southside Park and marked what was thought to be the first major-league spring-training doubleheader. The opener featured the Yanks against the Reds, with Brooklyn taking on Walter Johnson's Washington Americans in the nightcap. Jacksonville was giddy with excitement, and to help pack the stands on a Monday afternoon, Mayor John Martin gave city employees the day off, and urged business owners to close shop as well.

"I truly feel there is but one satisfactory and convincing way for our people to show their sense of obligation," Martin wrote in an open letter in the *Times-Union*, "and that is to overflow the grand stand and bleachers [so] that ground rules will have to be adopted, and even the blasé and sophisticated reporters of the great daily papers of the 'Big Towns' North will sit up and take notice. Knowing the great value in advertising and other material benefits secured for this city by its selection each year as a training camp by major league ball clubs, I feel that this is the proper time for our people to show their appreciation."

They had built it, so they came—some 4,800 squeezed into the park that Monday, paying $2 for a box seat, $1.50 for the grandstand, and $1 for the bleachers. They saw an entertaining opener featuring 15 runs, 26 base hits, and three home runs from Yankee bats—Meusel sending the team's first of the spring out of the park in the second. And though Ruth didn't go long, he doubled in the ninth and scored the winning run on Lewis's two-bagger. The final: New York 8, Reds 7.

Spoiling the sudden optimism was one unfortunate bit of business—a threatened player strike against the $1,000 share earned by the Yanks for their third-place finish in 1919. In doling out the funds, Huggins had allotted shares to the team's groundskeeper, trainer, two assistant secretaries, and two former Yanks traded the previous season to Boston, a decision met by shrieks of protest from the other players, who argued they deserved the whole wad.

Their ultimatum reached the boiling point before game time at the Burbridge when Del Pratt, Shawkey, and Peckinpaugh cornered Huston and Ruppert, saying they represented the players, who wouldn't play that day unless the finances were refigured to give each of them another $70. The owners were appalled, particularly at Pratt, the ringleader, but they relented and paid the extra allotments from their own pockets. But the incident left bruised feelings all around. "[They] didn't make much of a hit with the fans at home when this piker conduct became known," wrote Vila in a *Sporting News* dispatch that sounded like a talk-radio rant of today. "But the selfishness of the men wasn't strange in view of the characteristic greediness of their profession in general."

Pratt was said to be on his way out the door. But the irony was that Fewster's beaning had left the Yankees in need of dependable infield help, so he stuck. A former baseball and football captain at the University of Alabama, Pratt was a 10-year major-league veteran with a track record as a steady hitter, solid glove man around second base, and a hothead. He joined the St. Louis Browns in 1911, hit .302, but ran into trouble when Browns' owner Phil Ball accused Pratt and teammate Doc Lavan of laziness and throwing games. The players sued and the case was settled, but their futures were elsewhere, with Lavan unloaded to Washington, and Pratt, in 1918, becoming a Yankee. Pratt couldn't get along with Huggins either, and although the Yankee manager benched him for a spell in 1919, the infielder still played in all but 14 games and batted .292.

Maybe the excitement got to Ruth, for on April 1, he pounded his first home run of the spring—a two-run, first-inning shot over the center-field fence, 415 feet away, off Al Mamaux. "Hitting a ball out of the lot here is a feat which could be done only by Ruth," the *Times* reported. "No other man in baseball could have lifted a ball that far." The home run, which helped the Yankees to a 6–2 win over Brooklyn, their third straight, was immediately dissected by newspapermen, who dutifully reported that the drive would have also cleared the center-field wall at the Polo Grounds, 385 feet from home plate.

The Yanks beat the Dodgers again on April 3, 2–1, in the final game in Jacksonville before the two teams packed up for their traditional Pullman trip back north, which featured five more tune-up games against one another in Columbia, Greenville, and Chester, South Carolina; Winston-Salem, North Carolina; and Lynchburg, Virginia, followed by two more back home at Ebbets Field in Brooklyn.

How wonderful it was for the fans in small Southern towns to enjoy an exotic dose of big-league baseball. Visit small towns in the South today and you'll still meet old-timers who remember the big day when commerce stopped and the mill shut early so everyone could head to the ballpark to watch the big leaguers, and if they got lucky, see the Babe crack one, and maybe catch a glimpse of him close-up at the railroad station.

Playing before overflow crowds in rickety little ballparks did more than create warm memories that lasted a lifetime, however. In Columbia, South Carolina, the cold weather, a steady sandstorm, and a hard, rocky infield caused managers Huggins and Robinson to take out their first-stringers after only a few innings to keep everyone healthy. Maybe the sand clogged the Yankees' arms and legs—they lost 9–3. "Small boys ran around barefooted and apparently enjoyed the climate," Runyon wrote. "Naturally, it was the coldest day of the Spring. . . . Not infrequently it is the coldest day in 20 years. That fellow wasn't around today however."

The Yankees lost again the next day in Greenville, but won in Chester, thanks to Ruth's double and a triple. The Babe did himself better in Winston-Salem, where, with Shore pitching strongly in a 3–0 win before 5,000 of his hometown comrades, he crushed perhaps the longest double in baseball history. In the sixth, Ruth's slam cleared the center-field fence, kept going, and landed at a nearby racetrack some 600 feet away. But because people were ringing the field, the umpires specified before game time that all balls hit into the crowd would be two-baggers; umpire Bill Dinneen called Ruth back to second after the blast. Ruth argued, but a rule was a rule, and he went back to second, scoring a minute later on Duffy Lewis's single. "[But] this ball did not go into the crowd," Runyon wrote. "It went away beyond it. . . . It was longer than a peace treaty. It carried farther than Al Mamaux's singing voice. If you don't think this is far, ask the top-floor tenants when Al is singing in a hotel lobby."

The Yankees and Dodgers wended their way north. In Lynchburg, Pratt homered, Ruth and Lewis smashed triples, and the Yanks won, 6–2. Back home and playing at Ebbets Field for the final two games, the two teams traded wins—Brooklyn winning 3–2 in 13 innings and the Yankees pounding the Dodgers in the last spring game, 11–0, in an afternoon most notable for how many of the 16,000 Brooklynites there heckled the Babe all day, particularly in the fourth when Al Mamaux caught the big guy on a called third strike. But as Ruth was prone to do, he rose to the moment—rifling a triple in his next at-bat and finishing with two hits and three runs.

Has any other player ever created that level of intense excitement—by striking out? Probably not. No wonder baseball fever was so high in New York, and not just with the Yankees, but with the surprising Dodgers and John McGraw's pitching-heavy Giants too. "At no time since New York was first represented by three teams in the major league pennant races have all three been held so highly," the *Times* opined. As for the Yankees, "this 1920 aggregation has plenty of color, which other Yankee teams have lacked," the paper continued. "It has the most powerful array of hitters ever gathered on one Yankee team, and its pitching staff ranks with the best. . . . The pitching staff had no Carl Mays a year ago this time and there was no Babe Ruth to strengthen the attack. Pennants have been won by teams that did not carry the strength of the 1920 Yankees, and this might be their year."

FOUR

"A Sofa Cushion on Grant's Tomb"

Play Ball!

Miller Huggins wasn't catching much of a break on the evening of his team's scheduled season opener, set for Wednesday, April 14, at Shibe Park against the Philadelphia A's. He and his team were facing numerous problems, starting with another in a series of labor stoppages that had been plaguing the country since the end of World War I. In this case, an outlaw railroad strike, which Attorney General A. Mitchell Palmer blamed on the Industrial Workers of the World as part of an international Communist conspiracy, postponed departure of the Yankee train, forcing secretary Harry Sparrow to quickly find other accommodations. So instead, the players, many grumbling loudly at the situation, piled into day coaches and left earlier than expected—5 P.M. Tuesday—to make sure they reached Philadelphia in time. The team even took the extra precaution of hiring 12 autos and a baggage truck to stand by if they couldn't catch a coach. But they did, and the Yankee traveling party checked into the Aldine Hotel in Philadelphia that evening.

Complicating Huggins's burden was Carl Mays, who after all of nine months as a Yankee was proving to be a player with baggage. Mays stayed behind in New York because of an outstanding warrant for his arrest dating to May 1919, when as a member of the Red Sox he had been accused of hurling a baseball into the Shibe Park stands that clocked a city official named Bryan Hayes. Hayes, a customs official and boxing instructor, had been sitting behind the Boston dugout, where people were rooting for the Sox by banging loudly on the dugout roof, when Mays suddenly leapt out of the dugout and hurled a ball at the fans. The ball grazed a woman's head, and then struck Hayes, puncturing his straw hat and leaving him dazed. He wasn't badly hurt—fortunately, his hat had absorbed most of the impact—but the incident angered him. After the game, won by Boston 6–4, he lodged a complaint at the A's office. Connie Mack pleaded with him not to take legal action, but Hayes wasn't listening: he went to the local police station, where a warrant was issued, but Mays and the Red Sox had already left town.

In the interim, things hadn't improved much for the A's. After three A.L. pennants in five years, the last in 1914, the A's had sold off their best and brightest and headed right to the sewer, finishing dead last for five years straight. Even so, the privilege of seeing Babe Ruth in his Yankee regular-season debut drew 12,000 fans, many of whom wore heavy coats and furs to fight off temperatures in the 40s.

At least the A's looked sharp, thanks to spiffy new home uniforms with blue pinstripes and the famous blue elephant, previously on the left sleeve, but now on the left breast. The elephant replaced the large *A* that had been there since they had started play back in 1901. And on the mound for the Philadelphias was Scott Perry, so coveted by Connie Mack that he'd gone to court to protect the right-hander after buying him from the Boston Braves in 1918. Perry somehow scraped together 21 wins that season (21–19) for an A's team that won all of 52 games, prompting the Braves to claim he still belonged to them. The case dragged into the courts, and with Ban Johnson's help, Mack won. But in 1919, Perry had dropped to 4–17.

Huggins countered with Bob Shawkey, the Yankee ace. Elsewhere, the lineup was set, with Wally Pipp at first, Del Pratt at second, Roger Peckinpaugh at short, Bob Meusel at third, Muddy Ruel catching, Duffy Lewis in left, and Ruth in center. Playing right and leading off was the rookie left-handed hitter Frank Gleich, coming off an impressive spring and replacing Bodie, still suspended. Meusel was at third to replace Aaron Ward, out with a knee injury, and would move to the outfield later in the regular season. All in all, it was a solid but not yet great team that, bolstered by veterans and infused with some new blood, could have a shot at the first Yankee pennant.

As in Brooklyn, Ruth was the draw for many of the Philadelphia fans, particularly the leather-lunged ones. Hitting fourth, the Babe stepped to the plate in the first inning following a solo home run from Wally Pipp, the first Yankee in 15 years to hit a homer on Opening Day. The partisans greeted Ruth with cries of "Pipp's crabbing your act, Babe," "He's stealing your stuff," and "You haven't got a hit in your bag." But Ruth fooled them, slashing a single to right in his first Yankee at-bat. But the hit was wasted when A's pitcher Scott Perry fanned the next hitter, Duffy Lewis, for the third out.

With the Yanks still hanging onto a 1–0 lead in the fourth, Ruth batted again with the fans screaming for a strikeout. This time, he obliged them, stranding Pipp on second. Then, in the bottom of the eighth with the score tied at 1–1 and Philadelphia runners on second and third with one gone, the A's Joe Dugan lifted a routine fly ball to center, and it appeared at first as though Shawkey was working himself out of trouble. But, drifting back to make the catch, Ruth dropped the ball. The two base runners scored easily and the A's jumped ahead 3–1 to the glee of the fans. The score held up and the 1920 Yankees had started the season on a gloomy note. As for Ruth, his error pointed to perhaps his only flaw that season—fielding. The Babe spent most of 1920 in right field (although he still played in center occasionally), and his 19 errors that season led American League right fielders; it would be the most errors he'd ever commit in a single season. Two years later Ruth had cut his errors in half.

The next afternoon, with home plate umpire Dick Nallin set to yell "Play ball!" a small boy appeared at home plate with a large hatbox with ribbons, and informed those present that he had a gift for "Mr. Ruth."

Nallin called time, and called for the Babe. The dugouts emptied and both teams gathered around home plate, and many of the 8,000 fans stood to see what was happening. Ruth delicately removed the ribbons and twine, opened the box, and removed a brown derby, the gift of a Philadelphia hatter named Fred Mackin. The gesture, a symbol of the era for making a big mistake, wasn't lost on anyone.

Ruth could have been miffed. Instead, he grinned broadly and lifted his new hat, about seven sizes too small, to the top of his head, "where it reposed like a sofa cushion on Grant's Tomb," the *Times* reported. His magnanimous acceptance of the gag won the fans over, and the insults that had met him the day before quickly became cheers. Mackin even became a friend of Ruth's in time. The episode didn't help him on the field, however, and the big slugger went hitless in five at-bats, striking out three times, including in the seventh with the bases loaded. But thanks to a double and a triple from the hot-hitting Pipp, and five innings of one-hit ball from 35-year-old Jack Quinn, the Yanks won anyway, 4–1. So despite everything, Huggins had the season's first win.

Then it rained, postponing the series' last two games, and the Yankees pushed off to Boston, where they were rejoined by Carl Mays for a Patriots' Day doubleheader against the Red Sox at Fenway Park. While much of the razzing of Ruth in Philadelphia had been good-natured, Red Sox fans cheered the Babe—preserving their venom for Mays, the player who had ditched them less than a year before.

Following the custom, the doubleheader was a morning-afternoon affair with separate admissions charged for each game. Only 6,000 fans showed for the first game, taken by the Red Sox, 6–0, behind Waite Hoyt. Hoyt gave up only five hits, two to Ruth, and the Sox scored two in the third and iced the game with another four in the sixth off George Mogridge.

But the opportunity to hurl abuse at Mays, set to pitch game two, attracted 22,000 for the afternoon. Happily for Boston, the Yankee right-hander hadn't pitched for a week, and the lack of work was telling. He had trouble getting loose and was erratic, giving up hits in bunches before Huggins lifted him after seven, with the fans jeering him as he left the field. The Yanks lost 8–3, and lost again the next day, 3–2, when the Sox scored two in the bottom of the ninth off Bob Shawkey. After five games, the Yankees were 1–4, and Ruth, although he was hitting for average, was suffering a power drought. Headed to New York for the home opener against the A's, the Yankees were a team in need of a jolt.

"Usual Ceremonies Mark Inaugural Program," the *Times* dryly noted in the headline announcing the Yankees' April 18 home opener at the Polo Grounds. But for New Yorkers, tired of a long winter without baseball and anxious to gaze at Babe Ruth in pinstripes, the home opener's pomp was fun. With memories of the Great War painfully fresh, most of the pregame ritual involved soldiers, as U.S. Army Lt. Gen. Robert Bullard, who led the First Division in France, threw out the first ball. Elsewhere in the ballpark, flags flew, John George Frank's 60-piece band entertained, and 25,000 fans got down to the business of seeing what Ruth could do.

It hardly mattered that the day was overcast, chilly, and damp. Opening Day always drew a healthy crowd—virtually all of whom took the subway to reach the quirky, horseshoe-shaped showcase of a big-league ballpark fashioned back in 1891 to wedge into a plot of land between the rocky crevice of Coogan's Bluff and the banks of the Harlem River in northern Manhattan. Modernized by Giants owner John T. Brush after a devastating fire in 1911—this time with steel and concrete—the park held 38,000, with several hundred more likely to watch the game from atop the bluff.

Riding the 3rd Avenue elevated train, known as the "El," cost a nickel. It dropped off its cargo at 155th Street, its last stop and a block's walk from the ballpark. The dark-green wooden subway, with its open windows and long, thin seats, was surprisingly efficient—whisking riders from deep in the bowels of Grand Central Terminal on 42nd Street in Midtown the more than five miles uptown in all of 12 minutes.

Some fans bought tickets from the speculators yelling for attention just outside the ballpark's entrance. Most were content to line up at the ticket windows abutting the steep, rocky hillside just beyond the plaza in back of home plate. In February, the baseball magnates had not only raised ticket prices, but made them uniform in all big-league parks: $1 for the grandstand, 75 cents for the upper deck or pavilion, and 50 cents for the bleachers.

Once in the park, spectators had plenty of chances for further spending on items such as scorecards, available for a nickel from young boys strolling through the stands. The invention of Harry Stevens, a Scottish immigrant turned Polo Grounds superstar vendor, scorecards were made of crude stock paper, displayed the batting order for both teams, and had room for scoring the game and a whole slew of ads for products like Beeman's Original Pepsin Gum ("Good for Digestion") and Chesterfield cigarettes ("Sold on the Ground"). Scorecards really helped fans follow the game, with players still a decade or so away from wearing uniform numbers. In 1929, the Yankees would become the first big-league team to don numbers.

Despite the weather, things were looking spiffy indeed around the ballpark—they always did on Opening Day. One incongruity of sorts was that the coats of arms that lined the top of the Polo Grounds grandstand did not even include the Yankees. Each of the National League teams were represented instead—the Giants as well as the Brooklyn Dodgers, Philadelphia Phillies, Boston Braves, Pittsburgh Pirates, Chicago Cubs, Cincinnati Reds, and St. Louis Cardinals. The Yankees were merely the tenants of New York's National Leaguers.

Head groundskeeper Henry Fabian's lush green field was considered baseball's finest. It matched the color of the pea-green outfield walls aligned in an array of dimensions—only 279 feet to left and a cozy 256 feet to right, but a mammoth 483 feet to center—that gave the ballpark the look and feel of a lopsided horseshoe. Not that the size of the field really mattered all that much before 1920. Prior to Ruth, few players were capable of consistently hitting a ball that far.

The Polo Grounds featured other oddities, like an immense amount of foul territory, making it in the tradition of the dead-ball era a true pitcher's park. Both bullpens were in fair territory, in left-center and right-center field. The outfield was slightly sunken so that a manager, standing in the dugout, could see only the top half of his outfielders. Already, fans were buzzing about the short distance to the right-field fence, which seemed to suit Ruth's powerful uppercut left-handed swing, the one he fashioned after Shoeless Joe Jackson's. Also helping Ruth was the upper deck's overhang in right, which enabled high fly balls hit, say, 240 feet or so, to be home runs.

Like Ruth himself, the Polo Grounds was big, brassy, and loud. Right up to game time, trains constantly screeched to the stop outside, depositing more passengers before rumbling back south for more. Vendors brashly hawked Stevens's hot dogs, once called hot "dachshunds," but given their current name by Runyon's pal, the witty newspaper cartoonist Tad Dorgan. Unfortunately, those hot dogs generally arrived at a spectator's seat not wrapped in paper or foil and passed along by hand. The only drink available was watered-down orange soda.

The pavilion seats offered spectators a decent view of the landscape beyond the outfield—the steel girders of the MaCombs Dam Bridge over the Harlem River, and beyond that, the emerging riverfront industry of the South Bronx. And every seat had a good view of the oversized left-field scoreboard, which provided scores of the other big-league games through numbers that young boys put into slots, each corresponding to an inning.

From the get-go, Ruth was anxious to impress. Descending a flight of stairs from the center-field clubhouse and heading to the batting cage for pregame swings, Ruth acknowledged the smattering of applause that greeted him. The Babe was easily recognizable adorned in the crisp, white uniform with blue pinstripes and navy-blue cap with the interlocking "NY" in which owners Ruppert and Huston had outfitted the Yankees since 1916.

But trying to slam offerings from Rip Collins into the outfield grand-stand in batting practice, the Babe swung savagely and missed, with the force twisting him completely around. Ruth's bat dropped with a thud and the big slugger's hands clutched his right side, where he had badly torn a muscle inside his rib cage. Stepping behind the batting screen, Ruth dropped to one knee and was escorted by teammates to the dugout, where trainer Doc Woods massaged his rib cage. Ruth went back to bat again, but after one swing sat down. He started the game anyway, and in his first at-bat sent two foul balls down the first-base line off the A's Rollie Naylor, before swinging and striking out.

That was that for the Babe's debut as a Yankee at the Polo Grounds. After the inning, Frank Gleich ran out to center field, and Ruth, leaning on catcher Truck Hannah's shoulder, limped off toward the center-field clubhouse. "How do you like that?" said a disappointed fan. "I come all the way from Red Hook and they take him out five minutes after the game starts." The crowd cheered Ruth anyway as he left the field, and he smiled. Thank goodness for Duffy Lewis, who had followed Ruth's strikeout with a single, driving in Pipp. It got the Yanks going, and behind Quinn and three hits from Meusel, they took a sloppy 8–6 game.

"If this isn't hard luck, what is it?" wrote Joe Vila in the *Sporting News.* "The Yankees' owners had been patiently waiting for Ruth's appearance at the Polo Grounds for the purpose of getting back some of the dough paid to the Red Sox for [Ruth's] release. . . . The old Hoodoo, however, spoiled everything, and now the Yankees' followers are disconsolate. Baker in retirement; Fewster probably disabled for the rest of the year, if not permanently; Aaron Ward suffering with water on the knee; Ruth under the watchful eye of the surgeons! Can you beat it? And yet some of the croakers are trying to blame Miller Huggins, who, they say, isn't a real manager."

Doctors said Ruth would be out as many as 10 days. So Huggins considered his options—use the untested Gleich in center, or bring back Bodie, "Ping the Prodigal," as the newspapers had taken to calling him. He chose Bodie, suspended for a month now, and the decision paid immediate dividends. That Saturday against the A's, showing no ill effects from his inactivity, Bodie sent a screaming triple in the third to deep right center at the Polo Grounds, delighting the 17,000 partisans. He scored a minute later on Muddy Ruel's single. In the tenth, Bodie walked and then lumbered home on a single from Sammy Vick to win it for the Yanks, 3–2. Even with Ruth gone, this one was a satisfying win: Mays went the distance for his first victory of the season, and Aaron Ward, back from a bum knee, went hitless but secured the Yankee infield's left side. Having the dependable Peckinpaugh at short and Ward back at third sent Meusel back to right field, where he belonged.

Ruth recovered quickly. Closing out the A's series Sunday with Shawkey taking a 2–1 loss, the team continued its homestand Monday by taking on Washington with the Babe making an odd but significant contribution to a ninth-inning rally to steal the game. Down 2–1, Meusel and Bodie opened the ninth with consecutive singles, at which point Huggins cut loose with some serious maneuvering: from his third-base coaching box, he signaled for the Babe to approach the plate to pinch-hit for Ruel. The move did more than send the intimate Polo Grounds gathering of 6,000 into a demonstration of joy; it was clearly meant to rattle Senators pitcher Eric Erickson. After a practice swing, Huggins sent Ruth back and brought up Ruel with orders to sacrifice the two base runners ahead. But Ruel popped up, sending the Babe back to the plate, this time hitting for pitcher Herb Thormahlen. The big slugger swung and missed at the first pitch, but crashed the next one to deep left center, where it was caught by Sam Rice, but advanced the two runners. Ward then walked, loading the bases, and with Peckinpaugh batting next, Washington catcher Patsy Gharrity tried nailing Bodie at second but threw the ball wildly into center, bringing home Meusel with the tying run.

Peckinpaugh then walked on four pitches, again filling the bases. Pipp followed with a line shot to shortstop, which Senators rookie Jim O'Neill speared but then dropped. O'Neill threw to second for the force, but Peckinpaugh was safe at the bag, and Bodie ran home with the winner: 3–2 Yankees.

Two straight games postponed by rain gave Ruth more time to recover. That Thursday, Walter Johnson stopped the Yankees 2–1, limiting Ruth to a single and everyone else to four hits. A single was it for Ruth the next day as well against Boston, as Waite Hoyt mastered the Yanks again, 4–2, dealing Mays his second loss.

With the Yanks closing out April with a 4–7 record, scribes were wondering when the team, and particularly Ruth, would get on track. On Saturday, May 1, the Babe answered, finally, with his first home run of the season—a monstrous shot off Herb Pennock on the first pitch of the sixth. The ball carried completely out of the Polo Grounds, 30 feet over the right-field stands, and landed in a nearby field. Only one other batsman, Joe Jackson, was thought to have hit a ball out of the park.

It was a "mighty homer," W. O. McGeehan declared in the *Tribune*, not to mention "somewhat reassuring in view of the fact that the morbid-minded were inclined to believe that the 'Babe' might have lost his wallop after the injuries received on opening day."

The home run, the 50th of Ruth's career, rattled Pennock, who gave up a home run to the next batter, Duffy Lewis, which sailed over the left-field wall and helped to ice a 6–0 Yankee win. It also had the curious effect of actually calming the team, several of whom—Mays, Shore, and Frank O'Doul—were all tossed in the fifth for jawing at Dick Nallin, their old umpiring friend for whom Ruth had displayed his brown derby. The guilty three were angry at the narrow strike zone granted to Bob Shawkey, who somehow survived and went the distance in pitching a four-hitter for his first win of 1920.

After the Yankees traded wins with Boston the next two days, during which Ruth connected for his second home run of the season, the Yankee bench jockeys decided to give the umpires a run for their money. But this time, Dick Nallin had a novel idea of how to handle it. On May 4 in the series' final game, a 6–1 Yankee win, with things skimming along at 1–1 in the fifth, the umpire, upon hearing one comment too many from the Yankee bench, summoned Huggins. "The fans thought he was going to wish him a Merry Christmas," joked the *Times*. Instead, Nallin ordered Huggins to clear the bench of all the team's substitutes. So before a bemused Red Sox infield, 10 Yankee players marched en masse across the field and toward the center-field clubhouse. After that, the dugout's only inhabitants in addition to the Yankee starters were Huggins, coach Charley O'Leary, and trainer Doc Woods.

Among those who remained in the game was starting pitcher Jack Quinn, who gave up a lone run on only five hits for his third win. With the Yankees still struggling, the 35-year-old veteran right-hander was emerging as not just the team's most effective starting pitcher, but its glue. By the time May was done and the Yankees had turned the corner, Quinn had won four more.

Jack Quinn was an improbable star. At 6 feet and weighing nearly 200 pounds, Quinn was husky, broad-shouldered, and, by using very little motion in his delivery to the plate, seldom injured. Steady and with good control of his low-breaking spitball, he gave up only a few home runs and owed his longevity to a strong physique, hard work, and clean living.

Quinn was a native of eastern Pennsylvania, where he worked in the coal mines as a boy. Leaving his native Pottsville by hopping aboard a train, he traveled to western Pennsylvania, where he sat down on the edge of the woods to watch a semipro game. When the ball was hit out to where Quinn was sitting, he ran it down and heaved it, like a big leaguer, all the way back to the center of the diamond. Intrigued, the team's manager walked toward the stranger with the live arm, asking what position he played.

"I told him I was a pitcher," Quinn said, and just like that, he was on the team representing the hamlet of Dunbar, near Pittsburgh, and pitching that afternoon. Quinn won the game, earned $5 for his efforts, and became a semipro pitcher, while working on the side as a blacksmith.

Years later, Quinn was still telling that story, turning it into a tale that was more like *Tom Sawyer* meets *Field of Dreams*. "I had to fight to make my way," he said. "I got help from no one. I started out with only a dirty, ragged, unmatched suit of clothes to my back, a tattered hat, a strong pair of soles on my shoes and my two fists."

In 1907, Quinn entered organized ball with Macon of the South Atlantic League. A year later, he joined Richmond of the Virginia League and ran up a spectacular record—pitching 16 complete games and winning 14 without a loss. The other two were ties.

Taking notice, the Yankees, then called the Highlanders, signed him, and in 1909, Quinn went 9–5 in his big-league debut season. Quinn's performance was a pleasant surprise to the front office, but was as welcome as a plague to his teammates, who saw him as a threat to their jobs. "But I looked at them . . . and I knew I had as much stuff as they had," Quinn said. "So I hustled to make good. The players wouldn't let me be friendly with them for several months, but I didn't care a hang."

It was Quinn's first stint as a New Yorker, and he stayed four years—going 49–35, including an 18–12 record in 1910. Still, the Highlanders released him in 1912. A New York newspaper, in covering the transaction, reported Quinn wasn't 28 but 42, and that he had been let go because of his advanced years. Quinn saw an opportunity, and in all the baseball stops he made thereafter—with both Boston teams; the Baltimore Terps of the Federal League; the White Sox; Vernon, California; Rochester; the Yankees again; and the Philadelphia A's—he refused to give his age, adding an element of good-natured mystery to his durability. All the while, he just kept pitching, rejoining the Yanks again at Huggins's request in 1919, when he went 15–14.

All those years in the game had made Quinn a creature of habit. After each season, he always returned to eastern Pennsylvania and hiked the mountains to build up his legs. Then for several weeks before spring training, he'd head to Hot Springs to begin working himself into baseball condition. Jack Quinn's routine wouldn't change until he finally retired from baseball at 48 after 23 seasons in the big leagues.

On Sunday, May 9, Jack Quinn lumbered to the mound at Griffith Park in Washington with his team in a funk. The Yankees started their short five-game road trip to Washington coming off Quinn's last performance— the circus-like victory over the Red Sox five days before, which had finally put them above .500. But the Senators promptly throttled the Yanks, taking three of four, with the only New York win an inexplicable 7–1 shellacking of Walter Johnson.

If the team seemed distracted, they had a good excuse. At 6 P.M. that Thursday, Harry Sparrow, the team's popular, hardworking business manager, closed his office door at the Yankee headquarters on East 42nd Street and went home. Early the following morning, he was found dead in his sleep at home on West 127th Street, the victim of a heart attack brought on by influenza and pneumonia.

The 45-year-old Sparrow had been more than the man responsible for stocking the baseballs in the trainer's room. He was a New York sports fixture who had started as a concessionaire at Sheepshead Bay racetrack, and through a friendship with John McGraw became business manager of the memorable 1913 around-the-world tour of the Giants and White Sox. In 1915, Sparrow latched onto the Yanks in a similar role, and quickly established himself as Ruppert's detail guy. But it was his jovial, outgoing personality and beautiful tenor voice that people remembered most about Sparrow, and stamped him as a Runyonesque figure known at the racetrack, along Broadway, and throughout baseball.

So on May 9, the day that funeral services were held for Sparrow back in New York, Quinn got the tall order of trying to get his team back on track against Washington, facing Walter Johnson and the Senators. Once again, he delivered.

Luckily, Johnson was not yet himself, giving up 13 hits, including 3 each to Peckinpaugh and Pratt, a wild pitch, and only four strikeouts. Meanwhile, Quinn was himself—unflashy but good enough to get the job done, giving up 10 hits and walking only one in eight and two-thirds innings. The difference came with the score tied 1–1 in the fifth, when the Yanks clumped together three runs with a single, a Senator error, another single, and some more sloppy fielding by the Senators. The 5–3 final made for Quinn's fourth win, and a good way to finish up as the Yankees headed home for a long 15-game homestand against the cream of the American League: Chicago and the first-place Indians, along with St. Louis and Detroit. Two games under .500, and already a distant sixth, it was time for the Yanks to get into the race.

Chicago White Sox owner Charles Comiskey called his team the greatest ever assembled. He had a point, even though the heavily favored Sox had been inexplicably and soundly trounced by the Reds in the 1919 World Series, prompting immediate whispers that they might not have played to their best. True, the White Sox came to the Polo Grounds weaker than the 1919 team that had taken the A.L. flag—first baseman Chick Gandil had retired—but they still had a collection of talent that was the envy of baseball.

Second by a nose to Boston in 1916, the White Sox had won it all in 1917, breaking the Red Sox's string of two straight championships by beating the Giants in a six-game World Series. After an off year in the war year of 1918, when the Sox lost several stars to military service and the team dropped to sixth, Comiskey replaced manager Pants Rowland with Kid Gleason, the wily veteran of the baseball wars. Gleason, with 20 years' experience as a big-league pitcher and second baseman, and six more as a Sox coach, was tough but fair, a man respected by his players and the glue that guided them to the A.L. pennant in 1919.

The Sox had jumped to an early A.L. lead in 1920, thanks to their all-star lineup. Playing second was the slick-fielding Eddie Collins, the finest infielder of the generation. At third was Ruth's friend Buck Weaver, a career .300 hitter and a fielder of extraordinary range and quickness. In the outfield was the incomparable Shoeless Joe Jackson, celebrated as perhaps the game's greatest natural hitter, and Happy Felsch, fast, a solid fielder, and a lifetime .290 hitter. Their pitching staff featured balance—veteran spitballers Red Faber and Eddie Cicotte, along with hard-throwing left-hander Claud Williams and their wisp of a lefty, Dickie Kerr, who had come from nowhere in 1919 to go 13–7 and win two games in the Series.

It was enough to worry Joe Vila, even in May. "Huggins' men, having failed to mop up the earth with the Red Sox, Athletics and Washingtons, now will be subjected to a real test," he wrote in the *Sporting News*. "If they can't win a majority of the coming games in Harlem with the White Sox, Clevelands, Browns and Tigers what will happen to them [after the home-stand] when they go West?"

FIVE

"The Most Alarming Menace"

Ruth and the Yanks Hit Their Stride

On Wednesday, May 12, the 15,000 spectators at the Polo Grounds had barely taken their seats before the Babe, batting cleanup in the first, clocked rookie Roy Wilkinson with a towering smash into the right-field bleachers. Pipp was on first, and the Yanks were ahead 2–0. Ruth's home run was only the second to ever reach that part of the big ballpark, and it sent a bleacher mob of several hundred on a mad scramble for the souvenir—hauled in by a freckle-faced kid who quickly got to his feet and bolted from the park with his prize. "He is probably the happiest lad in town," the *Times* figured, "and will make all the kids in his neighborhood jealous when they hear about it."

The newspaper was half right: the happiest person in town at that moment was probably Miller Huggins, who was already having to defend his team against accusations that they were overrated. In the third, Ruth tripled to center field to spark another two-run Yankee rally, lending further credence to the idea that this was a team that had just gotten off to a slow start. Then, in the fourth, in his third at-bat, Ruth homered again, this time off Dickie Kerr, for his fourth of the season. The solo shot followed a home run by Peckinpaugh and gave the Yanks enough to win 6–5, behind a shaky Carl Mays. "Ruth cost the Yanks $125,000," the *Times* wrote. "If he has many days like [this one], he will bring that much into the doctors' pockets treating laryngitis patients."

The next afternoon, the Babe smacked another home run, his fifth. This one, in the fourth off Claud Williams, landed barely fair in the upper deck of right field. At the time it was a big home run because it tied the score at 4 and contributed to an all-out Yankee slugfest that included 20 hits—

4 from catcher Truck Hannah and 3 each from Ward, Meusel, and Lewis. It hardly mattered that pitcher Bob Shawkey wasn't sharp; the Yanks cruised to a 14–8 win, their season record reaching .500 for the first time since mid-April.

The Yanks were heating up with the weather, and the turnstiles were clicking. That Saturday, following two rainouts against the White Sox, 25,000 were at the Polo Grounds for the Yankees' first meeting of the season with Cleveland and its outstanding three-time 20-game winner and spitballer Stanley Coveleski. But if the Yanks were winning the slugfests, they were proving they could win the close ones, too, thanks to the steady hand of Jack Quinn.

It was Quinn's turn, and, as expected, he and Coveleski matched not just spitballs but zeros. In a game of control pitching and crisp fielding, the two starters matched zeros through seven innings. In the eighth, the Indians' Doc Johnson finally touched up Quinn, sending a double to left center and taking third on Steve O'Neill's groundout. But when Jack Graney rifled a low liner toward left center, the ball was speared in a sensational stop by Ward, playing short for the injured Peckinpaugh, out since midweek after being drilled on the shoulder in batting practice. Ward then wheeled to third and threw out Graney, which held Johnson and preserved the shutout.

With the game still scoreless in the ninth, Bodie singled, and up stepped Quinn. He took two quick strikes, and then lofted the next pitch toward the right-field seats, a ball that seemed to drift and drift until it disappeared into the corner seats for a home run and an improbable 2–0 Yankee win.

Quinn's surprise walk-off home run—he would hit eight in a 23-year career—toppled the Indians from first place and went a long way toward erasing evidence of the old Yankee hoodoo. "Something like that was bound to happen to a team that takes a game on a home run by a pitcher," mused Tris Speaker, the Indians' center fielder.

The Yankees were hot, and New York was taking notice. On Sunday, May 15, a throng of 38,600 squeezed into the Polo Grounds to see Carl Mays try to get back on track against the Indians' Jim Bagby. It was the largest crowd ever to see a game at the stately old park, bringing the attendance total for the four-game homestand to 90,000, and causing Yankee officials to raise the fire curtains in center field for the first time all year.

Those who made it into the park were the lucky ones. The scene was reminiscent of the memorable 1908 mob that descended on the park to see the Giants and Christy Mathewson take on the Cubs in a playoff game. A half hour before the game's 3 P.M. start, the Yankee front office announced that the game was sold out and closed the gates, leaving perhaps 10,000 fans without tickets to roam around outside the park and scramble for a good viewing spot on Coogan's Bluff on the heights.

Mounted policemen tried to keep the surging crowd in check. Newspapermen arriving 15 minutes before game time gained entry to the park by presenting their credentials and scaling a fence, because to open the gate would have incited those without tickets to make a dash for it. Even Red Sox owner Harry Frazee, intending to see his old adversary Ruth, couldn't get into the park at first; finally recognized, he was let in a few minutes before game time.

Too bad the game was over so quickly. The Indians were another in a series of A.L. teams who hated Mays, the result of a beanball battle two years before when the pitcher played for Boston. Cleveland jumped on Mays from the get-go: Graney lined the game's first pitch to center field for a single, and shortstop Ray Chapman followed by dumping a pitch into right, sending Graney to third. Ward then bobbled center fielder Speaker's slow roller to third, which scored Graney. Right fielder Elmer Smith then beat out an infield hit, and second baseman Bill Wambsganss, mercifully known as "Wamby" ("W'sganss" in the box scores), lined a shot off the wall for a double. The Indians nailed the Yankees for five runs in the first, sending Mays to the clubhouse after only two outs. By the time the afternoon was finished, Chapman had three hits, and O'Neill and the old Red Sox pitcher turned outfielder "Smokey" Joe Wood had two each. The Indians, behind Bagby, romped 8–2 to push their record to 17–7, and slid back into first, just ahead of Boston.

That suited Cleveland. Not only did several Indians dislike Mays personally, but they usually couldn't hit him with a sledgehammer. For the most part, Mays had mastered the Indians, and in his first three years in the league had run up a 12–2 record against them. "Clevelanders know by this time that whenever Mays performs the Indians might just as well leave their bats in the clubhouse," Henry Edwards of the Cleveland *Plain-Dealer* had written back in 1918.

The teams took Monday off, and traded victories in midweek. The Yanks, behind Shawkey, held the Indians to three hits on Tuesday in an 11–0 romp, and Coveleski came back from his loss over the weekend to six-hit the Yanks Wednesday 5–0 and drop the New Yorkers back to .500.

Tuesday's game brought both good and bad news. Coming back was the gritty Peckinpaugh, who had two hits. But leaving was Ruth, out again with a slight muscle strain, the result of his batting—although the injury was not serious and the slugger was expected back after several days. So with Ruth gone from the lineup and Coveleski throwing zeros, about the biggest excitement Wednesday came when a lost soul wandered down from the stands and deposited himself in front of the Indians' dugout. Smiling but refusing to leave the field, the stranger left only with a firm push through the nearest exit by home plate umpire Brick Owens. So who was this mystery visitor? "Probably a diamond salesman who has read in the papers that Cleveland is likely to be in the World Series," the *Times* figured. "He wanted to sign them up."

The Indians weren't the only players with an intense dislike for Carl Mays. For a pitcher who staked his reputation on pinpoint control—he averaged less than four walks per nine innings—Mays hit his share of batters, many of whom called him a no-good headhunter. In 1917, Mays led the American League with 14 hit batsmen, and his unorthodox submarine delivery meant pitches often came inside, humming directly at a batter's head.

Long was the list of American League players with a grudge toward Mays. There was Ty Cobb, with whom Mays had an ongoing feud, the result of several Red Sox–Tigers games when Mays threw at the temperamental Tigers' star. Vowing revenge, Cobb bunted down the first-base line, trying to get Mays to field the ball and cover the bag. It worked, and when Mays arrived at the bag Cobb lunged for him, his spikes cutting into the pitcher's leg. Mays doubled over in pain, and with blood spurting from his wound, Cobb leaned over and issued a warning: "The next time you cover the bag, I'll take the skin off the other leg."

But if opponents loathed Mays, his teammates detested him. "Mays is one of those unlucky fellows who seem to have a special knack for getting in wrong," said Yankee co-owner Huston. Added a Yankee teammate: "He was sulky. He was not congenial. You would ask him a question and he would brush you off. I was never on a club that a fellow was so disliked as much as Mays." Even Huggins, almost always with a soft spot for his current and former players, had no use for the pitcher.

Mays himself was mostly to blame. On the mound, he was perpetually bad-tempered—glaring at infielders he felt had made a poor throw, or umpires when things didn't go exactly the way he wanted. When he hit or came close to beaning opponents, Mays just shrugged. Pitching high and tight and intimidating batters, he said, was the way he played; it was just baseball. Mays's crankiness extended off the field as well, and he seldom hung out with teammates, disapproving of those who liked to drink, hit the clubs, and chase women. As Mike Sowell writes in *The Pitch That Killed*: "He was intelligent and articulate, but he pulled no punches when pointing out the faults of others."

In 1913, Mays was just another sore-armed minor-league pitcher with a conventional, over-the-top delivery when he laid eyes on the sinkerball of former major leaguer Joe McGinnity. Then playing for Portland of the Northwest League, Mays looked on in wonder as the 42-year-old Tacoma right-hander, known as "Iron Man" from his days as a member of John McGraw's Giants, set down one Portland batter after another with his unorthodox delivery.

Thinking that such a delivery could work for him, Mays asked Portland manager Billy Sullivan, a former White Sox catcher, for help in learning the sinkerball. The pitch was particularly hard to hit because the ball was thrown with the pitcher's hand practically scraping the ground, meaning it traveled upwards toward the plate as if shot from a cannon. Mays found it slow going at first, but even with his sore arm, he developed the motion and control needed to master the unusual pitch. He finished the season with 10 wins while pitching a workhorse 250 innings and walking only 54.

Mays rode his sinkerball all the way to the big leagues. Within two years, he was with the Red Sox, and aside from Jack Warhop of the Yankees was the only big leaguer who threw the pitch. By 1916, he was a star, and over the next three years won 62 regular-season games. Two more wins came in the 1918 World Series against the Cubs, including the clincher, a three-hit, 2–1 masterpiece.

Despite his success, Mays was disliked by his teammates. Tris Speaker certainly didn't like him because of his foul temper and tendency to belittle his infielders. Nor did Harry Hooper, who called Mays "an odd bird." About the only Red Sox teammate Mays didn't jaw with was Ruth, who towered over the pitcher and could probably have inflicted serious damage if the two ever came to blows. Mays just shrugged at the universal dislike thrown his way, and seemed, as Sowell writes, to "wear it as a badge of honor." Said Mays to *Baseball Magazine*: "It was long ago made very apparent to me that I was not one of those individuals who were fated to be popular."

Even Mays's 1919 arrival in New York was tinged with venom. Arriving at the Polo Grounds in the midst of the turbulent court case involving his services, Mays was greeted by his teammates, most of whom went over one by one to shake hands and say hello. But when catcher Truck Hannah hung back, Mays swung by his locker instead. When he did, Hannah suddenly turned and threw a punch at Mays, which knocked him back and into a row of lockers. Then Hannah leapt across a table and charged Mays, as if to continue the barrage, before suddenly stopping and extending his hand for a shake.

"Now we're all even," Hannah said, grinning. Mays just nodded.

The odd encounter had roots in a years-old feud between the two. A stickler for neatness, Mays always arrived at the ballpark with several pairs of shined cleats. But whenever he came to bat, the Yankee catcher would spit tobacco juice on Mays's shoes. Mays returned the favor, and with the concept of an eye for an eye, baseball style, routinely flattened Hannah with a brushback pitch in his first at-bat.

So it went with Carl Mays, the man who couldn't seem to catch a break from opponents—or from teammates. His constant grouchiness made him a hard man to like. Even Huggins, who Mays said had borrowed his car during spring training and not bought gas, fell under his scorn. "It is true I had never been popular [among teammates] but this had ceased to bother me," Mays would say later in the year. "And if I was not popular, I was at least rated as a successful pitcher."

Stuck in fourth place and in need of a spark, the Yankees looked toward the latter half of the long homestand against inferior opponents—three games each against the St. Louis Browns and Detroit—before heading back to Boston and coming home again to play the Senators.

Thank goodness then for Jack Quinn, the workhorse, who went to the mound May 20 and, with Ruth still out, won his sixth game of the season, an 8–3 shellacking of St. Louis sealed with three throwing errors by their spitballing starting pitcher Allan Sothoron. Long an American League doormat, the Browns were a tad better than usual in 1920, thanks to the potent bats of their talented first baseman George Sisler and an all-.300-hitting outfield—Jack Tobin, Ken Williams, two years from becoming baseball's first 30-30 player, and the exquisitely nicknamed Bill "Baby Doll" Jacobson.

Sisler, coming off a hefty .352 batting average in 1919, had signed his first baseball contract back in 1911 with minor-league Akron, but changed his mind and entered the University of Michigan, where he played baseball under coach Branch Rickey. Trouble brewed in 1915 when the sought-after Sisler graduated and turned pro: by then, his contract had been sold to the Pirates, but Sisler protested, claiming he'd been a minor when he signed his original contract, hadn't clearly understood the rules back then, and had yet to play for any professional team. Sisler wanted to play, not for Pittsburgh, but for the Browns, then being managed by his old skipper Rickey, and the case went to baseball's National Commission for a decision. The Browns won, which infuriated Pirates owner Barney Dreyfuss, particularly when Sisler became a star.

Batting against Quinn, Sisler drilled two doubles and fielded flawlessly. "[He is] one of the most graceful performers in all [of] baseball," the *Times* wrote, "and Sisler at the bat is as good as the best." He didn't have a hit the next day, however, but it didn't matter because the still-Ruthless Yanks could do little against the Browns' top pitcher, Urban Shocker, in a 2–1 loss before a hefty Saturday gathering of 25,000. Shocker, born Urbain Jacques Schockeor, limited the New Yorkers to only six hits, and survived a ninth-inning rally thanks to a terrific game-saving catch of a Del Pratt drive that the leaping Williams caught deep in center.

But the roar heard Sunday, May 23, reverberating across the Harlem River was both a heartfelt welcome back from 18,000 souls to Ruth—missing for what seemed like an eternity, though it had only been a week—and a plea to pick up where he'd left off. Behind 2–1 in the sixth, Wally Pipp plopped a bloop single into right off Carl Weilman, setting up Ruth for a chance to make his return dramatic. Ruth stepped to the plate, wielding his 52-ounce bat, and the crowd rose, urging him to belt one.

From the first-base coach's box, Charley O'Leary yelled encouragement of his own. "Show 'em you're normal, Babe. They think you're sick."

Weilman reared back and sent a curve that was intended to break outside. But it didn't, and Ruth reached out and drilled the ball on a long, majestic arc well over the top of the big right-field grandstand. Writers described it as the longest ball ever hit at the Polo Grounds. Ruth wasn't just hitting longer and longer home runs—for the first time in dead-ball history, he was using the long ball as a weapon to win games in crucial spots. Pipp scored, then Ruth trotted home, and the Yankees had suddenly taken a 3–2 lead. Ruth's sixth homer of the season sent the writers into more superlatives: "From the moment of contact, there was no doubt about it being a home run," the *Times* dutifully reported. "Bedlam in its wildest hours had nothing on that crowd which had seen a ball hit only as far as Ruth could hit it."

Ruth-related bedlam meant the introduction of a new custom at the Polo Grounds. Fans celebrating in the upper deck would remove their straw hats and fling them toward home. Most hats didn't reach the field, however, and rained down instead on the fans below. The cheers picked up again when the inning ended, and Ruth popped from the dugout and headed back to right field. And they picked up again when Bob Shawkey got the day's final out. Ruth's home runs were not only dramatic, they were winning games. The score held up and the Yankees' record was 15–14.

Taking in the Sunday game at the Polo Grounds were several members of manager Hughie Jennings's Detroit Tigers, the New Yorkers' last opponent on the homestand. Always a draw with the hated Ty Cobb, a regular target of New York boobirds dating back to Hilltop Park days, Detroit was having a dreadful time of it in 1920. A respectable fourth place and 20 games above .500 in 1919, the Tigers came to the Polo Grounds as losers of their first 13 in a row—still a team record—and 21 of their first 28 to stand dead last in the American League.

The Tigers were a relatively young team in 1920. They had talent, but had fallen into a rut. The great Cobb, having just won his 12th batting title in 1919, was hitting only about .200. As for Hughie Jennings, the once-great Baltimore Oriole who had taken over as the Tigers' fiery manager way back in 1907 and had won pennants in his first three years, the end was near. By then, Jennings, who went by "Ee-Yah" for the sound of the distinct yell he used to rally his team, had become a heavy drinker, "pathetically tired, ineffective, and with the old grin faded," Cobb would write in his memoirs. (In one of the quirks of baseball history, six big-league managers have been lawyers, five of whom—Jennings, Huggins, Jim O'Rourke, John Montgomery Ward, and Branch Rickey—are in the Hall of Fame. The sixth, Tony LaRussa of the St. Louis Cardinals, is probably headed there as well.)

Many nights, wrote Cobb biographer Charles Alexander, Jennings would sit in his hotel room and pour out his troubles to Cobb, insisting he take over as manager. Cobb would in 1921, but not before Jennings spent the rest of 1920 bickering with his players, and particularly the pitchers. It would be mid-June before the Tigers were finally supplanted in last by the A's. They remained in a sorry state: in September, Dutch Leonard quit the team and returned to his California fruit ranch, and Jennings suspended Harry Heilmann for indifferent play.

But the Tigers' dismal start didn't interest fans at the Polo Grounds much. They were there to see the two teams' stars—Cobb and Ruth, two men whose style of play symbolized baseball on the cusp of change. Here was Ruth, the fence-buster who specialized in blowing open games with one blast, against Cobb, who scored runs the old-fashioned way, slashing singles and doubles and moving around the bases by stealing and any other means necessary.

Score one for the dead-ball era in the series opener, as Cobb singled and later scored, and the Tigers' gangly right-hander Howard Ehmke cruised 5–1 to beat the hard-luck Mays. Ehmke's only blemishes: Ruth's two hits, a triple and a single.

Like many good hitters, Ruth held his own against the league's top pitchers, but he feasted on the second-liners. He reserved particular pounding for Detroit hurlers, with whom the Yankees often enjoyed true, old-fashioned slugfests, and against whom Ruth would hit an astounding 123 home runs—the most in history by a player off a single team. On Wednesday, with Wally Pipp on base, Ruth deposited the first pitch he saw from Dutch Leonard into the upper deck of right field at the Polo Grounds for his league-leading seventh home run of the year. It put the Yanks up 2–1, and Jack Quinn did the rest, holding Cobb hitless and the Detroits to three runs. The New Yorkers won it 4–3 in the ninth when Roger Peckinpaugh's single drove in Muddy Ruel.

Ruth's heroics were becoming routine. In the series' final game, he homered again to the upper deck in right field, now christened "Ruthville," and again off the first pitch thrown him—this time in the second off Hooks Dauss. Score another one for the new, long-ball kind of game. As if to accent the change, Cobb went hitless, and George Mogridge gave up only four hits for his first win as the Yankees cruised 4–1.

The series did more than launch a two-game win streak for the Yankees heading into another series at Fenway Park against the surprising, league-leading Red Sox. It was a passing of the guard, a validation that one swing of the bat could change the game more than anything could in dead-ball days. Although Cobb's hitting would pick up—by early June he was above .300 and would finish the season at .334—his star was being eclipsed by the Babe. A nasty, moody man, Cobb relished feuds and fights with everyone from rival players to hotel porters and waitresses. Indeed, he remained openly hostile toward Ruth for years, and it was only after the two had retired that they got along, even for a time becoming golfing companions.

"Ruth has become the most alarming menace big league pitchers have ever bucked against," the *Times* wrote. "An extra outfielder stationed in the upper grand stand may be necessary to curb the clouter. But that wouldn't stop Ruth, for they would also have to plant another outfielder out in Manhattan Field, and maybe before the season is over another would have to be scouting flies out in Eighth Avenue."

The newspapermen could hardly contain themselves. Ruth's latest home run had put him far ahead of his pace from the previous year, when he didn't sock his eighth until July 5. He was called "Big Bertha," "the Son of Swat," and the man "who made sick ball games well." Everything about him projected excitement, and he was attracting bigger crowds than the Yankees had ever seen. "Ruth looks good when he makes a home run," one Polo Grounds fan said to another. "Huh," said his friend. "Ruth looks good even when he strikes out."

In a year crowded with big events, America needed a diversion, a tonic, and somebody to take their minds off hard times. It needed Babe Ruth.

Less than two years from the end of the Great War, coming off its deadliest flu epidemic in history, and beset with labor difficulties, the United States that year was living proof that those who say the old days were kinder, simpler times should not become historians.

America hadn't planned on entering the Great War, which European nations had kicked off back in 1914. But in 1915, 128 Americans were among the 1,198 killed by a German U-boat torpedo attack of the British ocean liner *Lusitania* off the Irish coast. The attack prompted predictable outrage across the country against the German war machine. Then, in January 1917, Germany, by then suffering from a British blockade, declared unrestricted submarine warfare. Less than a week later, the United States cut diplomatic ties with Germany. War was formally declared that April, with the first American troops reaching Europe late that June.

By July 1918, more than 1 million American troops were in Europe. Finally, that November the war ended, and although U.S. casualties were minimal next to the carnage suffered by Europeans, they were still extensive with more than 53,000 Americans killed in action and another 63,000 dying of disease.

Even more devastating was the "war" back home—against a fast-moving, lethal strain of influenza believed to have sickened U.S. troops in France and then spread through the nation as soldiers traveled to and from Europe, laying waste to staggering numbers of Americans. The flu sickened more than 25 percent of the U.S. population and killed 548,000, raw numbers that devastated populations from the biggest cities to the smallest hamlets, and indescribably targeted the youngest and healthiest. The death curves in the great flu epidemic were W-shaped, with peaks for three groups in particular—babies and toddlers, the elderly aged 70 to 74, and young adults 20 to 40. The navy estimated that 40 percent of its servicemen got the flu in 1918; the army said that 36 percent of its soldiers got sick. Countless young children were left orphaned, and many families were destroyed.

The epidemic during the closing days of World War I was perceived by many as yet another wartime nightmare, similar to the horrors of the trenches and mustard gas. And then, as mysteriously as the flu appeared, it went away about the time the fighting stopped. And when it was finished, humanity had been struck by an illness that killed more people in a few months' time than any other illness in the history of the world. Every family it seemed had a child, a brother, or an aunt who died of this grisly illness in which the lungs filled with fluid, essentially drowning its victims. It was the Black Death come home to nineteenth-century America.

The war's aftermath proved no easier for many of the country's labor force. The years 1919–1922 saw more than 10,000 strikes involving some 8 million workers—4 million in 1919 alone. Strikes that year rolled from the California citrus fields to Southern cotton mills, El Paso laundries, Tampa cigar factories, and into the silk factories of New Jersey, New England's telephone companies, and even the Boston police force. In February 1919, a general strike in Seattle mobilized 100,000 workers, who ran the city for five peaceful days, then called off the strike as troops dispatched to "restore order" neared the city limits.

Much of the turmoil focused on union organizing, which had taken off in the years of the Great War. By 1920, membership in the American Federation of Labor was nearly 4.1 million, and total union membership exceeded 5 million. Almost 20 percent of industrial workers belonged to a union. With labor's growing ranks came a heightened call for labor activism. In January 1919, New York unions formed the American Labor Party, calling for restoration of civil rights and the "democratic control of industry and commerce by those who work." By 1920, American Federation of Labor unions and the railroad brotherhoods supported 23 state labor parties, which that July merged into the Farmer-Labor Party.

Labor's increasing powers created inevitable conflicts of assimilation. Racial conflicts divided workers and unions. In the summer of 1919, when race riots erupted in cities throughout the United States, many African Americans started forming unions of their own, dedicated to socialism and black liberation, the most prominent of which was Marcus Garvey's Universal Negro Improvement Association.

And with the growing radicalism of unions came the U.S. government's repression of labor activists, orchestrated across many fronts, including the U.S. Justice Department, which established a Radical Division—headed by a young agent named J. Edgar Hoover—to compile files on the most radical. In 1919, New York's Lusk Committee began investigating "un-American" activities, the first of many such initiatives. On the night of January 2, 1920, Attorney General A. Mitchell Palmer deployed federal agents in 70 cities across the country to arrest and detain 10,000 people identified in Justice Department files as aliens and Communists. Of those arrested, about 500 were deported, with the rest turning out to be citizens or immigrants without radical ties.

By 1921, 32 states had outlawed what was called "criminal syndicalism"—advocating illegal labor tactics or being a member of organizations that encouraged them. More than 100 detective agencies, meanwhile, gave companies the operatives to spy on employees suspected of union organizing, identify activists for firing, start fights at union meetings, and gang up on strikers—all tactics aimed at disrupting the growth of unions.

America certainly could have used a dynamic presidential candidate in such an atmosphere, but neither candidate in 1920 would help matters much, even as women prepared to vote for the first time after the passage of the Nineteenth Amendment. After eight years of a Democrat in the White House for the first time since the Civil War, the Republicans were solid in their dislike of Woodrow Wilson. Rejecting Wilson's farsighted world vision of a League of Nations, the forerunner to the United Nations, they unified around being everything the Democrats weren't: isolationist, anti-Bolshevist, and anti-Semitic. No wonder their candidate was the unimpressive Warren G. Harding, who on July 22 kicked off a front-porch campaign at his house in Marion, Ohio. Using as his model former president William McKinley, who had led a similar, successful campaign from his front porch back in 1896, Harding tried to look as presidential as possible—wearing a red carnation in his buttonhole, just as McKinley had done, and even bringing in McKinley's old flagpole from Canton.

Harding was simply an unspectacular man most notable for his ability to shake a lot of hands—"the most pleasant thing I do," he said. When he was done with that, he posed for photographs with his wife, a wealthy widow named Florence Kling DeWolfe, and looked on approvingly as delegations paraded through town serenading him with the catchy tune "Good Morning, Mr. Har-Har-Har-ding." But there was a major problem: Harding simply did not measure up to McKinley or anything remotely presidential. Lacking self-confidence, he stumbled when delivering a speech, saying, "I never saw this before. . . . I didn't write this speech and don't believe what I just read."

Conveniently overlooked was Harding's true passion—sexual dalliances with his mistress Nan Britton, who he even stopped to see at a friend's apartment after securing the Republican nomination, and who had borne him an illegitimate child. "His private life was one of cheap sex episodes," wrote Frederick Lewis Allen in the book *Only Yesterday*. "An ambitious wife had tailored and groomed him into outward respectability." Also overlooked was Harding's lackluster record as a senator—he had managed to miss two-thirds of all roll-call votes, including the one to send the Nineteenth Amendment to the states for ratification. In an odd way, Harding was exactly what America wanted, and how people loved it when he proclaimed, "America's present need is not heroics, but healing; not nostrums but normalcy."

The strategy would work, as would Harding's low-key campaign. With no clear front-runners themselves, the Democrats chose as their candidate the equally bland Ohio Governor James M. Cox, a choice more significant for his selection of running mate, Franklin D. Roosevelt of New York, Wilson's assistant secretary of the navy, a fifth cousin of former president Theodore Roosevelt, and a reformer with a reputation as a maverick. Cox and Roosevelt railed against Harding, calling him a "Happy Hooligan," but faced an uphill battle as the team running on the coattails of an unpopular president. "The day of supermen is ended in the Democratic as well as the Republican party," the *Providence Journal* wrote. "From Roosevelt to Wilson, we have dropped to two second-rate Ohio politicians."

No wonder Americans were happy to focus on Babe Ruth and his epic home run march of 1920.

Amidst the hoopla of Babe Ruth was another, quieter story that promised to pay big dividends for the New Yorkers: Bob Shawkey was finding his form.

If Jack Quinn had carried the burdens of the Yankee pitching staff in the early going of 1920, it was Shawkey, now at 4–4, to whom the team still turned. A Yankee since 1915, Shawkey had won 72 games as a New Yorker, and put together 20-win seasons in both 1916 and 1919, despite losing almost a full year in 1918 due to military service. At 5'11" and 168 pounds, the 29-year-old right-hander Shawkey was the rock, the dependable anchor of the staff, and a man Huggins would need to contend for the pennant.

He had taken to baseball on the sandlots of his native central Pennsylvania with no notion of becoming a pro baseball player. Educated as a boy in a one-room country schoolhouse, Shawkey spent a year at Slippery Rock Teachers College before deciding on a career change and going to work in 1910 as a tool dresser in the Pennsylvania oil fields, while playing semipro ball on the side. The next year, while working as a fireman on the Pennsylvania Railroad (the man who fired the engine by shoveling coal), he turned pro, signing with Harrisburg of the Tri-State League.

"I liked railroading," Shawkey said years later. "I liked going places. Even when I was earning good money in professional ball, I kept my job in the old Pennsy. I thought too, shoveling coal would make me strong."

So it did. In 1913, the 21-year-old Shawkey signed with the A's, and from the start displayed the attributes that would make him a success: a sharp curveball, an even sharper temper, and a will to win. His first start, in an A's practice game, was not memorable. "I was wild as a mountain goat," Shawkey said, "and my fastball was whistling by the ears and ankles of the batters, while my curve kept breaking into the dirt." Shawkey's temper exploded, and Connie Mack lifted him. Confused and frustrated, Shawkey approached teammate Chief Bender and asked for advice.

"Sure," said Bender, then on his way to a Hall of Fame career. "But first you have to show me that you can control yourself and also that ball. Never mind your smoke or curve. Learn to put that ball where you want it. Then come to me and I'll show you how to put stuff on it."

The mists of time obscure precisely what "stuff" Bender was referring to, but Shawkey proved himself a quick learner. He starred at minor-league Baltimore, earning a promotion to the A's in 1914. It was the great team's last year at the top, and Shawkey went 16–8 before Mack started selling off his stars and the A's hit rock bottom.

In 1915, Shawkey went 5–5 for the suddenly cellar-dwelling A's. Mack called him "a five inning pitcher," and unloaded him at midseason to the Yankees. The change did Shawkey good, for by 1916 he was both the team's ace and its workhorse, going 23–14 in 53 games. Perhaps most impressive of all, Shawkey pitched 21 complete games. All that coal shoveling had paid off.

By 1920, Shawkey had developed into a shrewd front-line pitcher, capable of mixing heat, control, and other tricks of the craft, like subtly moistening the ball as the situation dictated. Combining steady work habits and a willingness to toil long hours in the bullpen, he was also a Huggins favorite, and the Yankee manager liked giving him the ball.

His temper remained, and it infused his Yankee teammates with an overall disdain for anything umpire-related. A certain flair and style separated Shawkey from the pack: off the field, he was perhaps the team's most enthusiastic hunter, and typically went north after the season in search of deer and moose. "Most ballplayers are pretty good shots," he said. "They have a steady hand and a clear eye. If they did not, they wouldn't be successful as ballplayers."

Both off and on the field, Shawkey dressed fashionably, and always looked sharp. By inviting him to a formal party, as the *Daily News* once wrote, "you would suffer no fear that he would not be on intimate acquaintance with the proper rotation of the eating implements."

Shawkey's weakness for the wardrobe extended to the ballfield as well. He wore red flannel underwear, which drew considerable chuckles up in the press box. It was "the noisiest underwear in baseball's history," the *Daily*

News wrote. Shawkey said only that his choice of undergarments afforded him more warmth.

That was just fine with Huggins. He and the Yankees needed Bob Shawkey and his red underwear for the team to make a run for the flag.

Big crowds were turning out to see Ruth everywhere, cheering his every move even on the road, almost unheard of in baseball during those long-ago days. So it went at Fenway Park on May 27 in the first of a brief two-game series against the Red Sox, when Boston fans showered affection on their departed hero. They too wanted to see him clear the fences, and Ruth obliged by sending two moon shots—numbers 9 and 10 of the season—to help the Yankees to a 6–1 win, the team's third straight. The first homer, in the sixth off Harry Harper, landed high up in the right-field bleachers. So explosive was the ball in leaving Ruth's bat that Harry Hooper, the right fielder, didn't move a muscle when the ball started his way. Hooper, an old teammate, didn't see the need: he knew what Ruth could do.

Ruth's second shot displayed his true power. Facing rookie Benn Karr in the eighth, the Babe sent the pitch not to right but to the top of the 40-foot left-center-field fence, where the ball kept going—eventually disappearing into an upper floor of a neighboring parking garage. Ruth's three home runs in four days sent statisticians scurrying to again dig up the long-forgotten records of Ned Williamson, he of the one monster year back in 1884 as a Chicago Colt. It turned out that Ruth and Williamson were the only men to perform the feat.

Reporters were starting to focus on every aspect of Ruth's batting. His every swing was analyzed—yes, it did resemble Shoeless Joe Jackson's—as were his misses and even the way he trotted around the bases in his distinctive pigeon-toed gait. This was something no one had ever before seen. "Every swung strike left a trail of laughter, but backed by a chorus of respectful and awed 'Ooooooooohs' as the audience realized the power that had gone to waste and the narrow escape the pitcher had had," wrote *Daily News* sportswriter Paul Gallico, later the screenwriter for the film *Pride of the Yankees*. "And of course his home runs brought forth pandemonium, a curious double rejoicing in which the spectator celebrated not only Babe's feat and its effects on the outcome of the game, but also his excellent luck in being present and with his own eyes beholding the great happening."

But on this day in Boston, even Ruth's heroics weren't enough to hide the raw emotions that had developed between the Yankees and the game's two umpires, George Hildebrand and Billy Evans. It was the first time in 1920 that the crew was assigned to a Yankee game, which at first seemed like a good thing because tempers had flared repeatedly throughout the month between the New Yorkers and the umpiring crew of Big Bill Dinneen and Dick Nallin (umpires in those days were two-man teams). It had been Nallin who ejected 10 Yankees back on May 4. And it was Dinneen—a onetime star pitcher with the Boston Pilgrims, forerunners to the Red Sox—who on May 23 had called Ping Bodie out on a close play at first, prompting two pop bottles to find their way out of the stands, hurled in his direction. "A bottle thrower is never dangerous in May," said a bemused Dinneen, "but some of them acquire control in July and August."

In fact, Dinneen and Nallin had umpired so many games that the joke at the Polo Grounds became that they were likely to get their names into the new directory there. Unfortunately, it didn't get much better when George Hildebrand crouched behind home plate on May 28 in Boston to call the balls and strikes.

The Yankees, and especially starter Bob Shawkey, were cranky from the beginning. Shawkey grumbled repeatedly over the opening innings. Yet by the fourth he had built a comfortable 3–0 lead when the Red Sox loaded the bases with two outs. When Hildebrand called ball four on the next batter, Wally Schang, forcing in a run, an angry Shawkey bounded off the mound, strode halfway to home plate, and jawed at Hildebrand. Huggins emerged from the Yankee dugout, walked to home plate, and argued some more. Hildebrand listened, ordered everyone back to their positions, and signaled for the game to resume.

Pitcher Harry Harper stepped to the plate when Shawkey chose to continue his protest—this time by kneeling and tying his shoes with exaggerated gestures intended to embarrass the umpire. For almost five minutes, Shawkey tied his shoes, leaving Hildebrand—and everyone else in the ballpark—waiting. Then, Shawkey struck Harper out to end the inning. But as Hildebrand made the call, the pitcher removed his hat and bowed in a sweeping, exaggerated tone. Hildebrand just watched, but as Shawkey left the field, he told the pitcher that he was done for the day.

That pushed Shawkey over the edge. Fists cocked, he charged the umpire, swinging wildly. The two men brawled, and as they did, Hildebrand managed to pry his mask off and use it to clock Shawkey on the scalp, opening a gash behind his left ear. Billy Evans rushed in, trying to keep any others from joining. Nobody else did, and by the time Truck Hannah pulled Hildebrand away, the other players had grabbed Shawkey and the quick, violent altercation was over.

Everybody stood around for another five minutes, until a police lieutenant who moonlighted at the ballpark strode over and suggested everybody get back to their designated place so the game could resume. It did, with Shawkey replaced by Mays, who, despite loud jeers from the Boston faithful, held the Red Sox scoreless over the final five. The 3–0 score held up.

The fireworks overshadowed the Yankees' 4–3 win on Friday, May 29, the team's fourth straight. Embarrassed enough already by Ruth, the Red Sox twice issued him intentional walks, holding the Babe to a single in two at-bats. Ernie Shore lasted seven and one-third innings to pick up his first win and squeeze the Yanks past the White Sox into third place. Meanwhile, back at the Polo Grounds, where the Giants were playing the Phillies, every time another Yankee run was posted in the out-of-town portion of the scoreboard, a cry would go up as to Ruth's contribution. "One more for the Babe," a spectator would say. "There goes Babe Ruth," another would offer.

For a short while, Shawkey's outburst swiped the focus from Ruth. The Yankee pitcher and his red underwear were suspended for a week and docked $200. But the punishment was minimal next to the uproar over his behavior, as Joe Vila wrote in the *Sporting News*. "Shawkey's behavior spilled the beans," he wrote, "and attracted the attention of the entire baseball world to the methods of the New York Americans."

Vila used the incident to encourage baseball owners to do more in curbing what he wrote was the baseball establishment's tolerance of baseball rowdies who threatened to stain the game. "If the magnates prefer disorderly conduct to clean sport, let them change the rules accordingly," Vila wrote. "But so long as the rules prohibit kicking and fighting on the field, they must be enforced. . . . Rowdyism has been prevalent here and there in the big leagues and the time now has arrived to stamp it out."

He had a point. On May 26, Giants third baseman Art Fletcher was tossed from a game at the Polo Grounds for scuffing up a ball. He received a 10-day suspension, and became the baseball establishment's first victim of new rules designed to curb cheating. Little did they realize how much of an effect the ruling would have on Babe Ruth's ability to hit the long ball.

The new rules had been part of a sweeping effort back in February by the owners' joint rules committee to bar trick pitching. All foreign substances or other alterations of the baseball were banned, including resin, saliva, and talcum powder, which wily pitchers used to make the ball jump and hop. Those caught, like Fletcher, would be suspended 10 days.

Hygiene was the reason given for banning the spitball. But it seemed hard to believe that the moguls had suddenly become concerned that a baseball slathered with spit threatened the game's sanctity. Roger Peckinpaugh had another interpretation: "It wasn't the spitter exactly they wanted to bar," he told writer Donald Honig. "They wanted to get rid of all those phony pitches . . . in the disguise of the spitter. . . . The pitchers went to their mouths, but then they might throw you a shine ball or a mud ball or an emery ball. . . . The only way they could stop them fooling with that baseball was to bar the spitter, and not let him go to his mouth."

Historians credit one Elmer Stricklett, a journeyman pitcher, with being the baseball pioneer who dumped a smidgen of glop on a portion of the ball, held it tight so it slid off his two forefingers as he threw, and found that it veered and tumbled toward the plate "like a drunk," as one put it. Stricklett needed all the help he could get. Breaking in with the White Sox in 1904, he was traded to Brooklyn, where he spent three years, losing more games than he won each season, before finishing his career with a 35–51 record.

Just how difficult the spitball was to master can be seen by how few pitchers actually used it to achieve success. Before he faded away, Stricklett spread the gospel, teaching two future Hall of Famers—Jack Chesbro of the New York Highlanders and Big Ed Walsh, a teammate on the White Sox—how to throw a spitball. Stricklett ran into Chesbro at spring training in 1904, and the burly New York pitcher became the game's first master of the spitball. A 21-game winner in 1903, Chesbro used it to win a post-1900 record 41 games in 1904. That was just about the time that Walsh began throwing his spitball—and four years after Chesbro won 41 games, Ed nearly did, winning 40 for the 1908 White Sox.

To appease those whose living depended on using trick pitches, the magnates allowed each club to designate two spitballers, who in the coming season would be exempt from the ban. But when the 1920 season ended, baseball executives voted to allow 17 pitchers who used the spitball to continue using it for as long as they were in the big leagues, most notably future Hall of Famer Burleigh Grimes, who broke with the Pirates in 1916 and won 20 games six times before his 19-year career ended in 1934.

The spitball had been only one of a series of trick pitches used by frontline hurlers like Chesbro and Walsh at the turn of the century. Along with Christy Mathewson, Eddie Plank, Chief Bender, Grover Cleveland Alexander, and Walter Johnson, they were among the elite hard-throwing, rubberarmed, and wily star pitchers of the era who used a combination of spitballs, cut fastballs, and even knuckleballs to dominate batters and in effect christen the dead-ball era.

Nothing in the official rules of the time actually restricted pitchers from using any form of moisture to load up the ball. So they did—using spit, sweat, tobacco juice, and even dew from the damp grass to apply to the ball and deliver it to the plate. Some of the more cunning pitchers even cut their baseballs with razor blades hidden in gloves or by using belt buckles. Clark Griffith was a notable offender, going so far as to actually step from the mound and knock the ball against his spikes, presumably to pound out the dirt.

At the same time, the magnates ordered umpires to remove all scuffed baseballs from play, giving batters a cleaner ball to hit. The decison must have been painful to the rich but miserly owners—each ball cost $2.50. The *Sporting News*, after a game in which 36 baseballs were used, sympathetically wrote that the "constant inspections of balls and discarding and demanding of new ones takes time [which] interrupts play and wearies the fan. . . . It seems to have reached the point where a ball is thrown out if it gets as much as a fly speck on it. This should not be. It's not patriotic, for true patriotism still demands economy and conservation. Balls cost money."

Baseball officialdom swore that all the baseballs used in play were the same. But home runs flew off the bats with astounding frequency in 1920, making the claim difficult to believe. Major-league batters in 1920 pounded a remarkable 184 more home runs than in 1919, and there was constant talk of a "livelier" ball. The fact is it *was* livelier, the result of a decision back in 1919 by the A. J. Reach Company, the manufacturer of big-league baseballs, to use a more efficient yarn-winding machine that wound the yarn more tightly and gave the ball greater bounce.

The change marked the second time in a decade that the ball had been altered. The previous time had been after the 1910 season, when a new type of ball with a cork center enclosed in rubber replaced the all-rubber-centered balls in use for years. Not surprisingly, the A.L.'s cumulative batting average in 1911 jumped 30 percentage points, topped by Ty Cobb's remarkable .420 average.

This time, the changes capped a virtual revolution in cumulative batting average. Before 1920, the highest the American League had ever hit was .277, accomplished way back in its first season, 1901. But from 1920 through 1929, the league averaged .285. Pitchers suffered accordingly; in 1920, the cumulative A.L. ERA soared to 3.78, more than half a run higher than the previous year. "The various concomitants, plus the inspirational arrival of Ruth, made for a unique situation in baseball," wrote Donald Honig, "one that will probably never happen again."

Even so, some continued to insist that the ball was the same as it ever was. With Ruth and others like George Sisler and Rogers Hornsby bashing the ball at a prodigious rate through the 1920 season, a group of people identifying themselves as "friends of Babe Ruth" gathered a number of balls that Ruth had hit into the stands that spring and took them for testing to the United States Bureau of Standards in Washington, D.C. Bureau officials knew the drill, having tested thousands of baseballs back in 1917 and deciding the best buy for the government for use by servicemen during wartime.

Dusting off the machinery it had used three years before, the bureau put the new balls through the same battery of tests, using bouncing wells, impact walls, and propulsion tubes. On August 21, with Ruth well past his previous season's record, the bureau released its findings: nothing had been done to the ball to make it notably different from the one tested in 1917. But it *was* different, and with Ruth and others driving home runs out of big-league ballparks in dramatically higher numbers than ever before, the game would never be the same.

SIX

"They Have Never Seen His Equal"

Ruth Heats Up

With the Yankees headed home for a Memorial Day doubleheader against Walter Johnson and the Senators, Harry Fabian's groundskeepers at the Polo Grounds got busy. First, they tended to the usual things—sweeping the park clean, watering the lush outfield grass, and raking the smooth infield, considered the best in the game. But to leave no doubt about the inevitable Ruth drives expected to land in every corner of right field, they did something else—so that everyone could follow the flight of Ruth's home runs, they painted wide white marks on the friezes of the right-field stands.

It was good planning. In the morning game, Ruth went hitless, but his teammates didn't. They pounded three Washington pitchers—Jim Shaw, Leon Carlson, and Al Schacht—for 14 hits, including home runs from Lewis and Hannah, triples from Hannah, Meusel, and pitcher Mogridge, and a double from Peckinpaugh. Thanks to a five-run sixth, the Yankees withstood a three-run Washington rally in the ninth to win, 7–6. It was the fifth win in a row for the New Yorkers and halted the Senators' win streak at six.

The Yankee hot streak matched the weather, which was sunny and in the 70s. All in all, it was a glorious Memorial Day in New York, with big crowds—their memories fresh of the Great War just ended—turning out everywhere. They cheered as spiffy British, French, and Italian veterans, followed by the Royal Air Force Band, marched up Riverside Drive on the Upper West Side. The cheers got louder for the Americans—clusters of veterans not only from the Great War, but from the Spanish-American and even the Civil War. The 300 or so Civil War soldiers, most of them veterans of Gettysburg, Antietam, and Cold Spring Harbor, managed to push their bodies bent from age along the one-mile parade route in just under two hours.

More crowds gathered for parades in Brooklyn, the Bronx, and Kearny, New Jersey, where town officials accepted a silk American flag saved from the British battleship *Warrior* that had sunk in the Battle of Jutland. On Long Island, virtually the entire population of Oyster Bay turned out for ceremonies at the grave of their old neighbor former President Theodore Roosevelt, who had died the year before.

On Long Island, a crowd of 35,000 stormed Belmont Park, smashing the immense racetrack's single-day attendance record and filling every bit of available space from the edge of the lawn to the roof of the long steel stands. Several thousand more lined the Harlem River in northern Manhattan for the New York Rowing Association's annual Memorial Day regatta.

Meanwhile, at Ebbets Field in Brooklyn, 30,000 spectators saw the Dodgers sweep the Giants in a doubleheader. Feasting on the curves of Shufflin' Phil Douglas, the surprising Dodgers moved into a first-place tie with the Cubs, while relegating the Giants further into seventh in what was shaping up into a lost season for John McGraw.

Not so for Babe Ruth. In a scene reminiscent of the May 16 game against the Indians, 38,688 fans shoehorned their way into the Polo Grounds for the afternoon's Yankee game, anxious to see the Babe uncork home run number 12. On the mound for the Senators was a 21-year-old rookie stringbean of a left-hander, 6'4" Harry Courtney.

It was a wild game from the start. With the Yankees down 1–0 in the second, Pratt walked, Bodie doubled, and both scored on Lewis's two-bagger to left center. Then, with two outs, Peckinpaugh doubled, driving in Lewis—and driving out Courtney.

The Senators stormed back for three in the third, piling up hits of their own off a shaky Herb Thormahlen. In went Ernie Shore in relief, but the Senators jumped on him as well for two more in the fourth. With two gone in the fourth, Miller Huggins came out to fetch Shore, and in sauntered the 24-year-old rookie Texan, Rip Collins, for his first viewing by the Polo Grounds' faithful. Pitching to Red Shannon, Collins fired a strike, the crowd roared, and the scene was set: Collins retired the side by getting Shannon to bounce out to first.

So, down 7–3 in the fourth, the Yankees got busy. They shellacked Bill Snyder for two base hits, driving him from the box. Good-bye Snyder and hello to Walter Johnson, the American League's premier pitcher. Having shut out the A's only two days before, Johnson wasn't expected to pitch but was needed now, especially with the two teams facing another double-header on Wednesday.

Thirty-two years old, Johnson had been the American League's best pitcher for more than a decade, and just two weeks before—on May 14—had beaten the Tigers for his 300th big-league win. You had to go all the way back to 1909 to find a year when he had not won at least 20 games in a season, thanks to his bullet-like delivery and pinpoint control. And although the Yanks had beaten Johnson earlier in the month, the man nicknamed "the Big Train" had not given up a home run since 1918. (Unfortunately, Johnson would suffer both an arm and a leg injury in 1920, and uncharacteristically go 8–10 that season.)

Johnson stopped the Yankees in the fourth and the fifth, but in the sixth yielded singles to Hannah, Peckinpaugh, Meusel, and Pipp. And just like that, the score was deadlocked at seven, aided by zeros from Rip Collins. Johnson reared back and threw a hard curve that Ruth hit on the end of his bat, sending the ball on an arc toward right field. The ball struck against the facade of the right-field stand, and as the *Times* dutifully reported, "nearly tore away part of the roof."

As was becoming common at the Polo Grounds, the Babe's home run set off a public display of pandemonium. Straw hats again flew out from the stands, and people tore up programs and hurled them on the field, sending groundskeepers out to clean up the mess. Ruth basked in the adulation as he circled the bases, doffing his cap and grinning toward the grandstand as he headed back to the dugout with the crowd still shrieking its appreciation.

Ruth's home run, his 12th of the season, was more than just the first Johnson had given up in nearly two years. It was another dramatic shot in a season that was turning memorable. It gave the Yanks a 10–7 lead, which Collins held to get the win, increasing the team's streak to eight. And it helped close out a big month for the Yankees, in which they went 16–9 to secure third place in a tight A.L. race.

No wonder Johnson called Ruth "the hardest hitter in the game" in *Baseball Magazine*. "There can be no possible doubt on that point," he said. "[Ruth] hits the ball harder and drives it farther than any man I ever saw. And old timers whose memory goes back to days when baseball was little more than 'rounders,' tell me they have never seen his equal."

Johnson said something else that got to the essence of Ruthmania. "There was an odd angle to the [Memorial Day games] . . . which illustrate what a curious sport baseball really is," he said. "In the first encounter, Duffy Lewis smashed a home run into the stands, which tied up the score. There was very little commotion. A minute later, Truck Hannah drove out another homer, which won the game. The excitement was nothing unusual. [Then, in the second game, Ruth hit his home run] when the game is already won, and there is particularly nothing at stake, and the crowd gets so crazy with excitement, they are ready to tear up the stands. Strange, isn't it?"

What wasn't strange was how the other Yankee bats were coming alive, as if Ruth's magic was rubbing off on Meusel, Pipp, Lewis, Bodie, and Peckinpaugh. On June 1, the Yanks pasted Washington's Eric Erickson and poor Harry Courtney again en route to a lopsided 14–7 win, the team's ninth in a row, moving them back into second place. Bodie and Peckinpaugh contributed two home runs apiece, Meusel had three hits, and Ruth two, but no homers. Instead, Ruth saved his heroics for the mound, where he started the game, knowing that the team was due to play two doubleheaders later in the week. With Sammy Vick in right, Ruth gave up four runs and pitched into the fifth—just long enough to get the win.

Seeing Ruth on the mound was a novelty for Yankee fans. That wore off quickly the next afternoon, when in the final two games against the shell-shocked Senators, the Babe got back to hitting by pounding three more home runs—numbers 13, 14, and 15—off Tom Zachary, Carlson, and Snyder. Ruth's first two came in game one, which the Yankees took easily 8–1 behind Quinn, whose sizzling 8–1 record matched the final score. And although Mays got clocked again in the second game, which the Senators won 7–6 to stop the Yanks' streak at 10, Ruth's homer was all anybody seemed to want to discuss.

It wasn't enough anymore to report that Ruth had merely hit home run number 15. That the ball landed in the right-field stands, now dubbed "Ruthville," and hit a spectator who was about to leave the game and knocked off his brown derby, was, well, news. "Sir Isaac Newton would have found out much about the laws of gravitation if he had seen Ruth bang baseballs," the *Times* wrote. "He probably would have decided that there weren't any."

Ruth's three home runs capped a glorious baseball day in New York. Some 85,000 had jammed the Polo Grounds for the three-day midweek series against Washington—evidence, the *Times* wrote, that "business isn't interfering with baseball this season." Even former New York Governor Al Smith, serving as president of the New York Central Railroad as he angled for a chance to regain his seat, couldn't get in; he didn't have a ticket.

The home runs were jumping from Ruth's bat with such regularity that sportswriters were tripping over themselves with the superlatives, relegating the Yankees' rise to second place to a minor story. Readers were so ravenous for details about the Babe, how he hit his home runs and where they landed, that reporters had to dig harder and for more detail in looking for the story behind the story.

A case in point: Just after hitting his 12th, Ruth had told reporters that the first dozen were the hardest, after which he was just now finding his groove, which must have made American League pitchers shudder. Reporters took to covering all aspects of the Babe's play, to detailing that his 54-ounce bat was indeed baseball's heaviest to news that he was the A.L.'s only player to tape the end of his bat handle for a better grip.

"It's not only heavy, but long, about as long as the law allows," Ruth told F. C. Lane about his bat. "My theory is the bigger the bat the faster the ball will travel. It's really the weight of the bat that drives the ball. . . . I have strength enough to swing it and when I meet the ball, I want to feel that I have something in my hands that will make it travel."

Fans noticed the details too. Stepping to the plate at the Polo Grounds, Ruth would look briefly at the clock high atop the clubhouse in center field before facing the pitcher. "See that?" said one man to his companion. "He always does that."

Rival players were starting to catch on to the benefits of the long ball. After an injury-plagued season in 1919 and still rusty from time lost to military service, Ken Williams of the Browns followed the Ruthian philosophy of using a heavy bat (his was 48 ounces), gripping it tightly, and as he put it, "swing[ing] not only from [the] shoulders but from [the] feet."

"It's all a matter of taste and batting style," Williams said. "Babe Ruth is the model of all home run sluggers, so I guess I don't have to apologize for my own preferences." No, indeed: Williams would homer 10 times in 1920, but knock 24 in 1921 and a league-leading 39 in 1922.

The analysis intensified. Writers devoted whole columns to the distance and trajectory of Ruth's home run shots. With Ruth starting to feel more comfortable at the Polo Grounds, newspapermen noted that he was starting to hit not just to right, but also to the more distant recesses of center field, hitting the ball longer and farther with each clout.

The press hounded Ruth for exclusives. Early in the season, the United News, a subsidiary of United Press International, wanted to pay Ruth $1,000 for the season with a $5 bonus for each home run he hit, provided Ruth wired the sports desk each time he hit one out of the park and described the details. United News sent Fred Ferguson in an attempt to sign Ruth up, and Ferguson left messages all over New York for Ruth to call him. But the Babe never did, sending Ferguson down to Philadelphia, where the Yankees were playing the A's. Finding Ruth finally, in the midst of a craps game with six teammates at the Aldine Hotel, Ferguson kneeled down and joined in. Ferguson won, and only after he'd taken everyone's money did the Babe notice him. Thinking fast, Ferguson spit out his proposition, and the Babe signed up.

Assigned to take Ruth's wire copy and turn it into prose that would be read by people all over America was the 20-something Westbrook Pegler. But after a dozen or so home runs went by with no word from Ruth, a steamed Ferguson wired the Babe, asking what was happening. Two nights later, a telegram arrived from Detroit: "SOCKED ONE TODAY. FASTBALL. HIGH OUTSIDE. SEND CHECK. BABE."

Pegler tried catching up to Ruth as well. The young writer waited for the Babe in hotel lobbies or at the entrance to his home at the Ansonia Hotel on the Upper West Side, but Ruth always seemed to be coming or going in a hurry on his way to a date. "Oh, make up something!" he'd shout, brushing by in a cloud of cigar smoke. So Pegler did, spinning out columns that started in mid-April and ran through the season.

The columns were good enough. "There is a belief in some quarters that left-handed batters are helpless against left-hand pitchers, and some one also spread the report that I can't hit a slow ball," reported Pegler/Ruth in early May. "Herb Pennock is a southpaw. I am a left-handed batter. Saturday afternoon he pitched a slow ball to me that cut the outside corner of the plate. I knocked it over the grandstand."

Striding into the Yankee clubhouse before a game, Ruth was the central attraction: he wore the best-tailored clothes, had his nails done by a manicurist, and tried answering his voluminous mail. "Open these for me, will ya," he'd ask a teammate. "Keep the ones with the checks and the ones from the broads." Once, team trainer Doc Woods sifted through a wastebasket stuffed with Ruth's discarded mail and found $6,000 in checks and endorsements. "Born? Hell, Babe Ruth wasn't born," his eventual Yankee teammate Joe Dugan would say a few years later. "The sonofabitch fell from a tree."

In a sense, Ruth had been sprung from jail. The second child of a Baltimore saloonkeeper, Ruth at age 7 was declared "incorrigible" and sent to St. Mary's Industrial School for Boys, a reformatory turned orphanage that became his home, on and off, until the age of 18. The few frayed photographs of St. Mary's reveal a bleak, Dickensian-looking place. Ruth's family seldom visited, and the boy seemed destined to become a shirtmaker. But when Brother Matthias, the 250-pound, 6'6" giant of a Xavieran priest in charge of St. Mary's, took a shine to Ruth—recognizing his budding talent for baseball by hitting him fly ball after fly ball—the boy became a star. By 8, Ruth was on the 12-year-old's team and proving to be a natural at every position.

Ruth had grown up in an orphanage, but he wasn't an orphan. Ruth never talked much of his family, and not much is known of them. His father, George, and mother, Kate, would have seven other children, only one of whom—Mary Margaret—survived to adulthood. The Babe's earliest memories of home were mostly of street fights and outrunning the cops by dashing through the alleyways of waterfront Baltimore. "I learned early to drink beer, wine and whiskey, and I think I was about five when I first chewed tobacco," Ruth told writer Fred Lieb. "I didn't particularly like the taste, but I knew it was supposed to be bad. There was a lot of cussing in Pop's saloon, so I learned a lot of swear words, some really bad ones. That's why they kept sticking me back in St. Mary's."

Ruth admitted that he could be off the wall—"I have the same violent temper my father and older brother had," he told Lieb. As a youngster, he rarely attended school, was left mostly to his own by his overwhelmed parents, and received little direction. "I think my mother hated me," Ruth said many years later, and other than his comment to Lieb, he rarely mentioned his father, who died in 1918 at age 46 from injuries received in a brawl outside the saloon. His older brother died in a street fight as well. By then, his mother had died—in 1910, at the age of 34. No wonder so many thought Ruth was orphaned as a youngster; in fact, he was 23 and already a four-year veteran of the big leagues when his father passed away.

Years later, Ruth would talk with reverence of Brother Matthias's mentoring, how he would stand in one corner of the ballfield and clout towering home runs over the center-field fence. Ruth would spend hours playing catch with Brother Matthias, and even emulated his batting stance, the well-known pigeon-toed lean into the approaching baseball. Supplementing Brother Matthias's imposing size was a quiet but stern presence that earned him respect and the nickname "the Boss" from St. Mary's boys. Ruth remained a truant at heart—escaping the walls of St. Mary's from time to time—but he always went back and was met by Brother Matthias, who never scolded or reprimanded him. No wonder Ruth would call him "the greatest man I've ever known."

Once, during his last year at St. Mary's, Ruth slithered through an open window and was missing for three days before school officials found him. For punishment, Ruth was forced to stand on the road between the two athletic yards for five days during recreation. On the sixth day, Brother Matthias handed him a glove and a ball and said he could rejoin the games again.

Ruth learned to read and write—barely—at St. Mary's. Because of the school's vocational training, he also spent a lot of time in the tailor shop, and would probably have ended up as a tailor or shirtmaker, had there been no baseball. But by 1912, the 17-year-old Ruth's baseball talents were already legendary throughout Baltimore. He was the cog of St. Mary's "main" baseball team, the varsity for whom he starred as a left-handed catcher, using a right-hander's catcher's mitt. He also played some shortstop, pitched, and could hit the ball a country mile. This unusual ability to pitch *and* bat was earning him the attention of the school's newspaper, the *Saturday Evening Star*. In one game alone, Ruth caught, pitched, played third base, and got three hits, including a home run, and struck out six batters. Less than two years later, on a raw morning in late February 1914, Ruth walked out of St. Mary's as the property of the International League's Baltimore Orioles, run by a man named Jack Dunn. "Discharged. . . . He is going to join the Balt. Baseball Team," someone wrote as a final entry next to his name in the school log. Five months later, Babe Ruth was a big leaguer, ready to launch a career for the ages.

There was one more series, against the A's, before the Yanks left for their first western swing of the season. They beat the overmatched A's in the first two games—5–4 on Thursday, June 3, and 12–5 on Friday the 4th. And they again pounded home runs, but not Ruth this time. Bodie walked to the plate in the sixth on Thursday with New York behind 4–1 and three Yanks—Pipp, Ruth, and Pratt—filling the bases. A's left-hander Ray Moore threw and Bodie swung, sending the ball into the lower right-field stands for a grand slam. The four Yanks filtered across the plate, putting them ahead 5–4 much to the delight of Bodie, who raised his cap toward the stands, but not the film crew that rolled tape every time Ruth stepped to bat. Pressing, the Babe struck out twice. Shawkey went the distance, and the Yanks held on for the win. Asked for the secret to his home run prowess, Bodie smiled and said, "Oh, it's just a gift that me and Ruth have."

On Friday, the Yanks picked up from where they left off the day before. Facing Rollie Naylor with one down in the first, Meusel singled, Pipp walked, and Ruth beat out an infield hit, loading the bases. Up stepped Del Pratt, who cracked another grand slam, this one down the left-field line, that landed in the stands fair by inches. Before the day was done, Meusel homered too and the Yanks had pounded three Philadelphia pitchers for 15 hits.

"The heavy cannonading, due to the elimination of freak pitching and a livelier ball, is producing ball games such as they used to have years ago when Ed Delehanty, Dan Brouthers, and Pop Anson were breaking the fences," opined the *Times*. "The real hero of this season will be the man who can come along and pitch a no-hit game."

How true: In the past week, the New Yorkers had boosted their record to 27–16, a scant one game back of front-running Cleveland. In the last seven games, the New Yorkers had hit 53 singles, 19 doubles, seven triples, and 13 home runs. All the hitting was reflected in the Yankee batting averages. Peckinpaugh, 15–31 on the week, was hitting an unshortstop-like .329; Meusel, 16–32 during the week, was at .313; and Ruth, 10–28 with four home runs, .328. Not to mention Bodie was hitting .323, Pratt .285, Ward

.264, and Pipp .257. And to Ruppert's delight, the turnstiles were clicking at a team record, with more than 108,200 venturing to the last five games at the Polo Grounds.

Then, on Sunday, June 6, something miraculous happened: for the first time in years, the Yankees landed in first place. It happened when Cleveland split a doubleheader with St. Louis and the Yanks beat the A's again—this time, 12–6, behind Carl Mays. The barrage continued, with Meusel hitting his fifth triple in a week, Peckinpaugh cracking a base hit in his ninth straight game, and Ruth contributing no home runs but a triple, two singles, two walks, and four RBIs.

And then on Monday—on the eve of the team's 16-day trip to Detroit, Cleveland, Chicago, St. Louis, and Philadelphia—the New Yorkers split with the A's. The Yanks, behind Jack Quinn, took the first game, 3–1, but blew a two-run lead in the second game when Rip Collins gave up four in the eighth to lose 6–5. It hardly mattered that three A's pitchers finally shut down Peckinpaugh's hitting streak at 10 games, that Ruth did not hit home run number 16, and that the Yanks ended the day back in second place. They had been winning, and they had done so by hitting the long ball and changing the way baseball was played, drawing the kind of interest that made the magnates smile.

Roger Peckinpaugh's success surprised no one. He was 29, and along with the Indians' Ray Chapman and Boston's Everett Scott, comprised the elite of American League shortstops—a threesome that outdistanced the pack in both service and ability.

The smooth-fielding Peckinpaugh had reached the majors a decade before and been a Yankee regular since 1913. He was Huggins's kind of player—a student of the game and a hustler who made the others around him better. Possessed of the classical infielder's build—a big chest, broad shoulders, and slightly bowed legs, Peckinpaugh stood 5'10", weighed 160 pounds, had oversized hands, and a howitzer for an arm. He chewed Star Plug tobacco only when on the ballfield, and said he'd spit into his glove and rub the ball in the goop for two reasons.

"Star Plug was licorice flavored and it made my glove sticky," he'd tell the Cleveland *Plain-Dealer* years later. "It also darkened the ball and the pitchers liked that. The batters did not, but what the hell, there was [often] only one umpire."

Born in Wooster, Ohio, Peckinpaugh grew up in Cleveland, where he starred in football, basketball, and baseball at East High School. His family lived next door to Larry Lajoie, manager of the Naps, and when Lajoie, Peckinpaugh's idol growing up, offered him $125 a month to play ball in 1909, the year after the young player graduated from high school, he wanted to accept. But his father, John, a salesman and former semipro player, was standing in his way. The elder Peckinpaugh considered professional ballplayers a load of inebriated louts who lived in fear of real jobs, a theory that wasn't so far off the mark in those days.

So young Roger Peckinpaugh went to his former high school principal, Benjamin Ulysses Rannels, and asked him for advice. Rannels urged him to sign the contract but said to quit baseball and go to college if he couldn't make it to the majors in three years. Peckinpaugh made it in two.

In 1910, Peckinpaugh was the sensation of spring training with the Naps—that is, until Cleveland pitchers starting throwing curveballs. When that happened, Peckinpaugh's batting average promptly took a tumble from the .400 range, slithering right on down to the .200 level, and the young shortstop was dispatched to New Haven in the Eastern League.

When he emerged at the tail end of the 1912 season, it was to face Walter Johnson in his first official big-league at-bat. Years later, Peckinpaugh would recall Johnson throwing the ball so fast that the batter could hear it. He got the Cleveland batsman on a foul pop-up.

"I thought I had achieved something just hitting the ball," Peckinpaugh said. "I fouled his fast ball twice."

Peckinpaugh had spent most of the 1911 and 1912 seasons with Portland of the Pacific Coast League, fielding well, and he begged batting-practice pitchers to throw him curves. "I knew if I got back up to Cleveland, five of every six pitches I would see would be curves," he would say, "so I knew I had to learn to hit them. It took me a while."

But Peckinpaugh learned, hit around .250—his lifetime average—and in time developed a distinctive batting style featuring a space as large as six inches between his hands. Some said he was copying Ty Cobb, but Peckinpaugh disagreed, saying he developed the style very much on his own, after hurting his left wrist sliding.

"I had worked too hard to become a regular so I told no one," he said of the injury that led to his batting style. "You played hurt to keep your position. I kept experimenting until I found a style that would let me bat without hurting my wrist. I did most of the work with my right hand and got so I could punch the ball almost anywhere I wanted to."

Along the way, Peckinpaugh developed a wry, fatalistic attitude about batting. "Sometimes you can't seem to help it when things are coming your way," he told F. C. Lane, a writer with *Baseball Magazine*. "A batting streak is a great thing while it lasts, but it begins to wear on you. You try to keep it in the background of your mind and you might succeed if people would let you. But everybody you meet speaks about it, wishing you well. But the net result is that you have that confounded batting streak in your mind all the time. Naturally, it makes you a little bit nervous and not until you have made an out, can you breathe easily."

By 1913, Peckinpaugh had been christened as "Peck" in the box scores. And he'd captured the attention of Yankee manager Frank Chance, who knew he was expendable because Cleveland management already had a starting shortstop, Ray Chapman, who was exactly three weeks older than Peck and 100 points higher in batting average.

Peckinpaugh joined the Yanks on May 25 from Cleveland in exchange for Bill Stumpf and Jack Lelivelt, and four days later went 3–3 in his first Yankee start. He continued to hit and fielded flawlessly—becoming the glue that held an otherwise unsteady infield together and one of the few bright spots in a dismal Yankee seventh-place finish. Things got so bad by the following year—1914—that Chance quit the team in a huff, going back to his orange farm in California and leaving the Yankee front office to make a managerial change for the team's final 17 games.

Closing out the season as Yankee manager, the 23-year-old Peckinpaugh went 9–8, becoming the answer to one of baseball's best trivia questions: Peckinpaugh is the game's youngest skipper ever. The next year he returned to his infield duties only.

As for Cobb, Peckinpaugh called him the greatest player he ever saw. "Cobb was a wild man on the bases and he came with his spikes high on a lot of infielders," Peckinpaugh said. "But he never nicked me and I asked him why once."

"Because I respect your play," Cobb said.

Boarding a sleeper car the evening of June 7 at Penn Station for the more than 600-mile trip to Detroit, the Yankees were participants in a vanished part of baseball tradition that wouldn't die out completely until the 1950s, when the major leagues expanded to California. There was a romance to riding the rails on the long western swings that isn't there with modern-day air travel.

Traveling the New York Central afforded all members of the Yankee party—players, trainer, traveling secretary, Ruppert, Huston, and eight writers—a kind of intimacy hard to find today. Poker was the game of choice, and games between ballplayers and hard-drinking sportswriters provided, as longtime sportswriter Bob Broeg put it, "more than my share of bright moments as [the] train sped through the gloom of the night."

The long train trips gave ballplayers time to unwind and talk shop. It broke down barriers between the players and writers, most of whom were only slightly older and in some cases were actually paid more. For the writers, it afforded an opportunity to catch players for interviews, although there was still a lot left unsaid when it came to player behavior back in 1920.

Railroad food was scrumptious, thanks to the pride and talent of the galley, who considered it an honor to serve the big-name players and often stayed on hand to provide late meals or early breakfasts. For Broeg, the longer train rides were better than the shorter ones, in part because porters would gladly keep the club car open for the ballclub, or convert the dining car into an impromptu nightclub, using checkered tablecloths and dimly lit lamps to create the atmosphere for beer and pretzels and a late-night snack.

Stories of ballplayer train excesses are legion, many of them involving Ruth, who for a late breakfast typically ordered a pint of bourbon and a bottle of ginger ale, a porterhouse steak, four eggs, a double order of fried potatoes, toast, and a pot of coffee, followed by a king-sized cigar while traveling. Then there was the wild night when Ruth led a group of drunken Yankees into the compartment occupied by Ruppert and ripped the pajama tops off the Colonel's back.

Maybe this trip relaxed the Yankees, for in Detroit their hot bats showed no letup. Against the hapless Tigers, the New Yorkers tallied 36 runs and bashed 48 hits to sweep the four-game series. If anything, the series was good batting practice to prepare for the meat of the trip in Cleveland, Chicago, and St. Louis. With Cobb laid up with a bum knee and Manager Jennings absent for a death in his family, the Yankees pounded just about everything that Detroit pitchers threw.

But the best news for the New Yorkers came in the third game with the Tigers and did not involve batting. Helped by Ruth's 16th home run—a two-run shot in the third off rookie Frank Okrie, Carl Mays held on to win 7–5, and for the first time in the season exceed a .500 won-lost record (6–5). Giving up five runs on 11 hits was hardly a pitching performance for the record books, but it was downright masterful considering the skies, which dropped rain and hail through the game, and the wind, which held up at least two more Yankee homers. What kept the teams playing in such nastiness was anyone's guess, but umpire Brick Owens kept them out there. "It hailed—sweet sandwiches, how it hailed!" the *Times* reported. "Some of the hailstones were as big as eggs. Maybe not as big as big eggs, but as big as little eggs, anyhow."

After Rip Collins finished off the Tigers with a three-hit, 5–0 shutout in the final game of the series—the team's 18th win in its last 20 games—the Yankees traveled across Lake Erie by boat to Cleveland. Still trailing the Indians by percentage points, the team was facing its biggest field test of the year as well as a mob of excitable home fans intent on beating the big boys from the big city.

Clevelanders prided themselves on being among the most rabid but friendliest fans in the American League. But stung by recent abuse hurled by Cleveland fans at Joe Jackson, Ross Tenney of the Cleveland *Press* issued a stern warning on the eve of the big series:

"It's to be hoped that there'll be no repetition of ill-bred and uncalled-for booing in this series when Babe Ruth steps to the plate," Tenney advised. "A few fans did this without any excuse whatever when Joe Jackson was here early this season with the White Sox. Jackson merely answered them by pounding the ball all over the lot and making life miserable for Indian hurlers. So let's shut up anybody that tries to boo or jeer Babe Ruth."

The Indians were a hot team, led by the American League's top three batters—Tris Speaker at .397, first baseman Doc Johnston at .382, and new left fielder Charlie Jamieson at .380. A stickler for fundamentals and hustle, Speaker, the game's only player-manager in 1920, had his Clevelanders playing crisp baseball, marked by sharp fielding and aggressive baserunning that was paying off with a season for the ages.

That they were doing so was remarkable considering the loss of several top players, namely star pitcher Stanley Coveleski, whose powerful right arm had silenced the Yanks the previous month back at the Polo Grounds. On May 28, while preparing to pitch at League Park in Cleveland against the White Sox, Coveleski received a telegram with devastating news: his wife, sick for three years, had died suddenly at their home in Shamokin, Pennsylvania. A shaken Coveleski left that afternoon for home, and wouldn't return for several weeks, forcing the Indians to throw in a makeshift group of pitchers in his place.

Then, on Memorial Day, Jack Graney, a fixture in left field for a decade, who Jamieson had replaced earlier in the season, was diagnosed with tonsillitis. It was the beginning of the end for the fan favorite Graney, the team's all-time leader in games played, runs scored, and triples. He was batting only .250 in 1920, which was downright puny next to Jamieson's big numbers. Graney came back, but sparingly; two years later, he'd retire after 14 big-league seasons.

Cleveland fans ignored Tenney's call for civility. It rained until noon on the day of the series' first game, holding the Saturday crowd to 20,000, many of whom needled the Yankees from the get-go. They yelled at the New Yorkers from the moment they stepped on the field, calling them "bushers" and lending, the *Times* wrote, "more commotion and hullabaloo than there is at most world's series carnivals."

Quinn, owner of an eight-game winning streak, was on the mound for the Yankees. But on this day, the veteran spitballer wasn't sharp. Jamieson rifled a single over short to open the game, and reached third on Chapman's single. He scored on Speaker's single, although Chapman was thrown out on a close play at third, which third-base coach Chet Thomas protested with such vigor that he was tossed by umpire Billy Evans.

The Yankees clawed back, knotting the score at four, thanks to two runs in the fourth and again in the sixth off former Yankee Ray "Slim" Caldwell. A Yankee for nine years, the 32-year-old Caldwell had achieved some success—winning 18 games in 1914 and another 19 in 1915—but never reached his potential, thanks to a fondness for the bottle and a penchant for breaking training rules and clashing with managers like Frank Chance. Unloaded by Huggins in 1919 to the Red Sox, Caldwell went later that season to Cleveland, where in his first game for the Indians at League Park, he was knocked out by a bolt of lightning, but got up a moment later and pitched a complete-game victory. By 1920, he was trying to hang on, keeping batters off balance with pitches of varying speeds and a variety of deliberate delaying tactics on the mound intended to disrupt batters' timing.

Emotions nearly boiled over when, with the score tied and two gone in the sixth, Doc Johnston took Quinn deep with a triple to center. But when Johnston chugged around third and kept on going, Truck Hannah stood at the plate with the ball, thanks to fine relays from Bodie and Lewis. Out by 10 feet, Johnston slid hard anyway in a futile attempt to jar the ball loose from the Yankee catcher. As he slid, one of Johnston's spikes nicked Hannah on his little toe, causing the catcher to leap up with his fists cocked, poised for a fight. Out ran players from both teams to restrain the two men and bring the inning to a shaky end.

The score was still four-all in the eighth when Chapman walked, was sacrificed by Speaker to second, and scored on Larry Gardener's single up the middle. Caldwell held on for the 5–4 win.

The press overlooked the fact that Babe Ruth in 1920 didn't have much time for them, and didn't give a hoot about cultivating his image. It was taken care of for him—an easier process than today without the prying eyes of television cameras and reporters who actually ask questions about things beyond batting averages. Covering Ruth was suddenly important— and papers resorted to all measures, from ghostwritten stories to running as many photos of Ruth as possible. The *Daily News* even took to running parts of photos—a column where Ruth purportedly discussed his batting eye featured a close-up of just his eyes.

New York fans couldn't get enough. Babe Ruth was a genuinely unaffected, charismatic hero. Here was someone people wanted to know and read about—a welcome relief from unrelenting postwar news of labor unrest, Red scares, and the lingering ravages of the mammoth flu epidemic. Then, as now, New York was a great place to be a star provided you produced. Then, as now, there was the New York tradition of people moving to the city from somewhere else—and becoming both a winner and a New Yorker in the process. Nobody cared much that Ruth was from Baltimore and talked with a slight Southern twang; he was starting to personify the big team from the big city, as Joe DiMaggio from San Francisco and Mickey Mantle from Oklahoma would do in later generations. He was the big swinger in the big town, a man whose perpetual motion and restless energy matched his new surroundings.

By early June 1920, Ruth was a bona fide New York phenomenon, the prime topic of discussion in the city's 32,000 speakeasies during Prohibition. This was baseball as entertainment—as much a day's outing as the Hudson River steamer cruises that left weekend mornings from the Battery and for a round-trip fare of 60 cents (half that for children under 12) dropped off picnickers at Bear Mountain State Park.

There were an admittedly less-crowded bunch of entertainment options in 1920. With relief from the summer heat a big goal of many New Yorkers in those days before air-conditioning, roof dining was popular—so much so that the Strand at Broadway and 47th Street made it the main feature of their $1.75 "dinner de luxe," which came with dancing and "an entirely new and elaborate revue." Motion picture shows were gaining popularity as well, and giving the Broadway stage a run for its money with orchestra-led silents such as *The Wonder Man* starring boxer Georges Carpenter and Cecil B. DeMille's comedy *Why Change Your Wife?*

So what else could New Yorkers find to amuse themselves that summer? There was dancing at the year-old Roseland Ballroom off Times Square, a different class from the seedy dance halls where men could buy a dance for a dime. People looked for summer rentals to get away for the weekend, as they do today. Westchester County, now a northern suburb, was considered the country back then, where an eight-room house in Larchmont was yours for $1,200 'til Labor Day. Meanwhile, the Jersey shore and Brooklyn beaches were big destinations for those wanting to get away—visitors to the Hotel Shelburne in Brighton Beach could choose the $3 "European Plan," which entitled them to a room for the night with ballroom dancing to the music of Lieutenant J. Tim Brymn's military band. Meanwhile, New Yorkers could always go shopping, and choose from genuine South American Panama hats for $5.64 from Macy & Co. on Herald Square and men's suits for $37.50 from Leighton's on Broadway, just north of Times Square.

Ruth's extraordinary ability to cut through the abuse of a road crowd and win their hearts and minds was in full force that Sunday. Some 30,000 Clevelanders—the most to ever attend a game in the city—crammed into League Park. The crowd seemed ready all over again to call the Yankees whatever bad names that came to mind. But when Ruth put on a fierce display of power during batting practice, sending one shot clear out of the ballpark onto Lexington Avenue, he got the fans behind him.

So it went during the game. Indian left-hander George Uhle opened the game by getting Peckinpaugh to fly to center—Cleveland's highlight of the day. Meusel then doubled and Pipp doubled him home. It was 1–0 Yankees. Ruth and Pratt both walked and were followed by Bodie, who doubled, driving home Pipp and Ruth: 3–0. In came a new pitcher, Elmer Myers, who gave up a single to Lewis that scored Pratt: 4–0 Yanks. Hannah then flied out to left, scoring Bodie to make it 5–0. Shawkey then rapped a single, scoring Lewis, who slid into home to make it 6–0. The inning's only blemish: when Lewis slid, he badly wrenched his left leg, and would miss the next two weeks.

With their Indians out of the game, Cleveland fans turned their attention to Ruth and whether he could hit one out. As the game wore on, cries of "let him hit it" came tumbling from the stands, particularly when Myers appeared to be walking Ruth. With two down in the sixth, Ruth did hit it—home run number 17—cracking Myers's fastball clear over the right-field screen and over the roofs of houses on the opposite side of Lexington Avenue to make the score 9–0.

The final was 14–0, putting the Yanks .006 percentage points behind the first-place Indians. "I gave him only one fastball, and you saw what he did with it," Myers grimly told reporters in the locker room afterwards. At least Chapman seemed upbeat: "We'll get them tomorrow," he called out. "And the next day."

So they did. On Monday afternoon, the Indians pounded the Yanks for 15 hits, all but one off hard-luck Herb Thormahlen. On the mound was Coveleski, back after his wife's death and a subsequent two-week layoff, and he was effective in limiting the New Yorkers to five hits en route to a 7–1 win.

Chapman was right about the next day, too. The Indians scored five in the third, two from walks, driving Mays from the box. In came Collins, but he didn't do much better, and the Indians, behind Jim Bagby, coasted 10–2. Halfway through their road trip, the Yankees' bats were booming, but their pitchers, and Mays in particular, were showing signs of wear and tear.

Mays was still unglued, with his curveball, speed, and particularly his control seemingly vanished. Huggins said Mays, after missing the season's first series in Philadelphia and enduring a rash of early season rainouts, had never found his rhythm. Later, much later, Mays admitted there was something else on his mind that season: the spring training beaning of Chick

Fewster, one of his few friends on the team. Accustomed to working the inside part of the plate, Mays had been haunted by the beaning, and now seemed particularly reluctant to work close to the plate.

In Chicago against the White Sox, the Yankee bats kept on booming. The New Yorkers took three of four from the defending A.L. champs, with big crowds turning out to see what Ruth would do.

Even the heavens couldn't stop the Babe. For reasons known only to umpire Big Bill Dinneen, the series' opening game on June 16 was kept going despite intermittent rain, periodic claps of thunder, and a muddy field. "Dinneen, the human duck, didn't have sense enough to come in out of the rain, and, worse than that, kept the ballplayers out in the downpour with him," the *Times* wrote. "A policeman doesn't like to sleep any more than Dinneen likes rain."

With the Yankees up 3–2 after seven innings, it was raining so hard that Dinneen finally halted play. It rained hard for another 20 minutes, leaving the field a virtual mud pile. The game should have ended right then and there, but Dinneen resolved to continue. When the rain let up, out came an army of groundskeepers with brooms, sawdust, and ashes to get rid of the puddles. White Sox skipper Kid Gleason urged the men to work faster, knowing that the heart of the Yankee order—Pipp, Ruth, and Meusel—were due up in the eighth.

Trudging out to the mound to face the Yanks in the eighth was Sox starter Red Faber. "He should have worn rubber boots and a raincoat," the *Times* wrote. Pipp slapped a single to right and the rains resumed, coming down harder with each second. Then came a clap of thunder, and another. Still, Dinneen did nothing, and up came Ruth, stalking through the mud to face Faber. It was a delicious moment, like a scene from the film *The Natural* when even the thunder couldn't stop Roy Hobbs. But this was real life, and Ruth cracked a delivery from Faber on a long arc toward right field. Sox right fielder Eddie Murphy backed up to the fence, but the ball dropped into the crowd for a home run, Ruth's 18th. The shot upped the Yanks' lead to 5–2, and despite another rain delay and a White Sox rally, the New Yorkers, behind Quinn, Mogridge, and Shawkey, held on to win 7–4.

Ruth hit home run number 19 the following afternoon off Lefty Williams in the fourth. Ruth was showing no concern about weather conditions, blasting this shot into the teeth of a gale-force wind blowing in from center field and clear over the right-field bleachers onto Michigan Avenue. Ruth was decimating the competition with home runs, and giving people hope that his all-time record of 29 would soon be eclipsed. Best of all, Mays showed up and went the distance in holding the Sox to seven hits. The final was 7–2 Yankees, who remained a fraction behind Cleveland for first place.

Ruth and the Yankees, behind Shawkey, won again the next afternoon, piecing together a run in the ninth to beat Dickie Kerr 3–2. If that disappointed the 10,000 Sox fans, it was nothing next to the invective they hurled at Kerr, who in the ninth had the nerve to walk the Babe, preventing him from hitting one out. As Ruth trotted down to first base in what was only a one-run game at the time, many of the spectators actually got up to leave. Call it another powerful but subtle statement in the summer that Babe Ruth took America by storm.

The Yankees appeared to have had the game won the following afternoon when something freaky happened. Ahead 4–3 with two gone in the ninth and Shano Collins at second base, Chicago's Byrd Lynn batted for pitcher Eddie Cicotte and lifted what seemed to be a routine fly to left center, well within range of left fielder Sammy Vick. But in from center field thundered Ping Bodie, also hoping to make the game-ending catch. The two collided and the ball fell. By the time Del Pratt ran out and threw the ball toward the infield, Collins had scampered home with the tying run. The Sox scored two in the tenth to win 6–5 and spoil a good performance by hard-luck George Mogridge.

The loss was a hard one. It also took a toll on the Yankees' health. Vick had replaced Ruth in the second after White Sox third baseman Buck Weaver uncorked a throw toward first and plunked Babe, the base runner, in the noggin, leaving him dizzy and disoriented. Then Mogridge turned his ankle in the tenth, when he slipped on the infield grass while fielding a ball hit by Joe Jackson. Quinn promptly entered the game, and with two runners on base yielded a long smash by Happy Felsch down the right-field line that scored both runs and pulled the game out for the Sox. It also kept them in third place and within four games of the Yanks and Indians. A three-team American League race was emerging.

For George Mogridge, the turned ankle and the late-inning loss were emblematic of a frustrating year. Big things were expected of the 6'2",

165-pound beanpole of a left-hander in his fifth full season with the Yanks. Purchased by the Yanks from the White Sox in late 1915, the Rochester native endured three losing seasons in a row, but on April 24, 1917, he did something rare—pitching the second no-hitter in Yankee history in a 2–1 victory against Boston. (Tommy Hughes had pitched the first, holding Cleveland hitless in 1910 over 9 innings, and losing 5–0 in 11.) Mogridge's gem would be the first and only no-hitter by a Yankee left-hander for 66 years until Dave Righetti no-hit Boston in 1983. That is hard to believe considering all the great Yankee left-handers through the years, such as Herb Pennock, Lefty Gomez, and Whitey Ford. In 1993, Jim Abbot would join Mogridge and Righetti as the only Yankee lefties to throw no-hitters.

Mogridge's no-hitter was a slight harbinger of things to come. In 1918, Mogridge broke through—opening the Huggins era with a 6–3 Opening Day win over Walter Johnson and the Senators. Mogridge was a Huggins guy—a workhorse who pitched a league-high 45 games that season and posted his first winning season at 17–13 for the fourth-place Yanks. He followed with a decent season in 1919, going 10–7. Mogridge and the Yanks' other lefty starter, 23-year-old Jersey City native Herb Thormahlen (13–10 in 1919), provided the Yanks with enough lefty ability, if they were healthy.

At least Ruth's injury wasn't serious. So there he was in right field, and the Yankees, winners of 23 of their last 29 games, moved on to St. Louis, where on Sunday, June 20, another throng arrived at Sportsman's Park. There were 27,000, the biggest crowd to ever see a game in St. Louis. The fans filled every crevice of the grandstand, lined the aisles, and even hung from the steel girders. So many people were in the park that they spilled out onto the outfield, and the game was held up for several minutes until police, with the aid of ropes and pleadings from managers Jimmy Burke and Miller Huggins, managed to push them into the outfield corners, clearing center field. Umpire Dinneen let the game begin, but only after he imposed a special ground rule limiting a ball hit into the outfield crowd to a double.

St. Louis was agog over its Browns, winners of 10 in a row, the last 4 a sweep of the A's. Now only a game under .500, the Browns had emerged from the bottom of the standings and were threatening to overtake fourth-place Boston and fifth-place Washington.

But Ruth was the man the crowd came to see. He was the man of the hour, and could entertain even when he wasn't banging baseballs out of the park. Before the game, friends presented him with an oversized bouquet of flowers, and in the second he singled off spitballer Urban Shocker and scored when Bodie poked a home run into the right-field seats.

The score was still 2–0 when Ruth stepped to the plate in the fifth to face Shocker. Maybe it was the big crowd, or maybe it was just the heat and humidity of the St. Louis summer, but in a genuine theatrical moment, Shocker suddenly wheeled around and motioned his outfielders to move in, enraging Ruth. The veteran Browns' pitcher fired a pitch inside, and the Babe swung and missed. Shocker turned again and signaled the outfield to move in more closely. Again he threw, and again Ruth, gripping the bat tightly in his anger, swung and missed. Strike two. Shocker had his outfielders move in again. He uncorked the 0–2 pitch, and Ruth swung and missed for strike three. Steaming mad, the Babe turned and trudged back to the dugout. Shocker just laughed; he had shown up the great Babe Ruth. But the Yanks held on to win 4–3 behind Quinn, the workhorse, who won his 10th game despite giving up three hits to George Sisler and two each to Jack Tobin and catcher Hank Severeid.

But on Tuesday afternoon, just when Huggins was hopeful that Carl Mays had turned the corner, the erratic Yankee right-hander was pounded again, this time 9–3, as the Browns chased him from the box in the fourth after he gave up eight runs and nine hits. This time, Mays seemed unnerved by thunderstorms, which held the game up for more than an hour and had left the field muddy. He was shaky from the start, giving up a run in the first and three more in the third. In the third, he drilled Severeid in the ribs, enraging the batter, who threw his bat at Mays and rushed the mound. The two were separated, but Mays ran into more trouble in the fourth, loading up the bases and forcing in a run with a walk. In came Rip Collins, who gave up a double to Jimmy Austin for three more runs. The loss evened Mays's record at 7–7.

But as the Yankees were doing again and again, they bounced back the next day in the series' final game, beating Shocker 6–3. Shawkey earned his eighth win in a row, despite leaving the game with a strained back muscle. Most satisfying of all, Ruth got redemption, nailing Shocker for his 20th home run of the season.

What a road trip! Boarding the train for the long trip home, the Yankees had taken 10 of 15 games—"good enough as a road team to get real consideration as a pennant contender," the *Times* wrote. They had hit a ton and packed grandstands in every city they had played. With a 39–22 record, they were still only .042 percentage points behind the Indians, and were beginning to have the look of champions. Contrast that to the poor Philadelphia A's, who had headed west about the same time as the Yanks and dropped all of their 15 games, the majors' longest losing streak of the season.

Could the Yankees' first pennant become a reality? With Ruth, anything seemed possible.

SEVEN

"What Counts Is Socking That Ball and Giving It a Ride"

Ruth Becomes the Sports Phenomenon of the Age

On June 17, 1920, in Chicago's Wrigley Field, home of the National League Cubs, a team from Manhattan's High School of Commerce beat Chicago's Lane Tech High School 12–6. On the surface, that event seemed ordinary, except for several things, starting with the fact that the New York high schoolers, most of whom had never traveled more than 50 miles from home, had gotten to meet former President William Howard Taft, also aboard the Pullman that had delivered them to Chicago. Taft, now a Supreme Court justice, was a big baseball fan and had inaugurated the presidential tradition of throwing out the first ball of the season, and wished the boys well.

Notable as well was the name of the 16-year-old Commerce slugger who had delivered the game's decisive blow—a ninth-inning grand slam that sailed over the right-field wall and onto the porch of a house fronting Sheffield Avenue. The youngster, according to the *Times*, was named "Gherrig." The paper wrote of his home run that "the real Babe Ruth [had] never poled one more thrilling."

The ballplayer was in fact named "Gehrig"—Lou Gehrig. He would join the Yankees just 3 years later and stay with the team 17 more, playing in 2,130 straight games en route to a Hall of Fame career. But the real impact of Gehrig's home run could be measured in another way—by comparing any slugger to Ruth, the *Times* was bestowing on the Babe the new mantle of home run king.

Ruth's home run hitting was becoming the sports phenomenon of the age. Interest was so intense that it almost seemed that the 38,000 seats in the Polo Grounds were not enough to hold the crowds sure to cram the ballpark all summer to see what Ruth would do. "Anybody gets a big kick out of taking a cut at the ball and hitting it on the nose," he said. "Why, you take a 60-year-old golfer. Nothing in the world gives him such a thrill as clipping that golf ball on the button with a full swing. They'll tell you the science of fine shots is what counts. But that's all baloney. What counts is socking that ball and giving it a ride."

Sportswriter Grantland Rice rhapsodized, "Man o' War, 'Babe' Ruth, Jack Dempsey . . . Has Dame Nature suddenly decided to build up a new world kingdom of greater power in place of the more or less effete collection she has used until this trio stepped forth?"

Rice, a courtly Southerner and among the press box giants of his age, shrewdly saw that Ruth was no flash in the pan. "There is little truth in the rumor that Colonels Huston and Ruppert have requested 'Babe' Ruth to desist from knocking the ball out of the park until the cost of baseballs comes down a bit," he wrote in early May 1920.

By midsummer, Rice was devoting more than humorous throwaway lines to Ruth's slugging. He was writing poetry, such as this excerpt from "The Crime of the Ages":

Why is the mad mob howling?
Hurling its curses out?
Why is the wild wind yelping?
What is it all about? . . .
Maybe you've guessed the answer.
Hung to the bitter truth—
Only the rival pitcher,
Starting to walk Babe Ruth.

In the *Tribune*, W. O. McGeehan extolled Ruth's performance as well— doing so through the use of the archaic, annoying, and slightly racist voice of immigrant wise guy Izzy Kaplan, a fictional character speaking in dialect for the common man.

"I chust been up to the Polish Grounds, looking at Baby Ruthstein when he is making run homes," McGeehan wrote early in the season, an acknowledgment of the staggeringly high immigration rates that had made

New York almost 30 percent Jewish. "All the time he is hitting the baseballs out of the lot instead of knocking them into the stands, where, maybe, you could get some of them back."

Later, Izzy wondered if the livelier ball had something to do with Ruth's long-ball capabilities. "When all these fellows like Baby Ruthstein is hitting run homes at the Polish Grounds," McGeehan wrote, "my brains is asking me what is the reason that baseballs should go further this year when a dollar wouldn't go for a quarter as far."

Everyone had their theories about Ruth, including Miller Huggins. "Take all the adjectives there are in the language which could be used to describe a slugger, plaster them all on and then wish there were a few more for good measure," he said. "You can't describe him, you can't compare him with anybody else. He's Babe Ruth."

He was indeed. Ruth's legend was building. His titanic blasts were so utterly different from what anyone was used to that he was changing the game every time he sent another ball beyond the outfield fences. That he could do it after staying up all night doing things most of us only read about made him even more popular. "Fans everywhere loved him no less for his infractions," wrote Cobb's biographer Al Stump. "Vicariously, they were right with him."

Every Ruthian blast fueled the legend—creating a completely new game, based on clout versus the traditional scientific game favored by Ty Cobb and John McGraw. Sportswriters focused on this new game, calling it "a whale versus a shark." Said Phillies' right fielder Casey Stengel, who would finish near the top of the National League home run race in 1920 with nine: "Nah, it's a bomb against a machine gun."

Walter Johnson cited Ruth's batting eye and physique as clues to his greatness. "He is tall, heavy and strong," the Big Train said. "His weight is in his shoulders, where it will do him the most good. He is a tremendously powerful man. . . . He grasps the bat with an iron grip and when he meets the ball, he follows it through with his full strength and weight. For his size, Joe Jackson is as hard a hitter as Ruth, but that margin of 30 pounds in weight and enormous reserve strength enables Ruth to give the ball that extra punch, which drives it further than anybody else."

Of all the baseball writers of the era, Ferdinand Cole Lane may have come the closest to describing the essence of Ruth's greatness. Trained as a biologist and equipped with a healthy wanderlust that had taken him from his native Minnesota to Italy and several stops in between, Lane joined *Baseball Magazine* in 1910 and by 1912 had become its editor, a position he held for the next 27 years. The New York–based monthly magazine gave Lane both the space and the forum to pursue in-depth features and profiles, many of which are collected in his only book, *Batting*, published in 1925 with a plain brown paper cover and costing $1. Although Lane (34 years old in 1920) was ambivalent about the slugging game that Ruth personified and still considered Ty Cobb baseball's premier player, the Babe recognized his baseball knowledge and confided in him on all aspects of the game.

"Do you see those mud hooks?" Ruth asked Lane one day at the Polo Grounds, extending his enormous, powerful hands to provide more evidence of his abilities. "There's a lot of strength in those hands," said the Babe, gripping the handle of a bat. "And do you notice anything about those hands?" he added, extending his palms to reveal they were covered with calluses. "I got those from gripping this old war club. The harder you grip the bat, the faster the ball will travel. . . . When I swing to meet the baseball, I follow all the way around. . . . In boxing, when you hit a man, your fist generally stops right there, but it is possible to hit a man so hard that your fist doesn't stop. When I carry through with the bat, it is for the same reason."

Ruth's analogy spoke to a larger truth: a reservoir of breezy confidence. Never one to remember a name, Ruth was nonetheless struck by a onetime Red Sox teammate, a prospect who had done well in spring training and headed north, where early in the regular season he revealed a fear of the high and tight fastball. Ruth wondered if he'd been beaned. Pitchers caught on to the prospect's fear, and continually drove him away from the plate. By July, he was back in the minors, never again to be seen in the majors. Ruth's point, as articulated by Lane: "Don't let them get your goat."

Cobb was convinced that time would catch up to Ruth and he would soon fail. He figured pitchers would soon adjust to Ruth's big uppercut of a swing. He considered Ruth undisciplined at the plate, too much of a guess-hitter, and unable to master the curve. Besides, Cobb knew more than most about the stories of Ruth's prodigious appetites off the field. One morning, with the Tigers in New York for a series, Cobb was out at 6 A.M. for a run along Park Avenue when he bumped into Ruth returning home after a long night.

"Been having a good time?" Cobb asked.

"Pretty damned good," replied the Babe. "There were three of them."

In time, Cobb would come to admire Ruth, and the two would become golfing companions. When it became clear that Ruth was anything but a flash in the pan, Cobb began to appreciate his gifts, and get to the essence of what made him special. "After Ruth had been around awhile and no longer pitching, I could see what made him so different," Cobb said in later years. "His pitching made him a hitter [of home runs]. As mostly a pitcher, he didn't have to protect the plate as I did and the other regular hitters had to do. He could try this and that. Experiment. Learn timing. As a pitcher, if he flopped [at bat], nobody gave a damn. Pitchers always had been lousy hitters. . . . Once [Ruth] got smart and grooved his cut, he had a whole new career."

Like Ted Williams, Ruth was enormously disciplined at bat. He knew the strike zone—in 22 years, he *never* led the American League in strike-outs—seldom swung at bad pitches, and drew an enormous number of walks. Brooklyn (and later Cleveland) left-hander Sherry Smith recalled pitching for the first time against the Yankees—he walked Ruth four straight times, but only once intentionally, setting off "an awful howl from the stands," as he told F. C. Lane. But Ruth's eye was so good that Smith had little alternative: "If Babe got balls somewhere near where he liked to hit them, he would bat .450," he said. "He seldom gets a good ball. A pitcher is foolish to give him a good ball, especially with men on bases."

Pitcher Smith knew his subject. Walks for Ruth were fast becoming a way of life. The Babe would walk a league-leading 148 times in 1920, and also lead the league in 11 of the next 13 years.

Like Cobb, John McGraw regarded the excitement greeting Ruth's every trip to the plate with disdain. Long the toast of New York, that is until Ruth arrived, McGraw and his Giants had just finished a mediocre 7–7 homestand and were stuck in seventh place, six games under .500 and behind everyone but the lowly Phillies. McGraw hated losing, despised being out of the limelight, and took his wrath out on Ruth. The feisty Giants manager was old-school, a man who made his name with the great Baltimore Orioles teams of the 1890s and established his genius by playing dead-ball rules to the extreme—bunting, hitting behind the runner, steal-ing bases, and shooting for the single run. Like Cobb, McGraw looked at Ruth's ability to hit the long ball with derision and a touch of resentment.

McGraw and the Giants were having a wretched time of it in 1920. Ten games into the season, Frankie Frisch, the sensational 21-year-old shortstop from Queens by way of Fordham University, underwent an emergency appendectomy after being taken sick on a train bound from Boston. In May, McGraw was suspended for five games after arguing a little too strenuously with umpire Bill Klem in Pittsburgh. At about the same time, his longtime star pitcher and now coach and closest friend Christy Mathewson was diagnosed with tuberculosis, and departed for treatment in upstate New York.

But McGraw was having more than just a lousy season. After years as the city's top dog in the baseball world, he and his team, long the choice of the New York establishment, were being upstaged by the Yankees of Jacob Ruppert, the very man he had urged to buy the team back in 1914. Making it doubly painful was that this seismic shift in the New York landscape was happening on the Giants' turf—the Polo Grounds, which the Giants and Yankees had until now peaceably shared since 1911.

The Yankees had made noises about finding a home of their own for years. One of the team's original owners, Frank Farrell, tried for years, even secretly buying lots in the Spuyten Duyvil section of the Bronx back in 1909 for that very purpose. But Farrell and his former companion Bill Devery ran into financial problems and had to sell the team before they could do anything about it.

After Farrell and Devery sold the team in 1914—about the same time Hilltop Park was torn down—the Yankees' effort to find a new home became the province of Ruppert and Huston. It didn't much matter that the team remained at the Polo Grounds for the next four years because the Yankees were a mediocre outfit and drew peanuts next to the Giants. But the need to move became a full-blown issue in 1919 when the Yanks, under Miller Huggins, showed promise and took third. And in 1920, with Ruth stealing attention, gate receipts, and the hearts of fickle New York fans, McGraw took a stand: the Yankees and their $65,000 annual rent would have to go.

McGraw had been thinking of that for some time, having fired the opening salvo of the latest skirmish back on May 14 when, through Judge Francis McQuade, the club's treasurer and Tammany Hall bigwig, the Giants announced that the Yankees would not be permitted to play at the Polo Grounds once their lease expired at the end of the season.

In Pittsburgh to face the Pirates, McGraw again left the talking to others. McQuade's announcement was brief and said nothing beyond the basics. Giants President Charles Stoneham, who in 1919 had bought the team with McGraw and McQuade as partners, offered a little more, saying that "it would be better for the sport if the Yankees had their own grounds.

"New York is a big city and there is ample room for another plant of this kind," he said. "I remember once talking to [Ban] Johnson about it, and he agreed with me that the two baseball parks in Chicago have been a good thing for baseball. I think the same holds good for New York."

Especially galling for McGraw and other baseball officials was the Yankee–Red Sox pipeline, and how effortless it seemed for Ruppert and Huston to tap their drinking pal Harry Frazee for top-flight ballplayers. There were Ruth and Mays, and rumors ran rampant that Red Sox catcher Wally Schang was openly maneuvering to get himself sold off to the Yankees. Nothing could really be done, and in time, the other owners had every reason to be miffed, as a virtual parade of Red Sox went to New York, all to pay for Frazee's theatrical productions.

Ruppert fired back at McGraw immediately, claiming that in 1916, as part of the Federal League peace settlement, he had received a verbal assurance from former Giants owner Harry Hempstead that the Yankees would have a long-term lease at the Polo Grounds for as long as the team desired. Hempstead had assumed the presidency of the Giants in 1912, after the death of John Brush, his father-in-law.

"However, if the Giants do not want us any longer on the Polo Grounds, there is no use trying to stay around where one is not needed or wanted," Ruppert said. "I do not know how successful the Yankees will be this season, but we will probably be able to find a home somewhere for 1921."

To do so, he'd have to work quickly. Prospective sites for a new Yankee ballpark were bandied about. One plan had the team relocating at the corner of Amsterdam Avenue and 137th Street, opposite City College in Harlem. Another possible location was at 11th Avenue and 57th Street on the West Side, and two others were in Queens, both near the 59th Street Bridge. But nothing was definitive.

The Giants had every legal right to evict their tenants, but their position struck a sour note in New York circles after years of relative peace between its two major-league teams. "The argument that two parks will help baseball may be true of Chicago, but it has not been true of St. Louis, Philadelphia or Boston, the other cities where two clubs play major league games in different parks," the *Times* wrote. "There is a suspicion, too, that in Chicago, the Cubs would draw better at Comiskey's South Side park than on the North Side while the White Sox are away. Until such use can be found for a ballpark while the home team is away, there seems to be no convincing answer for two fields, with their huge overhead expenses."

But in the end, it was a brouhaha that blew over. A week later, with the Giants in Chicago, Ban Johnson called McGraw, Stoneham, and McQuade into his office and told them to settle their differences with the Yankees. The eviction order would be rescinded, and the Yankees would keep their home at the Polo Grounds in 1921 and beyond—but their rent was upped to $100,000 a year. A month or so later, Ruppert agreed to the terms.

For a man like Jacob Ruppert, a rent increase was a minor annoyance to running what suddenly had become a profitable business. Big crowds were regularly descending on the Polo Grounds to see the Yankees play, making this former stepchild of a team an enormous success in the battle for the hearts and minds of New York baseball fans, and proving that an investment in baseball could be successful after all.

After five frustrating years of ownership under Ruppert and Cap Huston, the Yankees were winning, and the turnstiles were clicking at a record rate. The question wasn't whether the Yanks would break their all-time home attendance record of 619,000, set the year before—it was how many more they'd draw, and if they could break the American League record set by the 1917 Chicago White Sox (684,000) and the major-league record of 708,000 set the year before by the Giants. Could the Yankees draw 1 million? What a turnaround from the team the two had purchased, with A.L. President Ban Johnson's considerable help, back in December 1914.

At the time, there were all kinds of rumors that the team was on the block. In 1914 the Yankees had finished seventh in the eight-team A.L., 30 games behind the pennant-winning A's. The rumors were confirmed on December 9, when a New York *Sun* reporter caught up with Ban Johnson as he stepped off a train from Chicago at Grand Central Terminal.

Seldom had the blustery Johnson shied from a reporter's notebook or a camera. But there was no bluster this time—only minimal comments for the record. In this case, Johnson's trip from Chicago was one of quiet purpose, a mission intended to secure new Yankee ownership. "Now that the news has leaked," he admitted, "I will confess that my recent mysterious visit to this city was made in connection with the contemplated sale of the New York club. I will say further only a difference of opinion as to value has kept the proposed deal in the air."

The prospective suitors, Jacob Ruppert of Manhattan and the improbably named Tillinghast L'Hommedieu Huston of Havana, were polar opposites. On the surface, they were similar men. Both were rich and came prepared to shell out large amounts of cash and use their considerable business abilities to jumpstart the Yankees and lead them from the wilderness of baseball mediocrity.

Both were military men. For starters, Ruppert was a colonel and Huston a captain who later became a colonel. Both men preferred to be addressed by their military monikers—good news for Huston because it spared him from being called "Tillinghast." Ruppert had earned his rank in the National Guard, and Huston from service as a captain of engineers in Cuba during the Spanish-American War. During World War I, Huston became a colonel for service in France building roads and railways under heavy German shell fire.

"The Yankee Colonels [as they became known] were the strangest pair of men I have ever known in baseball," wrote Ed Barrow, who began his long career with the Yankees in 1920 as the team's business manager. "When [they] agreed to buy the Yankees . . . it must have been the only time they ever did agree."

Otherwise, they were dead-ball baseball's version of the Odd Couple. Ruppert was the solid conservative, and Huston was the slovenly, erratic adventurer. As an aristocratic New York gentleman of leisure and business, the cerebral 47-year-old Ruppert would be out of fashion today. The first baseball team he had managed was composed of neighborhood boys his age on the Upper East Side, and although he later admitted that his enthusiasm for the game far exceeded his ability to play it, he was elected captain anyway—after buying the uniforms and equipment.

A future in baseball didn't seem to be in the cards once Ruppert hurt his arm. He passed the entrance exams to the School of Mines at Columbia University, but decided he didn't want to be a mining engineer, choosing instead to join the Ruppert Brewing Company, the company founded in 1851 by his father, Jacob Sr.

The young Ruppert showed early that he had a knack for business. At 23, he was placed in charge as general superintendent of the brewery when his father went away on an extended trip, and he did so well that the position was made permanent. By his late 20s, Ruppert had become general manager of the company, and within several years had tripled production.

Otherwise, Ruppert led the life of a young, wealthy late-nineteenth-century man about town. A lifelong bachelor, he directed a fleet of servants that included a butler, maid, valet, cook, and laundress in a 12-room mansion on the northwest side of 5th Avenue and 93rd Street, two blocks from the brewery on 3rd Avenue. The mansion had spacious grounds in the back that featured a peach and apple orchard.

Ruppert was a man of many passions. At 32, he was elected to the first of four terms in Congress, where he served as a Tammany Democrat in the silk-stocking Republican Upper East Side. Ruppert attended the opera and the right parties. He collected first editions, racehorses, jades, and porcelains. And if that wasn't enough, he yachted and in 1933 sponsored the second Byrd Antarctic Expedition. At his country estate in the Dutchess County hamlet of Garrison on the Hudson River, Ruppert raised St. Bernards and Boston terriers, kept a racing stable, and even a score of monkeys.

In business, he was gruff and direct—always addressing people by their last name and with a German accent, which made his words sound slightly intimidating. "Ruth" came out "Root" and the Colonel, never one for speeches, often directed short barbs to players he meant to motivate. "Now go out and win 30 games," Ruppert told Lefty Gomez after a contract signing. And to Waite Hoyt, Ruppert once asked, "What's the matter with you? Other pitchers win their games 9–3, 10–2. You win yours 2–1, 1–0. Why don't you win your games like the others?"

Huston was different. A rumpled, earthy man with a jovial air, Huston did not collect jades or porcelains. Whereas Ruppert or a valet carefully selected his clothes each day, Huston often wore the same creased suit for days on end. His real passion was people and a need to connect—to his many friends, Huston was simply "Cap." He liked nothing better than hanging around with the writers at spring training and going on the road with his players. Huston's frequent companion, W. O. McGeehan of the *Tribune* had another name for him: "The Man in the Iron Hat," a reference to his single concession to fashion, his derby.

A Cincinnati native, Huston combined restless ambition with a knack for making a buck. He got rich by staying in Havana after the Spanish-American War, with little capital, setting himself up in business by building the docks and piers there.

Huston's special skill was dealing with politicians to ensure that lucrative contracts came his way. While in Havana, Huston directed improvements to harbors in Santiago, Cienfuegos, and Matanzas. "Never do anything you can hire someone to do for you," he said. "It's the one who tells the other fellow what to do who reaps the profits."

Huston stayed in Cuba for more than 10 years, and moved easily among the sporting circles of wealthy Americans who enjoyed visiting Cuba to gamble and play. John McGraw, who met Huston during one of his frequent excursions there with the Giants, became a close friend, and when McGraw and his wife, Blanche, vacationed at the Havana Country Club, the two men spent considerable time together.

After moving to New York, Huston resumed his friendship with the Giant skipper. And it was through McGraw that Huston met Ruppert at the Polo Grounds to watch the Giants.

Ruppert was the first of the two to discover baseball. Nearly two decades before, he had toyed with the idea of buying the Giants, but he gave up after Andrew Freedman rejected his offer and instead sold the team, in 1903, to John Brush. In 1912, the Colonel considered buying the Cubs, but changed his mind so he could stay in New York. "I wasn't interested in anything so far from Broadway," he said.

What Ruppert still wanted to own was the Giants. He brought in Huston and approached McGraw, who said there wasn't a prayer that the team was for sale because Brush's widow and daughters were determined to keep the team in the family. Running things would be Harry Hempstead, the late owner's son-in-law.

"But if you really want to buy a ball club, I think I can get one for you," McGraw said. "How about the Yankees?"

Neither man was interested. Own the Yankees, a pathetic stepchild and tenant of the lordly Giants, the toast of New York? No way. But McGraw's vision was broader than theirs, and he assured Ruppert and Huston that they could become winners provided they pumped a healthy amount of cash into new players. "The New York American League club would be a fine investment if a championship team could be assumed," he told them.

"I am sure that [you] are just the men to go ahead and get the necessary material."

McGraw was convincing as a lobbyist. When at last Ruppert and Huston relented, they found both Farrell and Devery receptive to a deal. The years of losing had taken their toll: Farrell and Devery had started out as friends, but were barely speaking to one another by 1914. The last few years had been particularly hard on Farrell, who had spent a lot of money on players that hadn't worked out and gambled away even more at the race-track. The Yankees' home crowds had grown noticeably thin as well, drop-ping to less than 360,000 in each of the previous four seasons. When Ruppert and Huston came calling, Farrell had considered pledging his stock as security for a loan, forcing his hand.

Sounding like a man who was ready to pack it in, Farrell said a deal came down to the right amount of cash. "It is purely a question of paying me my price," he said. "Every man has his price and I have mine. If the prospective purchasers meet my terms, I shall be willing to step down."

The suggested selling price was $500,000. Ruppert and Huston coun-tered with $400,000, leaving the two sides far apart. There were other problems—among them the catering contract of hot dog king Harry Stevens. It turned out that Stevens had taken out a 10-year lease in the spring of 1914 at the Polo Grounds. Ruppert wanted the catering contract for himself, but he yielded. The hot dog king capped his lease.

The negotiations dragged on—two days became three, turned into four, and then five. Not wanting to inherit a completely hapless team, Rup-pert and Huston were driving a hard bargain, asking that Ban Johnson guarantee them a name manager and five veteran players from other A.L. teams.

Finally, on December 31, the deal done, with Ban Johnson announcing that the Yankees had been sold to Ruppert and Huston for a reported $500,000. As part of the agreement, Ruppert was named Yankee president and Huston secretary-treasurer. The new owners even got their players—outfielders Hugh High of the Tigers, Walter Rehg of the Red Sox, and ex-Cardinal Elmer Miller, along with Rochester first baseman Wally Pipp and second baseman Joe Berger of the White Sox. If Johnson's intrusion seems unduly autocratic today, consider another transaction he made that winter—ordering star infielder Eddie Collins to transfer from the A's to the White Sox, a move that became integral to making Charles Comiskey's Chicagoans the class act of the American League.

Ruppert and Huston got their manager, too—Wild Bill Donovan, who had spent the previous two seasons managing Providence of the International League. "We will have to begin at the bottom with the process of reconstruction," Wild Bill said a couple of days later. "We will try to build up a harmonious club with all the men working together. That is an essential ingredient."

Then the new owners did something shrewd—they hired Harry Sparrow as the team's business manager. A longtime crony of both McGraw and Huston, Sparrow had served in a similar position for the Giants and White Sox on their 1914 world tour. From the get-go, he gave the Yankees the fiscal stability the team had lacked for years.

The final price, as Ruppert had suggested some weeks before, was $450,000 after all. True to a man of his bearing, Ruppert showed up with his lawyers and a certified check for $225,000, his half of the purchase price. Then it was the rumpled Huston's turn—reaching into his suit pocket, he pulled out 225 $1,000 bills, tossing them casually on the table. The Odd Couple indeed.

"For $450,000," Ruppert said, "we got an orphan ball club, without a home of its own, without players of outstanding ability, without prestige." Along the way, they got a franchise that for neither man had ever really been a long-term obsession and one Ruppert had seen play only a handful of games—and those "only because Walter Johnson pitched or Ty Cobb was a participant."

The new owners, as businessmen with deep pockets and a fierce hatred of failure, did add a dash of respectability to the beleaguered franchise. However, things didn't get better immediately. The Yankees, under former Tiger pitcher Donovan, won 69 games in 1915, one less than they did the year before. In 1916—thanks to 23 games won by former A's pitcher Bob Shawkey—the Yankees improved marginally to fourth place, six games above .500 for their first winning season in six years.

But that was as far as Wild Bill Donovan would go. In 1917, his Yanks didn't get much further, dropping to sixth place—nine games under .500—as several veterans started leaving to join the war effort. The 1918 team—playing an abbreviated schedule and now led by Miller Huggins—was more of the same: the team took fourth, but lost three more than they won. Only in 1919 did the Yanks finally find their groove. Shawkey, back from the U.S. Navy, won 20 and the writers had taken to calling the Yankee lineup "Murderers' Row"—a nickname curiously coined while Ruth was still with Boston and Frank Baker was the team's home run leader with 10. The Yanks finished in third place, only seven and a half games out, for their closest finish in 13 years.

By midseason 1920, his team's improvement had Ruppert's juices flowing. "There is no charity in baseball," he said. "I want to win the pennant every year." With Ruth now a Yankee, was that too much to ask?

With the Yankees home on June 25 for the first of four games against the Red Sox before going back on the road to Philadelphia and Washington, New York fans couldn't wait to see what they would do next. They didn't have to wait long.

It hardly mattered that in the first inning of the series' opening game, Boston's Harry Hooper tagged Jack Quinn for a long home run into the upper deck of right field to put the Red Sox ahead 1–0. In the bottom of the first, Roger Peckinpaugh continued his torrid hitting by knotting the score in a flash with a home run to the left-field corner off Herb Pennock.

Then, after Pennock retired Ward and Pipp, up came Ruth. The crowd of 20,000—"all keyed up . . . with home run fervor," the *Times* wrote—rose and cheered. Pennock threw a curve, which Ruth struck on the sweet spot of his 54-ounce bat, sending the ball deep into the stands in right-center field.

Just like that, Ruth had clocked his 21st home run. He had taken to marking a notch around his bat's insignia for each one. This homer had put the Yanks up 2–1, and just like that, the stands erupted in bedlam. "Twenty-one and eight to go," yelled a man from behind the Yankee dugout when the noise had subsided enough to hear a single voice. The newspapers called it the longest home run hit yet at the Polo Grounds, but what Ruthian blast wasn't?

The Red Sox tied the game at two in the third and took the lead in the fifth, with both runs coming off Quinn, who was lifted three innings later for a pinch hitter. Boston then padded their lead in the ninth with three more runs off poor old Herb Thormahlen. But the lead was soon forgotten in the bottom of the ninth when Ruth stepped to the plate against Pennock and clubbed home run number 22.

This homer was too little, too late in a 6–3 loss to the Sox, but it was memorable all the same—a crushing shot that hit the top facade of the right-field roof and bounced back onto the field. It was becoming commonplace for reporters to give lavish descriptions of the trajectory of Ruth's home runs: "But for the interruption," the *Times* reported, "the drive would have carried far into the runway to the 'L' station exit, where hundreds of fans had lingered to get another look at the mighty slugger." The next day's headline in the *Times* didn't mention the loss first: "Ruth Makes Two," it read, "But Yankees Lose."

On Saturday, June 26, the Yankees bounced back before more than 36,000 at the Polo Grounds. Everything they hit seemed to land somewhere. Peckinpaugh and Bodie each had three hits, and a parade of Yanks had two each, and although curiously there were no home runs, the Yanks cruised 14–0. Combined with the White Sox's 12–7 win over the Indians in Chicago, the Yanks were now a scant half game from the top.

The lively Yankee hitting was one story. The pitching prowess of young Rip Collins, filling in for the injured Shawkey and emerging as a star, was another. All that the Red Sox managed off this cool-as-ice 24-year-old rookie right-hander was a lone dinker of a single to center by third baseman Eddie Foster to start the second that Bodie stretched for but couldn't reach. It was Collins's third win, and second shutout—and people were starting to take notice.

A native of Weatherland, Texas, Harry Warren Collins was a character on a team of characters. An all-around athlete who starred at Texas A&M in football, basketball, and baseball, he had earned his colorful nickname from his fondness for Ripy Whiskey, particularly popular back in Texas.

The nickname fit. "When I was six years old, I could drain off a goblet of beer and smack my lips," an elderly Collins would tell the *Sporting News* years later. "Corn whiskey later took the place of beer."

Collins was a Texan through and through. An avid hunter, he said he couldn't wait for the baseball season to end so he could get back home "for the wild country and the call of the coyotes." He collected guns, and would eventually own 135 of them.

And while he claimed to dislike the nightlife and big crowds of New York, Collins sure made the most of it. "I hit all the high places in New York," he once recalled. "The lights weren't quite bright enough for me, so I made them brighter. Many a morning I rolled home about 5 A.M. I didn't realize it at the time, but Miller Huggins gave me more consideration than I deserved."

Collins's emergence came at a good time for the mostly veteran Yankee pitching staff, which was banged up and showing signs of overwork. Quinn was a workhorse and having a season for the ages, but he was almost 36. There was Mogridge's lame ankle and Shawkey's bad back to think about. Compounding the concern was Mays's inconsistency and both Shore's and Thormahlen's continuing ineffectiveness.

"Until Huggins can get his staff of sharp-shooters in trim, the Yankees probably will have to slug their way to victories or take a tumble, and though the Yanks have shown they can slug, remember that there are other teams in the American League who also can hit—and which have some pitching to boot," Joe Vila wrote in the July 1 *Sporting News*.

One of those teams, wrote Vila, was the White Sox, who despite collapsing in the 1919 World Series and amid continuing whispers that the team would occasionally lose on purpose, were barely hanging onto third place, thanks to steady pitching from Eddie Cicotte, Lefty Williams, and Dickie Kerr. "Along Broadway, where the wise men congregate," Vila wrote, "the impression prevails that the White Sox will make things extremely interesting for the Indians and the Yankees."

Indeed, the Yankee bats were primarily responsible for taking the series' final pair from Boston with considerable drama. Before 33,000 on Sunday, June 27, the New Yorkers rallied for five runs in the eighth to spare Mays in another shaky performance and pull it out 7–5. Down 5–3, the Yanks tied the score with Ruth's triple—a "howling triple" according to the papers—off sidearm spitballer Al Russell, which spanked against the right-center-field exit gate. Then Ruth scored the winning run on Meusel's double.

And although the Indians maintained their slim lead with a 4–1 win over the White Sox and Ruth hit no home runs, the game was still a treat for residents of faraway Atlanta, Georgia, and Galveston, Texas, where detailed play-by-play accounts were flashed on the sides of newspaper buildings and telegraph offices, scaled-down versions of the big board in Times Square, where thousands could watch the progress of the World Series. Everyone everywhere wanted to know when Ruth would hit one next.

It wasn't the next game, which the Yanks took with another late rally. The heroics were becoming almost commonplace. This time, they scored three runs in the ninth to pull it out 6–5 on consecutive singles off Sam Jones from Pratt, Hannah, pinch hitter Frank Gleich, and Peckinpaugh, followed by Ward's double. Then, with the score 5–5 and Pipp at bat, Sox manager Ed Barrow brought in Pennock. Peckinpaugh, representing the winning run on third, was sure to be off with anything Pipp could put into play. On the first pitch, Pipp did put something into play, sending a roller toward second. It was enough, for with the crack of the bat Peckinpaugh was off. He scored a second later, and the Yanks had pulled one out for Herb Thormahlen.

The Yankees were finding improbable ways to win, and as one spectator remarked, "are never beaten these days as long as there is any daylight." But the same could be said of the Indians, who took a doubleheader from St. Louis to stay on top of the American League. People still poured into the Polo Grounds, with more than 107,000 taking in the four games against Boston.

The next morning, June 30, at the Aldine Hotel in Philadelphia, where the Yankees were preparing for the start of six games in four days against the A's, someone reminded Babe Ruth that the only cities where he had not hit a home run so far in 1920 were Philadelphia and Washington.

Being a competitive man, Ruth resolved to do something about that. It didn't take long. That afternoon, in the ninth inning of the first game of a doubleheader, Ruth strode to the plate to face the A's rookie pitcher Lyle Bigbee, a native of Sweet Home, Oregon, with the intent of knocking the baseball into the next solar system. He struck Bigbee's curve on the nose, sending the ball way beyond the right-field wall at Shibe Park into the general vicinity of greater Philadelphia. Ruth's 23rd home run of the season put the Yanks up 6–3. It was enough, even after Jack Quinn gave up two in the ninth. The final: Yankees, 6–5.

In the fourth inning of game two, Ruth added another home run—this one off Scott Perry for number 24. It helped as Collins cruised and the Yanks won 10–6 to stay on the heels of the Indians. The Babe had hit 12 home runs in June and was a dizzying 17 home runs and two full months ahead of his record 1919 pace. Meantime, his batting average was at .372, among the league leaders. For Ruth, the question had become when—not if—he'd break his record, and how many more he'd hit after that. Fans were asking the same of the Yankees, who had just bashed and slugged their way to a 20–9 record for June. They'd hit a startling 27 home runs that month (they would hit a more-startling 38 in July). It was a question of when, not if, they'd catch Cleveland.

They got their answer the next afternoon—July 1. With the Indians idle, the Yanks beat up on the A's again, this time 9–5, to slink into first by the narrowest of slivers—.002 of a point. Ernie Shore replaced Mogridge, and pitched well enough for the win, his second. Ruth had no home runs, but still helped himself to two hits, as did Peckinpaugh and Meusel. After the game in the clubhouse, the Yankee players let out three cheers and a couple of hip-hip-hoorays.

"They were a jubilant troupe," the *Times* wrote. "The[y] exuded almost as much joy as if they had clinched the championship and were assured of a place in the world's series sun."

If the Yankees had anyone to thank, it was A's owner and manager Connie Mack. His last-place team was hapless, helpless, and oh so generous. They lost the last three games of the series to the Yanks, making it a clean sweep and paving the way for the New Yorkers' nine-game win streak. Thormahlen got the 7–4 win July 2 and Mays and Collins completed the sweep with a doubleheader win on July 3.

Mack did another favor for the Yanks while they were in Philadelphia. He talked with Bryan Hayes and convinced him to drop all charges against Carl Mays, who was still unable to accompany the Yanks to Philadelphia. So Hayes, the fan who said the pitcher had intentionally plunked him with a hard-thrown ball back in 1919, rescinded, provided Mays apologize.

The welcome news came July 1, and Mays caught the next train to Philadelphia. On July 3 at a meeting in Mack's office, Mays delivered his formal apology to Hayes, which he repeated to the 15,000 fans at the ballpark that day. Then he went out and shut down the A's 5–0.

Getting Carl Mays back full-time meant a lot to the Yanks, but as with everything else connected to the New Yorkers that summer, it took a back seat to Babe Ruth. How many home runs he had, how many he hit yesterday, and how many he had to go to break the record was all anyone seemed to want to talk about.

On July 4 in the first of four games at Washington, the Yanks fell from first place with a 5–2 loss to the Nationals and the Indians' 11–3 win at Detroit. But all any of the 15,000 spectators seemed to care about was whether Ruth hit a home run. He didn't—and had only a double. Nor did he hit one the next day, a Monday, July 5 doubleheader loss for the Yankees in which Ruth was injured before the largest crowd to ever see a game in Washington. The Babe sprained his left wrist in game one when he

Sixteen-year-old George Ruth, the left-handed star of the St. Mary's varsity team in 1911 *(National Baseball Hall of Fame Library, Cooperstown, NY)*

Ruth, star pitcher of the Boston Red Sox, World Series champions of 1916 and 1918 *(National Baseball Hall of Fame Library, Cooperstown, NY)*

It is April 22, 1920, and the newest Yankee demonstrates the pose that was about to set the baseball world on its head. *(Bettmann/Corbis)*

A shot down the third-base line at the Polo Grounds *(National Baseball Hall of Fame Library, Cooperstown, NY)*

The classic "Ruthian" pose. Note the airbrushing around Ruth's head, the result of a newspaper editor's tinkering. *(Brown Brothers)*

Ruth at Madison Square Garden for his new movie, *Headin' Home*, in 1920
(National Baseball Hall of Fame Library, Cooperstown, NY)

This photo from spring training in 1920 could be the earliest surviving photo of Ruth as a Yankee. *(National Baseball Hall of Fame Library, Cooperstown, NY)*

It's off the "El" and into line at the Polo Grounds, all to see Babe Ruth wreak havoc on A.L. pitchers. *(National Baseball Hall of Fame Library, Cooperstown, NY)*

Ruth batting with a view of his favorite target: right field at the Polo Grounds *(Brown Brothers)*

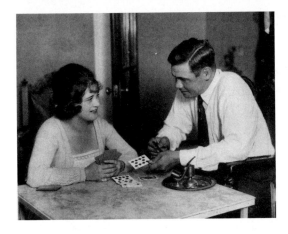

Ruth poses with his first wife, Helen Woodford. It's hard to believe that with all his carousing, Ruth was actually married. *(Brown Brothers)*

The physique that in 1920 launched 54 home runs. The famous beer belly would come later. *(National Baseball Hall of Fame Library, Cooperstown, NY)*

Red Sox owner Harry Frazee, the man immortalized for causing "the Curse of the Bambino" *(National Baseball Hall of Fame Library, Cooperstown, NY)*

Red Sox manager Ed Barrow
*(National Baseball Hall of Fame
Library, Cooperstown, NY)*

Roger Peckinpaugh
*(National Baseball Hall of Fame
Library, Cooperstown, NY)*

Yankee manager Miller Huggins (left) and the team's co-owner, Col. Jacob
Ruppert *(National Baseball Hall of Fame Library, Cooperstown, NY)*

Ping Bodie *(National Baseball Hall of Fame Library, Cooperstown, NY)*

Duffy Lewis *(National Baseball Hall of Fame Library, Cooperstown, NY)*

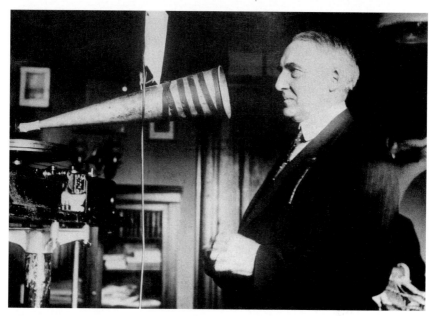

Ohio senator Warren G. Harding campaigning for president in 1920 *(Bettmann/Corbis)*

Bob Meusel *(National Baseball Hall of Fame Library, Cooperstown, NY)*

Wally Pipp *(National Baseball Hall of Fame Library, Cooperstown, NY)*

Del Pratt *(National Baseball Hall of Fame Library, Cooperstown, NY)*

Aaron Ward *(National Baseball Hall of Fame Library, Cooperstown, NY)*

Carl Mays *(National Baseball Hall of Fame Library, Cooperstown, NY)*

An anti-Prohibition march *(Bettmann/Corbis)*

Bob Shawkey *(National Baseball Hall of Fame Library, Cooperstown, NY)*

Jack Quinn *(National Baseball Hall of Fame Library, Cooperstown, NY)*

George Mogridge *(National Baseball Hall of Fame Library, Cooperstown, NY)*

The incomparable Damon Runyon, leader of newspapermen *(Bettmann/Corbis)*

Baseball Commissioner Kenesaw Mountain Landis with Damon Runyon and a group of baseball writers *(Underwood & Underwood/Corbis)*

The notorious Ty Cobb *(National Baseball Hall of Fame Library, Cooperstown, NY)*

Shoeless Joe Jackson, one of baseball's greatest hitters, was banned for his role in the infamous Black Sox scandal of 1919. *(National Baseball Hall of Fame Library, Cooperstown, NY)*

Cleveland shortstop Ray Chapman, whose life ended in tragedy at the Polo Grounds *(National Baseball Hall of Fame Library, Cooperstown, NY)*

George Sisler *(National Baseball Hall of Fame Library, Cooperstown, NY)*

Cleveland Indians player-manager Tris Speaker *(National Baseball Hall of Fame Library, Cooperstown, NY)*

A poster from the 1920 Babe Ruth film *Headin' Home (Author's collection)*

slipped after rounding second, but came back for game two, with his wrist heavily taped. Considerably worse off was Ward, badly spiked above the knee while scooping a throw at second on an attempted steal during game one. Ward would be out for perhaps two weeks, and was replaced by, of all people, Chick Fewster.

Nor, curiously, did Ruth hit any home runs the next day, when the Yanks pounded the Senators for 16 hits in a 17–0 drubbing that put them back into first. Fourteen of those runs came in one inning—the fifth— when every starter batted at least twice. With no ill effects from his wrist injury, Ruth had two singles to boost his hitting streak to 22 games. Even better, Carl Mays pitched a three-hitter for his seventh win—and finally seemed to be settling in with his new teammates.

Several story lines were emerging in the Yankees' season. Somehow they were winning, despite injuries to Lewis, Mogridge, Shawkey, and Peckin- paugh—while keeping pace with the Indians and staying just ahead of the underachieving White Sox, who continued to be dogged by rumors that they had deliberately blown the previous year's World Series. "The players are hustling for Huggins, and the mite manager is showing marked abil- ity in shifting his players about to meet the emergencies that have devel- oped through several accidents," the *Times* reported on July 5. "It is a team that is worthy of all the interest that New Yorkers are taking in it."

Then there was Ruth, who was exceeding all expectations while living life to the fullest. Home was a suite at the Ansonia on the Upper West Side along Broadway between 73rd and 74th Streets with his wife, Helen, and their adopted baby daughter, Dorothy. When he had planned the Anso- nia, West Side developer William Earl Dodge Stokes was influenced by the idea that Broadway would become an elegant boulevard, the Manhattan equivalent of the Champs-Elysées.

That hadn't quite happened—Broadway by 1920 was commercial and noisy—but the ornate 17-story Beaux Arts building, built in 1904, stood out anyway. Designed like a Parisian apartment building, the Ansonia was adorned with turrets, balconies, carved masonry, and extensive ironwork. Inside, it featured the latest in luxurious, big-city living, with dining rooms, a butcher shop, laundry, piped ice water, a private electric plant, and fil- tered air—and had become home to a number of prominent artists and Broadway types, among them Enrico Caruso, conductor Arturo Toscanini, and theater impresario Florenz Ziegfeld. Also staying there were most big-league teams, whose players could step out the front door, head one block south to 72nd Street, and catch the subway to the Polo Grounds. That was pretty heady company for the virtually uneducated kid from Baltimore, but Ruth was seldom there, and often stopped at the Ansonia just long enough to shave, shower, and eat before leaving again, all within a swirl of cigar smoke.

By then, Helen wasn't around much either, choosing to spend most of her time at the couple's farm in Sudbury, Massachusetts, near Boston. There were reports that Helen was lonely and increasingly discouraged about the couple's nearly six-year marriage. But Ruth wasn't paying much attention, basking instead in his pursuit of the fast life—partying and bedding as many women as he could find. "You should have seen this dame I was with last night," he told a teammate, more out of admiration than boasting, "What a body, not a blemish on it."

The Babe was also enjoying his new custom-built maroon Packard. It had a 12-cylinder engine and was nicknamed "the Ghost of Riverside Drive" by teammates, because Ruth loved driving on the sweeping curves of Riverside Drive early in the morning. Ruth was also demanding special privileges, among them permission to drive his car during road trips to Washington and Philadelphia. Grudgingly, Huggins granted him his wish.

Even at the ballpark, Ruth seemed impatient and anxious to move on. "Babe is not a good man to interview," wrote F. C. Lane. "He is big and buff and rather reticent. Even when he means to help you, [he] hardly knows how to go about it. And to many interviewers he doesn't mean to help. Ruth is cursed with a perpetual impatience. He is always in a hurry to get somewhere, it matters little where, so long as it is a different spot from the spot where he happens to be."

The pace easily outdistanced his teammates, but nobody seemed to mind. He liked the night life, Peckinpaugh said, "but he was always at the park early the next day." And while Ruth was famous for never remembering a name and having a poor memory, he could remember how a pitcher threw to him five years before or the circumstances of a home run he'd hit in 1915. Huggins did his best in trying to get his star slugger to behave, but it was a lost cause; Ruth merely ignored and mocked his manager, derisively addressing him to his face as "the flea" and "little boy." In later years, the two would reach a truce, but not before Ruth—who, according to Fred Lieb, "never could accept managerial discipline"—gave

Huggins "a miserable time." Said Huggins's sister and housekeeper, Myrtle: "Babe Ruth took five years from Miller's life."

Their relationship wasn't helped by the leniency Ruppert and Huston granted their star. When Ruth asked to stay at different hotels than his teammates on the road, the Yankee owners relented. In mid-June, when Ruth bought a new four-door touring sedan and asked to drive the car on the upcoming road trip to Philadelphia and Washington, they relented again.

In Washington, Ruth's home away from home became the Willard, where, as was his style, he set himself up with a flourish—lounging about in red slippers and a red robe, smoking a cigar. Dozens of visitors would stream in and out of his suite through the night, and Ruth even took to carrying a wind-up phonograph on road trips. He'd always be shaved by a barber—"that's what they're for, aren't they?" he'd say. Ruth particularly enjoyed singing, and even for a time took to carrying around a ukulele for such occasions.

At the Willard, when Joe Judge, the Nationals' first baseman, ran into Ruth coming out of the hotel, he asked where the rest of the Yankees were staying.

"They're over at the—the what's-it down the street," replied the Babe, gesturing vaguely. "But I'm staying here."

Judge laughed. "It must be nice to be rich," he said. "How much do they soak you for, Babe?"

"A hundred bucks for a suite."

"A hundred bucks a day!" Judge said.

"Well," the Babe gruffly replied, "a fellow's got to entertain, don't he?"

EIGHT

"They Came from as Far as Kokomo and as Near as the Bronx"

A Nail-Biting A.L. Race Captivates the Country

At 3 A.M., July 7, on a winding road east of Philadelphia, Ruth's devil-may-care lifestyle caught up to him. At the wheel of his new car on his way back to New York, and accompanied by his wife, Helen, catcher Fred Hofmann, outfielder Frank Gleich, coach Charley O'Leary, and a healthy supply of bootleg liquor, he rounded a bend near the hamlet of Wawa, skidded, and rolled into a ditch.

Bodies flew every which way. Remarkably, Ruth crawled from the car and began looking for the others. Helen seemed to be OK, as did Hofmann and Gleich, but not O'Leary, who lay unconscious in the middle of the deserted road.

Crouching beside him, Ruth was inconsolable. "Don't let him die," he wailed. "Lord, don't let him die!" Whereupon O'Leary came to and sat up. "What the hell happened?" he muttered. "Where's my straw hat?"

What happened was Ruth's extraordinary luck that no one was seriously injured. The Babe had banged up his knee in the wreck, and limped as the crew walked to a farmhouse nearby to get help. By daybreak, they had caught a ride into Philadelphia, where a newspaper, on hearing rumors of the crash, had rushed to print with the story that Ruth was dead. The Babe quickly called Ruppert with assurances that he and the others were OK, but later that day they arrived back in New York to another headline: "Ruth Reported Killed in Car Crash."

The news sent shock waves around the city, and many New Yorkers skipped work to gather around bulletin boards outside city newsrooms for further word, which came around noon and assured the multitudes that the Babe was indeed fine. In that week's *Sporting News*, Joe Vila focused on Ruth's luck, saying it may have underscored how well things were going for the Yanks.

"Perhaps this narrow escape has driven the Jinx away for the rest of the year," he wrote. "At any rate, Ruth will ride in railroad trains and trolley cars in future, rather than run further risks."

On Thursday, July 8, 20,000 fans showed up for the first of a welcome 21-game homestand against western teams. Against the Tigers, the banged up Yanks, with Ruth, Lewis, and Peckinpaugh recuperating on the bench, fielded a makeshift lineup that included Fewster in his first Polo Grounds start since his spring-training beaning. The Yanks had the lead but lost it when the Tigers scored three in the ninth off hard-luck Rip Collins to win 4–3.

On Friday, the Babe was back, as 18,000 watched before game time as the Knights of Columbus presented him with a diamond-studded watch fob, its centerpiece set in the emblem of the order. Standing with his team-mates at home plate during the ceremony was Ping Bodie, who later wise-cracked that "if anyone handed me a cluster of sparklers like that, it would be my luck to have them turn out to be ice. . . . The best I get for hitting home runs is a box of socks."

Then the Yankees went to work, jumping on Tiger left-hander Red Oldham for four runs in the third, three on Bob Meusel's home run into the lower right-field stands. Then, opening the fifth, it was the Babe's turn, and he took Oldham to the upper deck of right for his 25th homer of the season as the Yankees, behind Quinn, coasted 9–3 for their 50th win of the season against 27 defeats.

Huggins was relieved. For all the troubles his big slugger gave him, he needed a healthy Ruth if the team was to fight for a pennant. Ruth wasn't just hitting home runs; he was hitting them to win games, and wasn't going for more than a few days without adding to his total. And he was showing remarkably little regard for any type of pitcher—of his 25 homers, 12 had come off lefties and 13 off righties.

Nor did he care who was pitching. Red Oldham was the 12th pitcher he had homered off during the season, and although Ruth, as with many big sluggers, liked hitting off rookies, his victims had included some top talent: he had pounded Herb Pennock for three homers, Lefty Williams for two, and Urban Shocker, Dickie Kerr, and Jim Bagby each for one.

There was something magical about hitting home run number 25 on July 9, barely halfway through the season. On this date the year before, Ruth had hit number 10 off Shocker at St. Louis; he didn't reach hit number 25 until September 5. Yes, there was a pennant race, but the question on everyone's mind was when Ruth would break his record.

It was a wonderful fuss. Mail poured in offering get-rich schemes and outrageous requests. O'Leary took to keeping an extra locker for all the letters. Many he ignored, but some he answered, particularly those from young boys asking for an autograph. Ruth biographer Lee Allen estimates that in 1920, the Babe signed 5,000 photos and sent them to children who had written him, this at a time when the autograph craze was still far in the future.

That fact alone underscored the essence of Ruth's extraordinary appeal—that for all the gruffness, he always had time for kids. When a shoe company offered him a free pair for every homer, Ruth accepted, provided the company donate each pair to a Catholic orphanage in New York. "I never turn down a boy," he said. "It's the boys who make baseball." Although Ruth was receiving more publicity than a movie star, "the chances are that he made 10 quiet visits to see a boy in a hospital for every one that was publicized," wrote Allen.

Add to the list all the countless appearances that Ruth made for charity, showing up at clubs, schools, and church bazaars, particularly when it came to the Knights of Columbus and Catholic organizations. It was a deluge. Priests and nuns carting bats, photos, and requests for personal appearances waited for him everywhere he went. All over the country, baseballs autographed by Ruth were auctioned off by the Elks and the Knights of Columbus.

Some actually felt for the Babe, claiming, as one colleague said, "the priests milked him for everything they could get." Some hangers-on admitted as much. Westbrook Pegler, the writer, said he often delivered Ruth to private events, and pocketed most of the appearance fee himself, which Ruth never even realized. Why did Pegler do such a thing? He disliked the Babe, calling him on one hand "an unequaled exhibition, whose strength and accuracy with a baseball were of a pace with the madness for crazy pleasure, unheard-of-speed, and aimless bigness convulsing the nation," but on the other hand "unbelievably mean, foul-mouthed, and violent."

But Ruth was on a roll. Whereas many of the ballplayers enjoyed walking to and from the Polo Grounds on good-weather days, such simple tasks in public were becoming difficult for Ruth, who was followed just about everywhere he went.

"[Ruth] blocks the traffic going to and from the clubhouse," a witness said after watching the mob scene he attracted. "Men and boys fought with one another yesterday after the game to reach his side and grasp the mighty hands which clutch the home run bat. Girls and women make him pose for snapshots and proud fathers edge their lads up to him to lay his mammoth paws on their curly heads." Adding to the commotion were hawkers who gathered at the Polo Grounds gates to peddle photos of the Babe as well as sheet music of the latest popular song, "Oh You Babe." Even palm readers jumped in, asking if they might read the lines of those famous hands.

As the year wore on, Ruth took to leaving the ballpark through the back exits, catching a cab that he'd direct away from the main streets, just to keep from getting mobbed. It didn't matter where he was; as Ruth's popularity soared, kids everywhere sought him out, wanting to tag along, shake his hand, or ask for an autograph. Leaving Comiskey Park in Chicago, novelist James T. Farrell, then 19 years old, saw the Babe surrounded by more than 100 kids, "who pushed, shoved, scrambled and yelled so that Ruth could scarcely move.

"Wearing a blue suit, and a gray cap, there was an expression of bewilderment on his moon face," Farrell wrote of Ruth. "He said nothing, rolled with the kids, and the strange, hysterical and noisy little mob slowly moved on to the exit gate with Ruth in the center of it. More kids rushed to the edge of the crowd and they, also, pushed and shoved, Ruth swayed from side to side, his shoulders bending one way, and then the other. As they all swirled to the gate, Ruth narrowly escaped being shoved into mustard, which had been spilled from an overturned barrel. Ruth and the kids left the park, with the big fellow still in the center of the crowd of kids."

And that was just in the cities where Ruth played baseball. "One can only speculate on how this went over in rural and small-town America, where the daily newspaper, perhaps a weekly magazine, and the Sears, Roebuck catalog represented virtually the sole contact with the outside world," wrote biographer Kal Wagenheim. With every home run and every move, 1920 was becoming Ruth's year.

The Babe kept pace. On Saturday, July 18, he cracked home run number 26 to draw within three of the record. The Yanks were ahead 3–1 when Ruth, his left wrist still taped from the injury in Washington, stepped to the plate with one out in the third. "Crack it, Babe," yelled one of the 30,000 spectators. So he did, sending a pitch from Tiger right-hander Hooks Wiltsie far over the fence and into the alley separating the right-field grandstand from the bleachers. Moments later, straw hats littered the field in appreciation.

It was a good day all around. Ward and Peckinpaugh both returned from their injuries. Even Shawkey was back in uniform and seemingly recovered from his sore back as he tossed on the sidelines for the first time in weeks. On the field, Pratt and Bodie cracked home runs, and Ward, showing no ill effects of the spiking, fielded flawlessly at second.

On the mound, Herb Thormahlen ran out of gas, and with two gone in the ninth gave up three runs to knot the score at 6–6. So in trudged Mays, who retired Bobby Veach for the last out to send the game into extra innings. Mays set the Tigers down in the 10th, and then watched as Bodie ran home with the winner in the bottom of the 10th on Peckinpaugh's sacrifice to center. With under two innings of work, Mays got the win to improve his record to 8–8.

On Sunday, there was Mays again, starting before yet another Polo Grounds throng of 35,000. Opposing him was Tiger pitcher Howard Ehmke, with a surefire strategy for denying Ruth, now hitting .382, of his home runs: walk him. Ehmke walked Ruth in the first on four pitches, much to the derision of the big crowd. Then, in the third, with the Yanks up 3–1, Ehmke threw one in the general vicinity of home plate, and Ruth clocked it into the lower right-field stands for his 27th home run—two from the record.

Apparently, Ehmke learned from his slipup, but it came with a price. In both the fifth and the seventh, he walked Ruth on four pitches to more jeers. "Every last mortal in that gathering of 35,000 wanted to see Babe hit, and the idea of one man blocking the will of the populace was more than the crowd could bear," the *Times* wrote. "Ehmke reached a new mark in extracting jeers, hoots and hisses from a Polo Grounds crowd."

Poor Ehmke. By holding the Yankees to seven hits, his pitching was adequate, but five went for extra bases, including Ruth's home run and two doubles from Meusel, all of which contributed to a 6–5 Yankee win. Those two doubles extended Irish Bob's own streak—he was 11 for his last 20, including six doubles, a home run, and a single in his last three games alone.

But in the next day's papers, most of the attention was focused on Ruth and whether he could do the unimaginable—break his home run record at midseason in the upcoming five-game series against St. Louis. A lot of people would be turning up at the ballpark in the middle of the week to find out.

Midway through the 1920 season, the Yankees had all they could ask for: a nail-biting pennant race, a home run slugger performing feats never before seen, and enormous crowds. The team wasn't just outdrawing the Giants for the first time—they were attracting the greatest crowds in baseball history, outdrawing their fellow tenants at the Polo Grounds two to one, and typically attracting 15,000 or more on weekdays and 35,000 on Saturdays and Sundays. From Manhattan to Montana, the Yanks were on everyone's mind, but not only because of Babe Ruth—the team was clicking in large part because of a solid infield, a combination of veterans and rookies.

Wally Pipp, Aaron Ward, Roger Peckinpaugh, Del Pratt, Bob Meusel, and Chick Fewster were getting lost in the hullabaloo over Ruth. But they were hitting well, had plugged up the holes, and were doing so in a workmanlike, hustling way. Pratt may have been labeled a troublemaker back in his St. Louis Browns days, but now he, like the others, had become a Huggins guy.

Take Wally Pipp. Today, he's remembered as a trivia question: the guy replaced in 1925 by Lou Gehrig, who then went on to play a remarkable 2,130 games in a row. Even worse is the myth that surrounds the tale—that Pipp, the "man in the shadow," as the *Times* once called him, didn't play that day because he had a headache, a story that appeared *14 years* after the actual incident. No, Pipp didn't play that day because he was suffering from a headache—try a *fractured skull*, the lingering effect of a batting-practice beaning from hard-throwing Yankee rookie Charlie Caldwell, better known in later years as Princeton University's football coach.

Wally Pipp was a gamer both on and off the field, a Huggins guy before there were other Huggins guys. Twenty-seven years old in 1920, he had been the regular Yankee first baseman since 1915. So who was the first Yankee to lead the league in home runs? No, it wasn't Ruth; it was Wally Pipp, who in 1916 led the American League with 12, with Yankee third baseman Home Run Baker second with 10. Pipp led the league in 1917 as well, and although he hit only .251 in his first three seasons in New York, "he makes up for the infrequency of his wallops by their length," wrote *Baseball Magazine*. Indeed, it was in 1919 that the Yankee lineup first became known as "Murderers' Row," not because of Ruth, who wasn't yet on the scene, but because of Pipp, Baker, Bodie, and Lewis.

Born into an Irish Catholic family in Chicago, Wally Pipp grew up in Grand Rapids, Michigan, and attended Catholic University, where he decided to leave architecture for baseball. In 1912, he signed with Kalamazoo of the Class D Southern Michigan League, batted .270, and signed with the Tigers.

With precisely 68 games of minor-league ball under his belt, Pipp showed he was not a man to be treated lightly. Demanding a share of his purchase price, Pipp held out and threatened to go back to school rather than play for the Tigers. "Pipp may have been a pioneer for players' rights, but in 1913, he might as well have suggested that baseball be played indoors on a carpet," *Sports Illustrated* once wrote. His challenge went unheeded, and he soon ended his holdout, going 0–3 in his first big-league game on June 29, 1913, against the Browns. Pipp hit .125 in 12 games for the Tigers that year before getting shipped back to the minors, where in 1914 he broke through at Double-A Rochester, hitting .314 and leading the International League in homers.

Then, just days before the Yankees were sold to Ruppert and Huston, Pipp became a Yankee, largely because Ban Johnson ordered his American League owners to bulk up the floundering Yankees by selling them good players. Nobody paid much attention to the directive, except for Tigers owner Frank Navin, who peddled Pipp for the $7,500 waiver price. Only 21 years old, he was tapped as the team's starting first baseman.

Pipp hit only .246 in 1915, but by 1918, had shown pop in his bat, and was hitting .304 when the military called and he enrolled in naval aviation school at MIT in Boston. Despite playing only 91 games that year, Pipp was spared overseas duty when the war ended that November. In 1919, he enjoyed his best complete season to date by hitting .275 with seven home runs.

Years later, Pipp made a compelling case for the reason behind his relatively low home run totals. "In defense of my relatively measly record, I would like to point out that back in the dead-ball days, when freak pitches such as the spitball, emery ball, and shine ball were allowed, two of the greatest hitters, Larry Lajoie and Tris Speaker, each spent two seasons without getting a single homer. If hurlers were allowed to return to freak pitching, there would be a drastic slump in home run production."

Settling in for a Tuesday-afternoon doubleheader on July 13—the start of a five-game series against the Browns—Yankee players were startled to look up at the Polo Grounds' grandstand and see the fans still pouring in from the 8th Avenue El. On most other days, a midafternoon twin bill might draw 15,000, but these were not ordinary days, and by game time, 38,823—the Yanks' biggest home crowd yet—had somehow fit themselves into the park, bringing the year's attendance to more than 700,000, more than what every other A.L. club but Cleveland and Chicago would draw for the entire season. It was "baseball enthusiasm soar[ing] to undreamed-of heights," the *Times* wrote. "They came from as far as Kokomo and as near as the Bronx."

What they saw was the good, the bad, and the ugly. At the plate, they saw Ruth pressing to please the big crowd. He struck out five times and managed only a lonely single in six at-bats. At least the fans got to see the Browns' sensational young first baseman, George Sisler, who entered the game with a .416 batting average, have an equally frustrating day by going one for nine. And they saw the Yanks split with the Browns—Rip Collins dropped game one, 7–2, to Urban Shocker, but the Yankees took the second, 6–3, behind the welcome return of George Mogridge, his ankle sufficiently better.

Mixing a sharp curve with a spitter and the nearest thing to a 1920 version of the split-fingered fastball, Shocker smoothly struck out 14, including Ruth in his first three at-bats with not so much as a foul ball. Going back to Shocker's showy strikeout of Ruth back in St. Louis when he moved his infielders in—and Ruth's subsequent home run in his next at-bat—the two were developing a bona fide rivalry.

Nobody, except Ruth, seemed to mind that he was having a bad day. Even his strikeouts were entertaining, with the Babe taking mammoth cuts so forceful that he tended to end up in knots. "When Ruth fans, he fans right, and takes a healthy swipe at the ball anyway," the *Times* wrote. But when the big 6'5" left-hander Carl Weilman struck out Ruth in the fourth inning of game two, the Babe stalked back to the dugout, smashing his bat on the concrete steps in frustration. "I'll never strike out with that bat again," he said.

Ruth was still angry when he opened up the second inning against Dixie Davis on Wednesday, July 14, with only 12,000 in attendance. Before Davis knew what hit him, Ruth had pasted his 28th home run into the lower right-field grandstand. Davis wised up, and never threw anything else to Ruth that resembled a strike—walking him three times. He walked bunches of other Yankees too—six in all—but hung in there, giving up three runs on only five hits.

Opposing him was Quinn, who threw one-hit, scoreless ball into the seventh, when the floodgates opened. Sisler singled to left to open the seventh and went to second on Baby Doll Jacobson's bloop hit. Quinn then walked Ken Williams, loading the bases, after which Earl "Sheriff" Smith drove in Sisler with a dunker of a single to left. Wally Gerber then slashed a single to right, driving in Jacobson and Williams. Off trudged Quinn, and in ambled Ernie Shore, who gave up a double to Ernie Severeid, which drove in Smith for the inning's fourth run. Gerber then scored on Jack Tobin's sacrifice, and five runs had crossed the plate by the time the carnage was done. But the 7–3 final seemed insignificant next to the concern that Jack Quinn, having turned 36 only nine days before, was burning out.

Duffy Lewis was back on Thursday, July 15 for the first time in weeks, occupying his regular position in left field and allowing the Yankees to bring more stability to their wandering outfielders and allowing Ruth to get back to right. Maybe it was that, or maybe it was members of the hairy House of David touring baseball team—they of the long locks and bushy, flowing beards—on hand at the afternoon's festivities that drove the score up.

Neither starter—Herb Thormahlen for the Yanks, nor the Browns' Allen Sothoron—was on their game. Pounded early and often, both pitchers were driven from the box, which was unusual for games of the era. The

Yanks scored three in the first, but the Browns came back with six in the second, which the Yanks matched in the fourth. For all the game's hitting—Pratt would finish with four hits, and three Browns, Sisler, Williams, and Smith, each had three—all eyes were on Ruth, as he tried to tie his home run record.

He had a good shot in the ninth, when with the score knotted at 10–10 he stepped to the plate with one out against rookie right-hander Bill Burwell. How Ruth loved to tee off against rookies. But Burwell struck him out, and the game went into extra innings.

Burwell was still pitching and the score was the same when Ruth came up in the 11th, with Ward and Pipp on base with infield hits and nobody out. Now here was a situation: should the Browns walk Ruth to load the bases with no outs? Possible, but risky. So Burwell pitched to him as carefully as he could. The count went full. Figuring Burwell would have to throw a strike, Ruth was ready. It was a strike, and Ruth cracked it—the ball struck up against the top right-field frieze, perhaps three feet from clearing the roof, and plopped into the lower right-field stands, perhaps three feet fair.

Ruth had tied his record, with an extraordinary 61 games left to play in the season. In doing so, he had pounded the game's fifth home run—Pipp also homered for the Yanks—and driven in Ward and Pipp to win it dramatically, 13–10. The win kept the Yanks just percentage points behind Cleveland, which was busy pounding their third in a row from the hapless A's.

Ward and Pipp trotted home. Then came Ruth, absorbing the applause, but facing some added exuberance. This time, instead of just straw hats tumbling from the stands, several real, living, breathing people ran out onto the infield and pounded the Babe on the back as he rounded the bases after his record-tying blast. Amidst the celebration came another footnote of a record: Ruth's home run was the first time an American League batter had taken advantage of a new rule passed the previous winter by baseball owners allowing the batter in extra innings full credit for a home run when a lead runner actually wins the game. In years past, the clout was simply registered as a single.

Getting the win and a measure of revenge from his previous outing was Rip Collins, who relieved Thormahlen in the sixth and went the rest of the way, giving up just one run.

So could Ruth set the record on Friday in the series' final game? No. One reason may have been that just after the game started a little black dog wandered onto the field, which some said was a sign of bad luck. A more likely reason: the combination of good St. Louis pitching on the part of a 21-year-old left-hander from Pittsburgh named Bill Bayne, who struck Ruth out in the first and held him thereafter to a single, and some hefty hitting by George Sisler, who went three for five to pace St. Louis to a 5–2 win. In doing so, the Browns had beaten the Yankees three out of five games, and became the only road team that year to win a series at the Polo Grounds. Along the way, they had contributed to a full-blown Yankee pitching slump; this time, the culprit was Mogridge, who the Browns chased in the seventh. At least the Indians finally lost—5–4 to the A's.

Nor did Ruth set the record that Saturday, July 17, in the first of six games in four days against the White Sox, who appeared to be quietly rounding into form and were now crowding the Yanks for second in the American League race. Still clinging to first were the Indians at 54–27, followed closely by the Yanks at 54–29 and the Sox at 50–30.

With 36,000 on hand, Ruth had a double and two singles but no home runs as he and his mates roughed up Eddie Cicotte, who was looking about as hapless as he had in the 1919 Series. They chased Cicotte in the sixth and shellacked three Chicago pitchers for 21 hits, 41 total bases, and a 20–5 win for Carl Mays, who took his 10th win and fourth in a row. Every regular had a base hit but Ping Bodie. "And to think that I didn't get even a single when hits were as plentiful as snowflakes in January," said the "Pingless" one.

Mays gave up 15 hits but seemed to finally be returning to his old self. Doubly welcome for Huggins was news that Shawkey would be well enough to return within days. The day's real star was Aaron Ward, who combined a four-for-five performance at the plate with some slick stops at second. The 23-year-old Arkansas native had emerged from his spike wound as a star in the making—proving that he was not just a snazzy fielder, but a capable batsman, and aggressive enough for Fred Lieb to label him "scrappy."

Ward's whopper of a day against the White Sox lifted his batting average to .260. The hits were falling just in time, because while his glove had never been in question—he was now drawing regular comparisons to

White Sox hotshot third baseman Buck Weaver—his early Yankee batting averages were downright measly: .117 in eight late-season games in 1917, .125 in a military-shortened 25 games in 1918, and .205 in 27 games in 1919.

Despite the slow start, Huggins established early faith in Ward and never wavered. "I never met a more ambitious kid than Aaron," he liked telling anyone within earshot. "That boy wants to play so badly that he actually suffers when he has to sit on the bench."

Ward had felt that way from the time he developed a love for baseball as a youngster growing up in Little Rock. A true son of the South, his middle name was Lee, so named for the Confederate general. A ballplayer with a serious side, Ward worked in the Arkansas State Legislature as a page boy and graduated from Ouachita College intending to study law.

In college, the black-haired, dark-eyed Ward quarterbacked the football team and played shortstop for the baseball team. His range and quick hands earned him a contract in 1916 with Montgomery of the Southern Association, and in 1917 with Charleston, where the Yankees snared him in midseason. By then, he had become a second baseman and had developed a philosophical attitude about it.

"The backbone of the infield is undoubtedly at second base," he told *Baseball Magazine*. "For one thing, it's where most of the double plays originate. Then, second and short, between them, handle the great bulk of the infield chances. First and third are important; also, they are the wings of the infield and receive no such heavy battering. Weakness in a club anywhere is bound to show, but weakness around second base is likely to be fatal."

The Yankees were scoring runs in bunches again, giving fresh evidence that "inside baseball" was on its way to becoming a part of the past. Despite average pitching of late, "the enemy hitters have been outclassed by a mile, and the race this year is to the team that can slug the ball," wrote Vila in the *Sporting News*. "Not only do the Yankees slug, but they make their drives count, as their record of runs scored proves—and no one can deny that runs win ball games."

The Yankees seemed to come up with a different hitting star for every game. Whereas on Saturday, a hitless Ping Bodie trudged off the field muttering that "somebody will pay for this," on Sunday he did something about it. The "somebody" was Lefty Williams, who got into trouble from the get-go by loading the bases on a walk to Pratt, a double to Ruth—"half a home run," the *Times* wrote—and a walk to Meusel. Up stepped Bodie, who knocked a grand slam into the left-field bleachers to spot Rip Collins a quick four-run lead.

Bodie wasn't done. In the third, he doubled to drive in Ruth for the Yankees' fifth run, and later added a single, all coming in a steady downpour that most of the 33,000 spectators endured for a chance to see Babe Ruth take his shot at history. In all, the Yankees teed off for eight runs, more than enough for Collins, who went the distance, giving up only four. And although it was the Yanks' eighth win in nine games against the Sox, there was a twinge of regret: of Ruth's two hits, one was a double and the other a single. History was on hold.

"Only a stretch of bad weather can prevent the current week from being the greatest, from the standpoint of both attendance and enthusiasm in the baseball history of New York," the *Times* opined on Monday, July 19. "Pennant contenders hardly can be classed as novelties in New York, but the chase now underway in the American League has created an interest far exceeding that of the days when the Giants were making their numerous fights in past years."

The race was turning into a three-way dogfight. The Indians, due at the Polo Grounds for four games later in the week, were clinging to first, with the Yanks one and a half games back and the White Sox nipping at their heels. The crowds that turned out to see Ruth and the Yankees were so enormous—and with two doubleheaders in two days against the White Sox coming up, they were expected to keep drawing—that the drumbeat had again increased for a new ballpark, with Vila leading the charge.

Vila wrote that the team had abandoned the idea of building a park in Queens, and were interested in looking at a property near Broadway and 8th Street.

"A Yankee park so far downtown would be a novelty and a powerful magnet for fans who cannot leave business in time to reach the Polo Grounds," he wrote in the July 22 *Sporting News*. "Of course, nothing has been decided yet and in the end the Yankees may take their home to the Bronx. But it is better to locate on Manhattan Island if such a thing is possible."

More immediate was Ruth's chase of the home run record. Four homerless games weren't long in the great scheme of things, but for the 28,000 fans who showed up Monday on another wet day at the Polo Grounds, the wait seemed eternal. Compounding the anxiety was more rain, which had delayed the start of the scheduled 1:30 P.M. twin bill by a half hour.

The delay gave Ruth a chance to pay a rare compliment to a worthy opponent—Shoeless Joe Jackson—whose average, like the Babe's, hovered in the .380s. During batting practice, Ruth gave Jackson, the man whose batting style he had copied, one of his new bats. Ruth wished him well with the bat, but made Jackson promise that he wouldn't use it against New York. Shoeless Joe, a player of such prodigious gifts that he emerged from a South Carolina mill league to hit .408 in his first big-league season, accepted the bat with gratitude, rubbed in a few coats of tobacco juice, and a few days later used it for the first time in a game against the Red Sox and clubbed a 450-foot home run into the right-field bleachers.

Meanwhile, Miller Huggins gazed up at the sky and figured they'd be lucky to get in one game. But then the rain stopped, replaced by a burst of sun before dark, threatening clouds and a drizzle here and there set in for the rest of the afternoon—reason enough for both umpires and players to hurry things along before another downpour.

So when the Yanks broke it open early with a 6–0 lead off White Sox right-hander Roy Wilkinson after two innings, Huggins implored his team to step it up and work faster in an effort to get in the four and a half innings needed to make it a regulation game.

Many of the fans thought the extra snap and hustle in the race against rain was pretty funny. They took to cheering every groundout and putout that hurried the game along, and howled with glee when Eddie Collins fouled out to Ward for the final out in the fifth to make the game official, with the score now 8–0, all but assuring a Yankee win.

But in the first game of the twin bill, the only Yankee to go long was Ping Bodie, in the fifth off Wilkinson. Ruth added a double, and Pipp had three hits. But the best news was on the mound, as Shawkey, making his first appearance since tearing a back muscle on July 23, was his old self in limiting the Sox to nine hits for his eleventh win and the team's fifth in a row over the defending A.L. champs. They even made it through all nine innings. The final: 8–2 Yanks.

The rain held off, and the teams got to game two, with Herb Thormahlen facing Chicago's wisp of a left-hander, Dickie Kerr, whose two wins in the 1919 Series had been a Sox bright spot.

In his first at-bat, Ruth walked. Joe Jackson homered in the second to put the Sox ahead 1–0, which is where the score remained in the fourth when Pipp singled to right. Kerr then retired Pratt, and turned to face Ruth. The 5'7" lefty worked the count to 2–2, then uncorked a curveball that Ruth clocked squarely and convincingly into the lower right-field stands.

Number 30 had happened. Playing deep in right, Chicago's Nemo Leibold, his shoulders square against the fence, watched the ball disappear into the lower part of the grandstand, setting off a wild scramble to claim the ball.

Indeed, the Polo Grounds became a wild, waving collection of people celebrating a piece of history. Hats flew in the air and onto the field—it must have been a wonderful year for New York haberdashers—as Ruth, a wide grin creasing his face, circled the bases. After crossing home, he walked toward the dugout and doffed his hat at the multitude—the conventional form of acknowledgment. But the gesture had no apparent effect, as the cheers continued to ring out, so Ruth, now dubbed the "Wizard of Wallop" by the *Times*, bowed. Still the crowd cheered, so he bowed again. Minutes later, as he headed out to take his place in the outfield, the cheering resumed.

The blow put the Yanks ahead 2–1. But in the seventh, the Sox hit Thormahlen hard, piecing together three runs on a walk to Happy Felsch, singles to Shano Collins and Swede Risberg, an error at the plate by Truck Hannah, and two more singles by Nemo Leibold and Eddie Collins. The Chicagos tallied four more off Ernie Shore in the eighth, and despite another home run by Ruth—this one, number 31, in the ninth—held on for an 8–5 win.

"The big slam has arrived and a record which made baseball followers gasp in amazement less than a year ago has passed into the discard," said the *Times*. The home run record belonged to Ruth—again. Now, every time he went to bat, there was the possibility of a new record, and nobody else would hold the single-season home run record until Roger Maris, who wouldn't even be born for another 14 years. And it was only July 19. "Ruth was just as happy over his success as was the crowd," the *Times* wrote of home run number 31. "While the fans howled in glee, tossed hats around the stand in reckless abandon and made the big stand a mass of waving arms, Ruth completed his journey to the plate and then beamed back with a smile that spurred the crowd on to greater exertion, if that were possible."

After the two games had ended, a small boy worked his way into the Yankee clubhouse, found Ruth, and presented him with the record-breaking home run ball he had grabbed while sitting in right field. "I didn't throw it on the field, Mr. Babe, because I wanted to give it to you myself," he said. Ruth took the ball, smiled, patted the boy on the back, and gave him a season pass for the rest of the Yankee home games.

On July 20, the Babe knocked home run number 32 off Chicago's Red Faber in the fourth inning of the first of two, and put the Yanks up 5–3. There the score stayed until two gone in the ninth, when Shano Collins worked a tiring Jack Quinn for a walk, Ray Schalk singled, pinch hitter Eddie Murphy reached base on Pipp's error, and the floodgates opened. Then, Leibold, Eddie Collins, and Weaver all singled, and the Sox had scored four to go up 7–5. In the bottom of the ninth, the Yanks loaded the bases with nobody out, but failed to score. It was a hard loss.

Game two was better. George Mogridge went the distance, and the Yanks, with a homer from Pipp, perhaps atoning for his costly error from earlier in the day, nailed Cicotte again. The final was 6–3, which, combined with Cleveland's 9–8 win over Boston, left the Yankees two games in back of Cleveland as the Indians streaked to New York for a showdown in a five-game series.

The Indians series came at just the right time. The Yankees were hot, and Ruth's pursuit of the home run record helped set an all-time single-series attendance record. Another 32,000 had poured into the Polo Grounds for the final doubleheader against the White Sox, bringing the total attendance for the four days to 129,000—an average of more than 32,000 a day—far above what the Giants ever drew in even their greatest years. The figure was astounding, and was set despite several days of rain and bad weather. New York fans just couldn't get enough of their Yankees.

The Indians arrived in New York as a hot team themselves. Winners of 12 of their last 15, the Clevelanders were paced by their gifted player-manager, Tris Speaker. Speaker was batting .417, and along with George Sisler (.406) and Joe Jackson (.403) comprised the exclusive group of base-ball's only .400-plus batters. The next-highest A.L. batting average was Ruth's paltry .386.

So who better than Carl Mays to get the start for the New Yorkers in game one? Mays was on a roll himself—following his miserable start by winning his last six decisions, four of them complete games, to raise his record to 13–7.

Pitchers can often tell within the first moments of starting a game whether their stuff that day is good. Against the Indians, Mays appeared to be on his game. Through eight innings, he shut down the Indians on five hits and allowed only one runner to reach third base. Thanks to home runs from Meusel and Pipp, the Yanks had built a cushy 4–0 lead. So there was little cause for concern when Speaker opened the ninth by rattling a double to center, and then reaching third on Elmer Smith's grounder to Pipp.

Then the roof collapsed. Larry Gardner doubled to right, scoring Speaker, and Mays had lost his shutout. Next, Bill Wambsganss hit one to short that Peckinpaugh fielded and threw well over Pipp's head for an error, allowing Gardner to score. Doc Johnston singled, scoring Wambsganss, and just like that the score was 4–3 with the tying run on first.

When Steve O'Neill slapped a hard single past Peckinpaugh, sending Johnston to second, Huggins signaled he'd had enough: with Mays lapsing into another of his sudden, inexplicable bouts of ineptitude, the Yankee skipper signaled for a change. So off to the clubhouse went Mays, and in came Rip Collins to a big ovation from the 25,000 fans.

Collins slipped two quick strikes past pitcher Ray Caldwell, whom Speaker had allowed to bat for himself. But on the next pitch, Caldwell lined a single to center. Johnston was off with contact, and steamed around the bases. Out in center field, Ping Bodie gloved the ball cleanly and fired toward home. It arrived on one hop and right on the button: catcher Muddy Ruel tagged the sliding Johnston out at the plate. Two down!

Joe Wood replaced O'Neill on the bases at third. Caldwell was on second, and Huggins chose to intentionally walk the next batter, Charlie Jamieson. With the sacks jammed, up stepped Ray Chapman. He worked the count to 3–2, and then on the next pitch, with all three runners off on the pitch, he struck out. The game was over and the Yanks had held on, barely, taking it 4–3.

"An epidemic of blood pressure, high nervous tension and several other disorders swept over the Polo Grounds," the *Times* wrote in describing the action. It was a rattling-good win, typical of the nip-and-tuck games the

Yanks and Cleveland would play all year. Still, the Yanks took a laugher on Thursday, 11–3, with Collins coming back to go the distance for his eighth win, and won again on Friday, 6–3, behind Shawkey. By taking three in a row from the Indians, in addition to the previous four of six taken from the Sox, the Yanks had moved back in first place by a half game.

The series featured the debut of Speaker's special shift on Ruth. When the Babe came to bat, Cleveland infielders on the left side suddenly shifted right. It worked until the sixth inning of the Friday game, when Ruth smote the first pitch from Guy Morton into the upper deck of right field for his 33rd home run of the season. Things were going nicely as well for Peckinpaugh—his home run Friday gave him three in two days. Huggins lifted a tiring Shawkey after eight and one-third innings to give him a bit of a rest. But Bob's 12th victory signaled a continued strong return; he had not lost a game since early May.

The Indians squeezed back into first on Saturday, July 24, with a 4–2 win in the series' last game. Before another mob scene—there were 37,500 in the park, with thousands more following as much as they could from overhead on Coogan's Bluff—Big Jim Bagby gave up two solo shots to the Yanks and little else. Meusel went deep in the second, and in the fourth Ruth again defied the shift by sending a pitch off the flagpole on top of the right-field grandstand.

Ironically, it was Ruth who contributed to the loss after moving to first base in the eighth to replace Pipp, who had been tossed for arguing with the umpire. In the 11th inning, Ruth fielded a ball hit by Chapman but threw high to Mogridge covering at first. Later, when Gardner tripled to right, Chapman scored the winning run. In taking the loss, Mogridge had wasted another gritty performance by Quinn, who gave up two runs on six hits in eight innings, despite a strained side muscle.

Reporters marveled at the size of the crowds. More than 114,000 saw the four games against Cleveland, an average of just under 30,000 per game. And countless others had followed the games pitch-by-pitch with every detail flashed over the wires to bulletin boards that usually adorned the side of the local newspaper building.

Ruth's face was quickly becoming one of the best known in advertising. He and Ping Bodie posed on the dugout steps while carefully examining a package for a bacon company. When the Babe headed out to take batting practice, he was besieged by photographers asking that he sometimes smile, sometimes pose with his bat cocked, or even flex his muscles. Whether Ruth did or not depended on his mood and whether he trusted the reporter or photographer.

When an enterprising New York dealer offered him a pair of shoes for every home run he hit, Ruth quickly accepted, and donated each pair to a Catholic orphans' home, underscoring his genuine commitment to underprivileged children. To others, Ruth could be gruff.

One day, when a photographer at the Polo Grounds asked him to display his broad shoulders by posing in his undershirt, Ruth refused, replying curtly, "I don't wear undershirts."

"Perhaps you don't know me; I represent the ——," the photographer countered, mentioning the same name of his newspaper.

"I don't read newspapers," Ruth said testily, tightening his belt, grabbing his glove, and heading for the field.

He had good reason to be on guard. Attempting to capitalize on Ruth's popularity, a New York outfit called Educational Pictures rushed into theaters a series of one-reel Babe Ruth "Instructional Films," compiled from leftover newsreel footage of the slugger. Giving the films titles like *Play Ball with Babe Ruth* and *How Babe Ruth Hits a Home Run*, the company offered Ruth nothing as compensation. After the films opened, a lawyer convinced the Babe to file a $250,000 damage suit against Educational Pictures. But when the case reached the court, a judge ruled that Ruth was a public figure and could be filmed and photographed without his permission. The Babe had the last laugh, though: the film series flopped.

Ruth was about to make even more news. He inked a contract to appear in a film to be shot in August up the Hudson River in the Rockland County hamlet of Haverstraw. The film was called *Over the Fence*, later changed to *Headin' Home*, a silent with captions by Bugs Baer, featuring Ruth as the simple but dutiful iceman who becomes a star by whittling a bat from a tree limb and knocking a home run out of the local ballpark and through a stained glass window of the church.

The film was one of many offers that regularly piled into Ruth's increasingly crowded mailbox; his secretary, John Igoe, told F. C. Lane that Ruth once received 144 letters in a single day. Choosing the right offers was becoming imperative because there were so many. Eventually, a pay telephone was installed in the clubhouse next to his locker, as was a wastebasket. When a New York theatrical company offered Ruth the starring role in a play based on his career, he declined, preferring to stick with the movies. One proposition he chose to take was a December sojourn with an all-star team to baseball-hungry Havana, where it was said fans gathered around the newsstands for the latest scoop on the Babe's home runs. As it turned out, Ruth would play a lot of baseball in Cuba, but also find time to lose most of his earnings—about $30,000 worth—at the racetrack.

The next day, Sunday, July 25, Mays got the ball again against Boston, in town for a quick two-game series at the Polo Grounds before the Yankees headed west. This time, he had little trouble in limiting the Ruthless and punchless sixth-place Red Sox, to four hits, two by Everett Scott, and only two runs. It helped that the New Yorkers pounded future Yankee Waite Hoyt for two runs in the first and five more in the fifth, including a two-run home run from Ruth—number 35—that landed in the lower right-field stands. And it didn't matter that in the third, the Sox pulled off a triple play. The Yankees took the game 8–2 to give Mays his eighth win in a row.

Years later, in an interview in the book *Baseball Chronicles*, Hoyt remembered Ruth's fifth-inning shot. "I had reasoned the only way to stop him was to make him supply his own power," he said. "I threw him a high looping slow ball. . . . Ruth blooped my scientific pitch into . . . the right-field grandstand."

But just when everything seemed to be going well for Mays, he ran into trouble. Driving home to the Roger Morris Hotel atop Coogan's Bluff, Mays stepped on the gas, anxious to spend every moment with his pregnant wife, Freddie, who was due any day, and before the Yankees pushed off the following evening on another western swing. Driving down St. Nicholas Avenue over the speed limit, Mays was pulled over and issued a ticket for traveling 27 miles per hour over three blocks. His court date was set for August 20.

Maybe Carl Mays and the rest of the Yankees were looking ahead to the trip. On getaway day, the homestand's last game, they were a listless lot, losing meekly 9–0 to Boston's Sam Jones. The Yankees hit for only three singles all day, none from Ruth, who didn't even manage an official at-bat by walking all four times up. Yet, the Yanks had finished their homestand 13–8, managed to stick a half game back of the lead, and most important, showed both the Indians and the White Sox that they were legitimate contenders. And with that, the Yankees all piled into cabs for the trip to Pennsylvania Station and the long trip west to St. Louis.

Arriving in St. Louis for a five-game series, sportswriter Fred Lieb brought three Wyoming cowboys into the Sportsman's Park clubhouse to meet Ruth. Adorned in chaps, spurs, and cowboy hats, the men said they had ridden three days to a little railroad station in Wyoming to flag down a train headed to St. Louis to take in a couple of Yankee games before heading back home to their ranch. "Baby Ruth," one of them said, "I'd have ridden on horseback all the way to St. Louis to see you hit them home runs."

So the Yankees and Babe Ruth may have left home a second-place team, but heading into their second western swing of the season, they were the hottest story in baseball. Overflow crowds, "like addicts, craving more and more long smashes by the 'Prince of Pounder,'" one reporter wrote, were expected to see them play in every port of call.

In Chicago, a sportswriter peered out from the press box at the multitudes packing Comiskey Park and shook his head: "Never has such a ballplayer been such a hero outside of his own bailiwick," he said. The fans "were up on their toes waving their hats and yelling like Old Ned." And in Cleveland, Ruth was presented with an oversized tribute in acknowledgment of his record-setting season—a 15-foot wooden bat adorned with flowers. Meanwhile, interest in Ruth's every at-bat continued to increase throughout the country, solidifying his status as America's first sports superstar: in Worcester, Massachusetts, a pharmacist took to hanging a sign outside his shop that looked like a giant thermometer, but in fact it was measuring Ruth's home runs.

"The Yankees expect to clean up the Tigers in Detroit and the White Sox in Chicago," wrote Joe Vila in the *Sporting News* of the Yankee trip. "They have learned to respect the Browns, who recently beat them three out of five . . . and they realize that the Clevelands will be much different in their own grounds. . . . The Yankees will tell you that if they return . . . in the middle of next month in first place, nothing can keep them out of the World's Series."

In St. Louis, the Yankees had good reason to give due respect to the Browns, who were quietly and methodically compiling the A.L.'s best starting pitching staff. The mainstay was Urban Shocker, who continued to spitball the Yankees into submission. On Wednesday, the veteran shut them out 1–0 on only five hits, wasting another fine performance from Shawkey, who dropped his first game in nearly three months. Then, in the Thursday doubleheader, the Yanks and Quinn lost the first game, 4–3— Ruth ending it with the bases loaded by flying to center off Dixie Davis— but awoke from their mini-slump to take the second, 6–4, in satisfying fashion.

Down 4–3 in the eighth, with Meusel and Ruth both on base, Ward dunked a delivery from reliever Bill Burwell into the left-field seats to put the game out of reach and give Collins his ninth win of the season. In the midst of a three-game losing streak in which bats seemed wanting and arms wild, the Yankees needed that. Meusel's fourth-inning home run— his ninth—powered the Yankees to their 64th win of the year, serving as another declaration that the dead-ball era was headed to extinction.

Of growing frustration to the fans was the propensity of pitchers to issue bases on balls to Ruth, who as the *Times* said, was "getting foot weary from walking." It was about the only strategy opposing pitchers could use to keep him from depositing their offerings into the bleachers, but it was getting monotonous. Shocker walked Ruth three times on Wednesday— making it seven of his last eight at-bats in which he drew a walk—and struck him out in the Babe's only official at-bat. On Thursday, when a St. Louis paper carried the screaming headline "Come Out and Pay $1.10 to See Ruth Walk," 15,000 did and whistled when Browns' pitchers complied.

The wasted opportunities were getting on Ruth's nerves too. "It is pretty tough for me to be doing so much walking when I have a fine automobile rusting in the garage," he said. "If they won't let me use base hits as a means of transportation, they ought to furnish me with at least a bicycle."

But on Friday, July 30, the Babe proved he wouldn't need a bicycle. Against three Browns' pitchers, the Yankees rattled off 21 hits and 38 total bases to win 19–3—the kind of game the *Times* compared to "the annual picnic of the Longshoremen's Union when the married men play the single men." Pipp wore out the bases by himself with a home run, two triples, and a single. Meusel had four hits as well, including a home run and a double. The slow-footed Bodie added a home run and a triple, which must have been a sight. It all meant an easy day for Mays, who went the distance to improve to 16–9. But all paled next to Ruth's ninth-inning home run off Elam Vangilder—the longest shot ever at Sportsman's Park, which sailed far over the right-field bleachers and into a yard on the other side of Grand Avenue.

Maybe it was the steamy St. Louis air or just the new lively baseball, but on Saturday the teams hooked up in another slugfest, won by the Browns 13–8. It was the Yankees' fourth loss in their last six games, causing more worry to Huggins, who lifted an ineffective Collins in the third after he was touched up for six runs. Too bad for poor Huggins, who never got credit for Yankee success, but was always blamed when they lost, and had the added pressure of seeing his team crumble while Huston, who never liked him to start with, and his cronies accompanied the team. Again the culprit was the pitching staff—minus Quinn with his strained side muscle—which critics said didn't have depth enough to win a pennant.

At least the Yankee bats touched up Shocker, who went the distance for his 15th win but gave up those eight runs, including a first-inning Bob Meusel home run. And at least Ruth got back some measure of revenge against his nemesis, drilling Shocker for an eighth-inning home run, number 37, that again disappeared over the right-field bleachers and into the busy traffic of Grand Avenue.

Despite the losing, the Yanks remained in second place. And yes, the Babe really was enjoying himself in St. Louis, finding time to visit his favorite American League house of ill repute, where he reportedly took on the entire lineup. And there was a German restaurant in the city specializing in barbecued spare ribs that Ruth enjoyed so much that with the team ready to push off Saturday evening to Chicago, he stopped by the restaurant, ordered a batch of the spare ribs and some home brew, and lugged them back to the train. While in transit, he set up shop in a train washroom and sold the ribs to teammates for 50 cents a portion. He insisted on being paid, too, but included in the players' allotment all the beer they could drink.

Arriving at the Cooper Carlton Hotel in Chicago, the first thing Yankee players noticed were the lobby crowds, gathered to see the Babe and wish him well. It would be about the nicest thing to happen to the team in a trying weekend.

The Yanks lost three of four to the White Sox, victimized by a curious umpiring decision, shaky pitching, and a lack of timely hitting. They were devastating losses, and allowed the White Sox, implored by big, boisterous crowds all week at Comiskey Park, to continue their crawl back into the thick of the A.L. pennant race.

Chicago was baseball mad, and while they rooted hard for the Sox, the consensus was for the Babe to hit one out. "On the streets, in the restaurants and on the cars, Ruth is the one topic of conversation," the *Times* wrote. That Sunday morning, August 1, people even gathered in the hotel lobby to watch him go to church—yes, the Babe often attended church while on the road, plunking down $50 for the offering, "figure[ing] he paid up for all the sins of the week," recalled a teammate.

That afternoon, 40,000 stormed Comiskey Park—the park's largest crowd ever—to see Bob Shawkey and the Yanks face Eddie Cicotte's tantalizing knuckleball, the one that had so mysteriously disappeared in the 1919 Series. They saw a great pitcher's duel and an odd call that helped seal a Chicago win. With the Sox up 1–0 in the fourth, Ruth sent a knuckler to the opposite field that Joe Jackson sprang from left field to chase down. Tearing after the ball, Jackson disappeared into the first few rows of the spectators, only to be pushed out by a dozen or so in the big crowd, with the ball firmly planted in his mitt.

Shoeless Joe walked over to umpire Dick Nallin and informed him that he had indeed caught the ball, although neither umpire nor anyone else on either team had actually seen the alleged catch. Nallin signaled Ruth out, launching Huggins like a projectile from the dugout headed toward home plate umpire Thomas Connolly. The Yankee manager argued long and hard, contending that a ball hit into the crowd was a ground-rule double, and that the ball wasn't put back into play after Jackson claimed to have caught it. But Connolly sided with Nallin, and Ruth was gone.

That's how things went for the Yanks that day; they managed only five hits, and were again shut out, this time 3–0. Huggins was tossed in the seventh for arguing that Duffy Lewis's strikeout was a half-swing.

The Yanks got back on track the following afternoon, thanks to Quinn, who scattered nine hits in a 7–0 pasting to push his overall record to 14–7. With the Sox never in it, the 25,000 spectators—this one the largest Monday crowd in Comiskey Park's history—turned their collective attention to see what Ruth could do. In the fourth, when the Babe took Lefty Williams deep on a low line drive that landed in the right-field bleachers for home run number 38, they went dizzy with excitement. When he trotted out to right field in the bottom of the inning, they tossed him the ball to keep as a souvenir, and the Babe tossed up a new ball in exchange. It was a gracious moment on both accounts, and was seen by the writers as another way Ruth was building his legend as the most popular player ever—at home and on the road.

No wonder another crowd of 25,000 booed their own Red Faber the next afternoon when he walked Ruth three times, limiting the Babe to a single in his only official at-bat. Mays pitched well, but Faber, benefiting from the mysterious lack of punch from the Yankee bats, pitched better as the Sox won again, 3–1, behind Jackson's two-run triple in the first that sealed it. "The Yanks are a peculiar outfit on this trip," the *Times* reported. "One day, they fold up and the pitchers fail to pitch and the sluggers fail to connect. Next day, the pitching is great and the hitting would knock over a brick wall."

The grumbling could be heard all the way down Broadway: the pitching *was* shaky, and seemed to pose the biggest impediment to New York's pennant hopes. "Shawkey and Mays are dependable," wrote Joe Vila in the August 5 *Sporting News*, "but Jack Quinn, whose side was wrenched in a recent game . . . has let down, while Mogridge isn't reliable. Thormahlen looks like a total failure, but Rip Collins is likely to pull the team along in good style." There was even a rumor that the Yankees had purchased the contract of 37-year-old Chief Bender, gone from the majors for three years and now player-manager with New Haven of the Eastern League— a story that both Huston and Huggins denied.

Another obstacle was the schedule. The Yankees had all of 19 games left at the Polo Grounds and faced another grueling western swing in September. Meanwhile, they still had 19 games left against the A.L.'s best— 9 against Chicago and 10 versus Cleveland—whereas both the Sox and Indians could look forward to a majority of games against second-division clubs.

The Yankees' listlessness continued. In the Wednesday getaway game, the Sox pounded them again, this time 10–3, moving them into a virtual second-place tie with the New Yorkers. Things started well when the Yankees jumped on Dickie Kerr for two runs in the first, but the Sox stormed back in the bottom of the inning off a wild George Mogridge.

Mogridge had nothing. The Sox's first batter, Lefty Leibold, walked, and then Eddie Collins and Buck Weaver singled to load the bases. Joe Jackson's single up the middle scored the two lead runners, and Happy Felsch singled again to reload the bases. In came Rip Collins, who was even wilder: he hit John Collins, forcing Weaver home for the third run. The Sox scored their fourth when Collins walked Kerr, forcing home Felsch to make it 4–2 Sox. The game was essentially over.

Huggins did what he could, tinkering with the lineup by replacing a hit-less Pipp in the sixth with Meusel and sending Duffy Lewis out to left, but little seemed to work. Dickie Kerr shut the Yankees down without a hit from the second to the seventh, as Huston looked on with increasing impatience.

The next afternoon against Detroit, normally a team the Yankees found easy pickings, things got worse. This time, the fielding disintegrated: Harry Heilmann's home run in the fourth slipped past the normally sure-handed Bodie in center, and in the fifth Meusel let a routine fly drop, giving Cobb a double.

Ruth did his part. The first batter up in the second, he sent a pitch from Howard Ehmke on a line shot over a wire fence flush against the right-field wall. The ball bounced back onto the field, but was ruled a ground-rule home run, hardly a Ruthian blast, but number 39 all the same. His home run put the Yanks up 1–0, and would be their only run of the day. The final was 7–1 Tigers, with Shawkey pitching the entire dismal way. The day's only good news: Chicago lost and Cleveland didn't play.

Huggins kept tinkering. On Friday afternoon, he sent Duffy Lewis out to left in place of the indifferent Meusel, and the move worked. Lewis tripled home a much-needed three runs in the first off George Dauss. Catching was Muddy Ruel, replacing Truck Hannah, who had been sus-pended indefinitely for arguing with the umpire in Chicago. And Huggins moved Ruth up in the order from cleanup to third, batting Lewis fourth.

Not that Ruth needed a jolt, for despite the team's troubles, he stayed locked in his season-long home run groove. In the third, he pumped a solo shot off Dauss, number 40, into the right-field bleachers to break a 4-all tie. And in the sixth, with Ward and Peckinpaugh on base and two down, Dauss threw and Ruth swung, sending a moon shot that sailed clear over the right-field fence, out of Navin Field and across Trumbell Avenue into a garage, where, the *Times* reported, "a mechanic was talking kindly to a stubborn Ford."

The shot was Ruth's 41st home run of the year, sending the 10,000 Tiger fans into hysterics and the writers into new fits of hyperbole. In the next day's papers, the Babe was "the human howitzer" who "decorated the ball game [with] two man-sized home runs." And he didn't just "hit" home runs—he "thumped" and "blistered" them. And like so many of the sea-son's Ruthian blasts, they were big home runs, the second one capping a five-run inning that put the Yanks up 11–4 and assured them of breaking their losing streak and moving up on the Indians, who lost to the A's 2–1. Jack Quinn held on for his 15th win, and the Yanks took it 11–7.

On Saturday, Ruth had only one hit, a double, in the ninth. But so did every other starter, except Carl Mays, and the Yanks coasted 7–3. But with Ruth relatively quiet, Tiger fans turned their attention back to cranky hometown hero Ty Cobb, who was called out by umpire Big Bill Dinneen on a close play at the plate. Cobb disagreed, and jumped up arguing. That fired up the faithful, who spent the rest of the game jeering Dinneen, and surrounded him after the game, threatening all kinds of bodily harm. Only when he was flanked by fellow ump Brick Owens and Duffy Lewis was Dinneen able to cut safely through the mob and into the clubhouse.

Had the Yankees emerged from their slump? On Sunday, the series' fourth and final game, it was hard to tell. Looking more like Christy Mathewson, Detroit's Howard Ehmke used a devastating changeup in yielding only three measly hits, all singles, to the New Yorkers en route to a tidy 1–0 win. Before an overflow crowd of 28,000, which ringed the outfield and perched on top of the fence and even surrounding telephone poles, the Tigers tallied the game's sole lonesome run in the fifth when Cobb doubled and scored on Rip Collins's wild pitch. Too bad for Collins, who gave up only six hits but took his fifth loss. And too bad for Ping Bodie, who absentmindedly blew the Yankees' best chance of the game in the fifth when he was caught off base by second baseman Ralph Young with the hidden-ball trick, among baseball's oldest plays.

Bodie was mildly criticized for the play. Never a favorite of Huggins, particularly since the two had clashed back during spring training, "Ping must watch out," the *Times* wrote, "or he will be buying building lots in Long Island Sound." But it was Huggins who absorbed the real wrath of Yankee fans when the team slumped. Maybe it was his diminutive size, or the lack of respect he seemed to get from his players, but Huggins was the team's scapegoat—blamed for the Yankee pitching woes, for not benching Meusel sooner, and for executing just about every form of poor judgment going, short of his failure to solve world peace. "When the Yankees were beating Cleveland and the White Sox [in New York] recently, typewriters reeled off columns of praise for Ruth, Peck, Pratt, Bodie, and the many other favorites," Vila wrote in the August 12 *Sporting News*. "But there wasn't a word about little Huggins. Nobody gave him a bit of credit for the winning work of his men. In fact, Hug was entirely ignored. But as soon as the Yankees began to lose ball games in the West, Huggins was noticed."

Maybe the Yankees were looking ahead to their four-game series in Cleveland. Who could blame them? Their troubles had helped the Indians stake a four-and-a-half-game lead, and Cleveland sportswriters were calling the upcoming showdown between the two clubs "The Little World's Series."

Demand for tickets was intense, and by the time Bob Shawkey got set to face Guy Morton on Monday, August 9, the park was jammed with 15,000, with all the reserved seats having been sold out for days. Even threatening skies didn't keep away the crowds, who enjoyed an unusual pregame ceremony courtesy of Cleveland fan Maxie Rosenblum, who seized the moment to present Ruth with a 12-foot floral bat as a tribute to the slugger's home run prowess. "Babe Ruth—41 home runs," the inscription read.

"I hope you hit 100 home runs, if none of them are against Cleveland," said Rosenblum in handing over the oversized bat. Ruth grinned as he took the bat and posed for photographers. Not to be outdone, Cleveland owner Jim Dunn staged a ceremony of his own—"Golden Year of Baseball Day," which honored the first game ever played at League Park, 50 years before. Attending the game were 50 old-time Indians' fans, many of whom were more than 80 years old, and all of whom received golden baseballs to commemorate the occasion. To further mark the festivities, Dunn called on Indians' manager Tris Speaker, presenting him with another floral display, this one amidst an oversized Indian head.

Meantime, from downstate in Cincinnati came word of Common Pleas Court Judge Edward T. Dixon's vacation schedule—a trip with his baseball-mad son to Cleveland to see every Yankee game until Ruth had homered. "This youngster of mine, he is a 'bug' on baseball and a bigger bug about Babe Ruth," the judge said. "Some time ago, I promised the boy I would let him see Babe Ruth make a home run this season. . . . If Babe makes a home run the first day out, then we will be home that day. . . . But we will remain with the Yankees, going where they go until Babe makes a home run."

The floral tribute was about all Ruth got that Monday. Morton walked him three times, and he popped up and fouled out in his only two official at-bats. But not so the Babe's teammates, who jumped on Morton for four quickies in the first, with the big hit a double by Pipp. The lead gave Shawkey a nice cushion, and when the afternoon was done, the Yanks had cruised 7–3. Although the Indians' lead had melted to three and a half games, the Yanks fell into third place, thanks to the White Sox's double-header sweep of Washington back in Chicago.

It poured Tuesday, and the game was called after the second with the Yankees up 1–0, disappointing the big crowd of 25,000. Ruth was having a good day, however, as he got word late in the day that the diamond-studded watch fob he received from the Knights of Columbus and thought he had misplaced on the night boat from Detroit to Cleveland had been found at the team's Detroit hotel. The Babe was so relieved that he immediately sent $100 to the finder, a hotel chambermaid.

Picking up the following afternoon, the Yanks got a scare in the first when Ruth singled to center, and while trying to stretch it into a double, twisted his right knee sliding into second base. For a moment, Ruth tried banging his joint back into place with his fist. It didn't work, and he was carried from the field. His replacement in right was Bob Meusel, back from exile at the end of the bench.

But before another throng, this one numbering 27,000, accompanied by assorted brass bands, Carl Mays, winner of 10 of his last 11, was on his game. Except for one mistake—surrendering a grand slam to Elmer Smith in the third—Mays gave up little else. The bands' presence came in handy, blaring into action in celebration of Smith's grand slam, which put Jim Bagby and the Indians up 4–0. The band members barely had a chance to catch their breath before former Cleveland Mayor Harry Davis, back in town after winning the Republican nomination for Ohio's governor, unexpectedly sauntered into League Park, touching off another celebration and delay of game when Speaker and the rest of the Indians streamed from the dugout and leaned into the stands to shake hands with the former mayor.

You would think under the circumstances that Mays would have shown his tendency to self-destruct. Instead, he bore down, giving up a hit here and there, but no more runs. Things got tense in the bottom of the fourth when Mays threw a pitch that seemed headed toward Doc Johnston's head, forcing the Indians' first baseman to throw his arm up to protect himself. Johnston hit the dirt, and got a free pass to first base from home plate umpire Ollie Chill. If the hit batsman wasn't enough to incite the Cleveland bench, none of whom liked Mays to start with, the pitcher's protest that the ball had hit Johnston's bat solidified their dislike.

Mays made it worse for the Indians in the fifth when he doubled home Muddy Ruel in the midst of a three-run Yankee rally. The New Yorkers tied it in the sixth, and the game settled into a classic pitching duel between Mays and Bagby. In the 10th, Mays again delivered, smacking another double, this one deep into left center, and later going to third on Ward's infield single and scoring on Meusel's single. The Yankees tallied three in the 10th and held on 7–4. The come-from-behind win had narrowed the Indians' lead to two games over the White Sox, winners again against Washington, and two and a half games over the Yankees. Just like that, the American League pennant drive had again become a horse race.

The tightening of the A.L. race seemed to put everyone on edge. On Thursday afternoon, Ping Bodie missed a home run to right field by inches, and then was called out on strikes by Chill, prompting him to protest and be tossed from the game. Only when Pipp grabbed Bodie and led him away from the umpire did the temperamental player calm down. "The very thought of an umpire calling Ping out on strikes changes Ping into a raging lion," opined the *Times*.

Bodie's outburst came in the midst of a first-inning Yankee rally, which started when leadoff batter Aaron Ward singled off Stanley Coveleski. Ruth, who was back in the lineup, walked, and then Lewis tripled to the right-center-field corner, driving Ruth and Ward home. Next up, Pipp singled, driving home Lewis, and just like that, it was 3–0.

That was more than enough for Jack Quinn, who stopped the Indians on eight hits and one run. The Yankees were in control from the get-go, holding on 5–1 for their 70th win of the season to narrow the race and put the White Sox, winners again, at the top for the first time all season. The game's probable outcome was more than enough to dampen the spirits of the 18,000 fans, who made their displeasure more than apparent by booing and yelling at the Cleveland players, notably shortstop Bill Wambsganss, who was slumping at bat and in the field. Afterward, Speaker was furious at the crowd's behavior, claiming the next morning in the Cleveland *News* that "we haven't quit, as some few fans may have surmised. . . . My boys don't know the meaning of that word."

But Wambsganss didn't advance his cause the following afternoon when he stepped to the plate in the first against Shawkey with the bases loaded, and grounded out weakly to second.

In the third, Ruth walked with two outs and scored the game's first run when Pratt doubled him home. The Yanks added two more in the fifth for a 3–0 lead, which Shawkey held until the seventh when Ray Chapman's sacrifice fly to left brought home pitcher Ray Caldwell. The Yanks went up 4–1 in the eighth on a double by Pratt, who scored on Lewis's single. But when the Indians threatened in their half of the eighth off a fading Shawkey, Huggins looked down his bench and summoned Mays, who despite going 10 innings two days before had been warming up throughout the game. After Shawkey gave up a double to Wambsganss and a single to Johnston that scored two runs and narrowed the Yankee lead to 4–3, Huggins finally called on the underhanded ace. In he came and down went any hope of a Cleveland comeback: with one gone, Mays struck out Steve O'Neill, and Ruel pegged the ball down to Ward at second, which caught Johnston in the hit-and-run. In the ninth, Mays struck out Speaker to end the game and preserve Shawkey's 4–3 win.

By taking four straight, the Yanks had stormed back within striking distance of the lead, a half game back of the Indians and one behind Chicago. More important, they made any talk of a losing streak seem like eons ago. A quick two-game weekend series in Washington remained before the Indians and Yankees were to hook up again for a scheduled four-game series the following week at the Polo Grounds. Pushing off that Sunday in the Indians' Pullman car from Cleveland, Chapman had the last word: "Tomorrow, we ought to win pretty easily," he said of the Monday game when Mays would again be pitching for the Yanks. "I can't hit this man Mays, but the rest of the team sure can."

That Saturday, August 14, in Washington, Ruth managed to do about the only thing he had yet to do in 1920: his solo home run in the first off "Grunting" Jim Shaw, number 42, gave him a home run in every American League ballpark for the season. That set off a big ovation from the packed house, proving that Ruth continued to be the biggest drawing card in baseball—home and away. And it sent Common Pleas Court Judge Edward T. Dixon and his son home to Cincinnati, having finally seen Ruth homer after five games.

The big home run returned the media focus firmly to Ruth and the Yankees. Back in New York, John McGraw and the Giants had actually temporarily eclipsed the attention afforded Ruth and the tight American

League race—but not from anything on the ballfield, but from a brawl. Late on the night of August 7, McGraw, after an evening's drinking at the Lambs Club on West 43rd Street, slugged vaudeville actor John Slaven on the noggin so badly that the actor was hospitalized with a severe concussion.

The incident had occurred in the wee hours outside McGraw's apartment on West 109th Street, and gathered frenzied headlines for a week. McGraw, who had shared a cab with Slaven, claimed the actor had started it by inexplicably clocking him over the head with a water bottle back at the Lambs Club. The only problem was that it wasn't Slaven who had done the clocking—it was another actor, William Boyd. Eventually, the testy McGraw would be acquitted of all charges—including violation of the Volstead Act—before the incident was forgotten, and peoples' attention got back to baseball.

The Babe's blast in Washington was his first homer in eight days. It gave the Yanks an immediate lead, which was important because both Shaw and New York starter Rip Collins had good command of their pitches. The Senators tied it in the second, but the Yanks put the game away with two runs in the sixth when Peckinpaugh walked, Ruth singled, and both runners scored on Pratt's stinging double that sailed over left fielder Clyde Milan's head. Collins held on, and the Yanks won 3–2, which, combined with the White Sox's doubleheader split with the Tigers, put the New Yorkers back into second place.

On Sunday, the Yankee batters did their job, totaling nine hits for four runs off Eric Erickson. But George Mogridge was again wild, giving up a run in the second, three more in the third, and another in the fifth before being lifted with no outs. It was enough, and the Senators coasted 6–4. Combined with wins by both the Indians and the White Sox, the loss tumbled the Yanks back into third place as they headed, thankfully, back to the Polo Grounds for the rest of August. They were looking to bring the American League pennant to New York once and for all.

NINE

"An Accident Pure and Simple"

A Tragic Diversion to the Race

Monday, August 16, certainly started off as a baseball kind of day. For starters, there was the heat, which in those days before air-conditioning could be unrelenting. In New York that day, the humidity reached 94 percent and the temperature was in the mid-80s, which combined with virtually no breeze made it not just hot, but oppressive. But by the time the events of this memorable day were finished, it wasn't the heat or the result of that day's game between the Yankees and the Indians that were on people's minds. It was something far more important—a man's life, which hung in the balance.

Events started normally enough for Carl Mays, the day's scheduled pitcher. He rose in his apartment at the Roger Morris Hotel and followed his usual pregame routine, dining on a breakfast of ham and eggs. Then he spent some time with his wife, Freddie, and the couple's three-week-old baby. Before leaving for the ballpark shortly before noon, he reached into the icebox, took out a chicken leg, and stuck it in his pocket. Following another game-day ritual, Mays would gnaw on the chicken leg during the game to keep his mouth wet. Mays wanted this one—a win would give him career victory number 100.

The Indians, still smarting about the previous week's sweep by the Yankees, wanted it too. On the way to the ballpark on the elevated train from their quarters at the Ansonia, the players seemed tense—that is until shortstop Ray Chapman, known for his smooth, silky baritone, broke into song. That loosened his teammates up, and the Indians, suddenly as relaxed as they had been for weeks, descended the train platform and piled into the Polo Grounds' clubhouse. "Mays is pitching for the Yankees today," belted out Chapman as they entered the clubhouse, "so I'll do the fielding and you fellows do the hitting." Everyone laughed.

Raindrops didn't keep 23,000 fans from ignoring the heat and journeying to the Polo Grounds. Among them were players from four other baseball teams—the Brooklyn Robins and Boston Braves, who had an off-day, as well as the International League's Jersey City Skeeters and Buffalo Bisons, who hurried to the game in Harlem after their game was rained out across the river.

The rain was still falling when home plate umpire Tommy Connolly decided to start the game anyway. The Indians went after Mays from the start, with the leadoff batter, left fielder Charlie Jamieson, rifling a single to left. Up stepped Chapman, the league's best bunter, who everybody in the country knew would be trying to lay one down in order to sacrifice Jamieson to second. Imagine a batter today sacrificing in the first inning. Mays's counter-strategy: pitch him high and tight to make it harder to get the bunt down.

The first pitch whizzed in high and inside for ball one. Mays also came inside on the second pitch, which Chapman, in his characteristic crouched stance, squared around on and bunted a few feet in front of the plate. Out jumped catcher Muddy Ruel, who pounced on the ball and flung it down to first to nail Chapman, who had done his job: lead runner Jamieson slid safely into second.

But the Indians went no further that inning as Speaker and Elmer Smith both flied out to Ping Bodie in center field. But Cleveland took a 1–0 lead with one down in the second when Steve O'Neill drilled a home run into the left-field bleachers. They picked up two more in the fourth, when the rain stopped, as Larry Gardner walked, O'Neill singled, and Doc Johnston's sharp grounder to short sent Gardner home, crashing into Ruel as he crossed the plate a fraction of a second ahead of Peckinpaugh's throw. Ward then bobbled Wambsganss's grounder to third to load the bases, after which Stanley Coveleski's sacrifice scored O'Neill. Cleveland led 3–0.

In the bottom of the fourth, the Yankees came up empty. Peckinpaugh popped up to Gardner at third base, Ruth grounded to first, and Pratt fouled out to O'Neill. As the inning ended and Mays strode out to the mound to start the fifth, his thoughts turned to the inning's first batter, Ray

Chapman. Stepping into the batter's box, Chapman threw down one of the two bats he'd been carrying toward the dugout and looked out to the mound, ready to go. Thomas Connolly gave the signal to start and leaned down behind Ruel to make the call.

Out on the mound, Mays reared back and threw, sending his underhand delivery high and tight—again to stop Chapman from bunting to get on base. Ruel would say later that the ball, a fastball, seemed to be in the strike zone as he raised his glove in anticipation of catching it.

The pitch sailed toward Chapman's head, as if shot from a cannon. But instead of moving, the batter inexplicably remained in his crouch, as if frozen by the flight of the ball, which struck his left temple with a sickening crack that spectators later said could be heard throughout the park. Many would recall that Chick Fewster had also seemed frozen at the plate when he had been beaned, back in spring training by Jeff Pfeffer.

Mays heard the crack, and thinking the ball had struck Chapman's bat as it headed back toward him, he instinctively scooped the ball up and threw it to Wally Pipp at first. Only when Mays saw the look on Pipp's face, transfixed toward the scene at home plate, did he realize anything unusual had happened.

What happened was that Chapman, who had stood in place for a moment after being struck, with his head quivering and mouth agape, was slowly slumping to the ground. Ruel tried to break his fall, but Chapman fell to his knees. Behind Ruel stood Connolly, who knew right away that Chapman had been badly hurt. "We need a doctor," he shouted toward the grandstand. "Is there a doctor in the house?"

Out popped Dr. Joseph Cascio of nearby St. Lawrence Hospital. And from the dugout came a stream of Cleveland teammates, led by Speaker, who had been kneeling in the on-deck circle. He reached Chapman just as the fallen ballplayer struggled to a sitting position; it was a miracle he was still conscious. Moments later, nearly every Indian teammate was surrounding Chapman, bunched in so close that Speaker yelled at them to move back and give him air.

For several minutes, the doctor worked on Chapman, helping him to his feet. The ballplayer waved off an offer of assistance and started walking toward the center-field clubhouse to the polite applause of the fans. But as Chapman neared second base, steadied by teammates, his knees buckled. His teammates grabbed him and carried him the rest of the way to the clubhouse.

On the mound, Mays retrieved the baseball and focused on a rough spot on the ball, which he immediately pointed out to Connolly; he explained that the spot was what caused the pitch to carry farther inside than he expected. Examining the ball, Connolly removed it from the field, thereby getting rid of what could have been a crucial clue into what had really happened. Others insisted that it was the rain that had made the ball slippery and had accounted for Mays's loss of control.

Watching from the press box was Joe Vila, who later recalled the sound of the ball as it struck Chapman's skull. "The crack of the ball could be heard all over the stand and spectators gasped as they turned their heads away," he wrote in the *Sporting News*. But like a lot of others that day, he had seen Chapman get to his feet and even walk after the beaning, giving hope that the injury wasn't that serious.

After all, wrote F. C. Lane in *Baseball Magazine*, "the accident came with such lightning swiftness and so unexpectedly that perhaps no two of the 18,000 surprised spectators saw it alike and few of them realized its seriousness."

But Lane, sitting in the press box next to Al Mamaux of the Dodgers, did. At first, Lane thought the ball had struck Chapman's bat, but Mamaux, his ear trained to detect the velocity of a hit ball by the impact on the bat, knew otherwise. "No, the ball makes no such noise as that when it strikes a bat," the Dodger pitcher said. "It hit him on the head."

Play resumed as Speaker sent Harry Lunte to first base to run for Chapman and later take his place at shortstop. Speaker then sent a grounder to second that Del Pratt handled, forcing Lunte for the first out. Elmer Smith struck out, but afterward Gardner tagged one off Pipp's glove, sending Speaker to third. Then O'Neill slashed a single to right that grazed the top of Pratt's glove, scoring Speaker. Only then did Mays settle down, getting the last out, but the damage had been done: it was 4–0 Indians.

In the clubhouse, the doctors made a further examination of Chapman and decided that he should be dispatched immediately to St. Lawrence Hospital. Lending moral support was John Henry, a former catcher with Boston and Washington and one of Chapman's best friends, who was visiting from Boston for the series. "For God's sake, don't call Kate," Chapman told Henry, referring to his wife of 10 months, "but if you do, tell her I am all right." Then Ray Chapman lost consciousness.

In the sixth, Mays finally found his groove, and set the Indians down in order for the next three innings. But Indians' right-hander Stanley Coveleski already had a groove, and he matched Mays with zeros until the ninth, when Ruth singled to right, Pratt walked, and after Lewis flied out and Pipp grounded out to first, Bodie rifled a double against the right-field wall that scored both runners. Ruel kept it going by singling home Bodie, quickly making it 4–3. But 23-year-old pinch hitter Lefty O'Doul, in his second season and getting a long look from the Yanks, grounded out. The Indians had held on for a narrow but costly win, moving them a half game in front of Chicago and one and a half ahead of the Yanks.

Minutes later, Mays sat on a stool in front of his locker in the clubhouse, reflecting on his less-than-stellar performance. "I was wild as a hawk," he told Lane, who caught Mays just as he emerged from the passageway under the center-field bleachers and headed for the clubhouse. "I always am when I am saved up for a special game. I was never effective under such circumstances and I used to tell [Ed] Barrow so just as I have told Huggins. But when a manager calls on you to pitch, you have to do the best you can."

Then he paused, thinking of the Chapman beaning. "The ball was wet," Mays said, "which didn't make it any easier to control."

Only then did the pitcher emerge from his ruminations and ask Lane whether he had heard about Chapman's condition. Lane said he hadn't, but added that he did know that the injured player had been taken by ambulance to St. Lawrence Hospital, six blocks away. Mays didn't answer; he showered, dressed, and left for home.

Across the hallway, the Indians took little comfort in winning and moving back into first place. Team members dressed hurriedly and left en masse for the hospital, where Speaker telephoned Kate Chapman about her husband's condition. She departed from Cleveland right away on the Lake Shore Limited overnight train to New York.

After a few hours, Speaker sent his ballplayers back to the Ansonia to get some rest. An x-ray diagnosed the gravity of Chapman's injury—a depressed fracture to the left part of his skull, three and a half inches long.

By 9:30 that night, Chapman's pulse had plunged to 40 and he had suffered spasms on both sides of his temple, indicating to surgical director Dr. Thomas D. Merrigan that there was a laceration on his right side—opposite from where he had been struck.

The doctors decided to operate, but thought they might wait until Kathleen arrived from Cleveland. But with Chapman's condition steadily worsening, they decided around 10 P.M. to begin as soon as possible. With Kate still on the train, it was up to Speaker to give approval for the operation. After conferring with Indians business manager Walter McNichols, he did, and the operation started at 12:29 A.M.

The operation took 75 minutes, during which doctors removed a one-and-a-half-square-inch piece of Chapman's skull and found his brain so severely jarred that blood clots had formed. Immediately afterward, the operation seemed successful, and doctors told Speaker that Chapman had started breathing more easily and that his pulse had gone back to 90. Encouraged by the news, Speaker and McNichols headed back to the Ansonia and told the anxious Cleveland ballplayers, all of whom were still awake, that Chapman was improving.

But in the end, the injury was just too great to overcome. At 4:40 A.M., Chapman died, making him the first and only major-league player to die from injuries sustained in a game. The news was relayed immediately to the Ansonia, where many of his Cleveland teammates broke down in tears. Larry Gardner recalled, "I can still see him now coming behind me with that smile he always wore, and saying, 'You aren't mad, are you?'" The thoughts of others quickly turned to rage against Carl Mays, already the game's most detested player. Said Doc Johnston: "Mays should be strung up."

Stepping quickly into the festering controversy was Speaker, who tried to tone things down. "On the part of two or three of our players, there is some bitterness toward Mays," he said. "But I am going to do all I can to suppress it and any bitterness that might arise. For the good of baseball, for the good of the players themselves, and especially out of regard for the poor fellow that's dead, it is our duty to do that. I am going to do all I can to see that there is no bitterness."

That the culprit was Mays was unfortunate. As news of Chapman's death spread, so did the anger against the already disliked ballplayer on the part of players throughout the American League. Most prominent in their attitude were players from the Tigers, undoubtedly encouraged by Cobb, who didn't like anyone, and the Red Sox, still sore that Mays had ditched them back in 1919. That the upbeat Chapman had been so universally liked and admired by everyone didn't help matters; one rival player, Tigers short-stop Donie Bush, even volunteered to play the rest of the season with the Indians, provided the league sanctioned the move. It didn't and Bush remained a Tiger.

Several teams planned protests against Mays. The Red Sox, before tak-ing the field Tuesday at home against Detroit, at first decided to not suit up for any game in which Mays appeared, before cooler heads prevailed and they decided to see what Speaker thought. The Tigers did the same—they were due at the Polo Grounds for a four-game series starting Satur-day, a fact not lost on anyone. Also in the mix were the White Sox and the Browns, where resentment against Mays was also high due to what several players were convinced was his tendency to throw the beanball.

Speaker had other matters on his mind. Late Tuesday morning in his room at the Ansonia, he received Kate Chapman, just off the 10 A.M. train from Cleveland, who fainted on receiving news that her husband was dead. Then it was time to confer with Huston on Tuesday afternoon's scheduled game at the Polo Grounds, which nobody felt like playing. Hus-ton immediately postponed the game. Chatting with Huston, Speaker gave assurances that he would try to suppress any bitterness—and strikes by rival teams.

Weighing in was Connie Mack, who said he found it hard to believe that any pitcher would deliberately throw a ball to hurt a batter. "I, for one, believe Chapman's death was an accident pure and simple," he said. "The unfortunate part of it all is that it happened to be Mays who pitched the ball that hit Chapman."

Despite his dislike for Mays, Huggins agreed. "It was a fastball inside that hit Chapman," the Yankee manager said. "The way I look at it, some-thing must have happened to his left foot. No batter gets hit by a pitched ball so long as the forward foot is free and he can shift it. He can get out of the way when that's the case."

Also standing firmly behind Mays were the New York scribes. "Mays received a panning from persons in other cities who probably took it for granted that he had pitched a 'beaner,' " wrote Joe Vila in the *Sporting News.* "Because Mays had been accused of adopting such unfair tactics on previous occasions and remembering that a year ago he threw a ball at a spectator in Shibe Park, he became the target for unwarranted criticism."

Dan Daniel of the *Herald-Tribune* wrote, "If there were any proof of intent on the part of Mays to strike Chapman with the ball, he would merit trial for murder. No mere threat on the part of players of other clubs to refuse to bat against the pitching of Mays would be sufficient. But in the absence of proof that the accident was anything more than an accident, threats and accusations are de trop. Many a baseball player has been struck on the head."

F. C. Lane agreed, absolving Mays of any blame and choosing to focus on the unfortunate pitcher's personal crisis of his own, particularly his "misfortune to arouse a deeper feeling of enmity in his associates on the diamond than any other player who ever lived.

"I have discussed this enmity with perhaps 50 different players in the American League as well as with Mays himself," Lane wrote in *Baseball Magazine*. "But it still remains as deep a mystery as ever. Players of the utmost integrity and usually sound judgment have heatedly maintained that Mays was a tricky ball player: that he deliberately threw the bean ball, that he was thoroughly unscrupulous.

"Mays is baseball's man of mystery. Perhaps no one ever fully understood him. It is certain that the unfortunate episode of Chapman's death will make him more misunderstood than ever."

Speaker himself recalled the time in 1916 when he'd been seriously beaned. Others remembered Roger Bresnahan, plunked on the head the year before, and Chicago Cub great Frank Chance, whose career was cut short by one too many beanballs. It seemed improbable that Mays would want to hurt anyone, given his genuine friendship with beanball-victim Chick Fewster, a fact he and others brought up several times that week.

At 10 A.M. Tuesday, when Yankee secretary Mark Roth knocked on Mays's front door in Washington Heights to deliver the news that Chapman was dead, the pitcher took it hard. Some hours later, with the assistance of Frederick Grant, a lawyer with the Yankee counsel, Mays made a statement about it to the district attorney. Delivering the statement, his eyes grew teary.

"It was a straight fastball and not a curved one," said Mays, his voice cracking. "It was a little too close, and I saw Chapman duck his head in an effort to get out of the path of the ball. He was too late, and a second later he fell to the ground. It was the most regrettable incident of my career, and I would give anything if I could undo what has happened."

The statement was enough to convince the D.A.'s office not to pursue the incident. The office ruled Chapman's death an accident and pursued it no further. But by the time Mays arrived back home, the reaction had already taken an ugly turn: while he was gone, Mays's wife, Freddie, had received two threats from telephone callers, one who vowed to shoot Mays when he drove across the 155th Street bridge.

Pondering his next move, Mays considered contacting Chapman's widow to pay his respects, but Huston said no. He also considered visiting the James McGowan Funeral Home at 153rd Street and Amsterdam Avenue, where Chapman's body had been moved, but decided against that too, admitting later that "the sight of his silent form would haunt me for as long as I live."

Many others did visit the funeral home, however, including each member of the Indians and several Yankees. So did a lot of fans, many of whom had showed up for the Tuesday afternoon game, still unaware that Chapman had died and that the day's game had been canceled. In all, estimates Mike Sowell in *The Pitch That Killed*, some 3,000 fans visited the body that day.

That evening, the casket that held Chapman's body was delivered to Grand Central Terminal for the long train ride back to Cleveland, where burial was set for Friday. As the casket, enclosed in a white pine box, was carried through the terminal, many rush-hour commuters paused, removing their hats in respect. "Chapman at least is freed from further care and worry," wrote F. C. Lane. "But there are many who would not like to face Carl Mays' future."

Curiously, it was Ban Johnson of all people who did more than anyone to stop the immediate strike threat against Carl Mays. Despite all the lingering hostility between the American League president and the Yankees over the previous year's jump by Mays from Boston to the Yankees, Johnson decided to take no action against the pitcher, and in doing so ended any threat of a strike.

"I could not conscientiously attempt to make any trouble for Mr. Mays," Johnson said from Cleveland that Friday, on the eve of the Yankees-Tigers series. Then, he offered a prediction. "It is my honest belief that Mr. Mays will never pitch again," Johnson said. "From what I have learned, he is greatly affected and may never be capable temperamentally of pitching again. Then, I also know the feeling against him to be so bitter among the members of the other teams that it would be inadvisable for him to pitch this year at any rate."

That thought was very much on Huggins's mind as the Yanks and Indians, minus Speaker, who had returned to Cleveland on the train with Chapman's body, got ready to resume their series on Wednesday. The Yankee manager told Mays not to even think of going to the ballpark at least until his next scheduled start over the weekend.

So Mays stayed out of view for the next four days, leaving home only on Friday to pay the speeding ticket he had received a month earlier. In the meantime, Mays was still his cranky self, and in speaking to reporters, he only fanned the flames of the discontent against him by blaming umpire Connolly for the tragedy. "It was the umpire's fault," he said. "A roughened spot on the ball, sometimes even a scratch, will make a ball do queer things. Umpires are instructed to throw out balls that have been roughed."

Those statements showed Carl Mays to be in dire need of a lesson in public relations. A lot of people who disliked him to start with were angry that the ballplayer had not chosen to view Chapman's body at the funeral home. But blaming the umpire for the accident fanned the discontent to a near-boiling point, and Connolly, backed by fellow umpires Big Bill Dinneen and Bill Evans, fired back immediately with a statement that no pitcher in the A.L. "resorted to trickery more than Carl Mays in attempting to rough a ball in order to get a break in it which would make it more difficult to hit." Even though Mays was cleared of any wrongdoing by the baseball establishment, the anger from just about everyone in baseball would never really go away.

On Wednesday, flags at the Polo Grounds flew at half-mast and both the Indians and Yankees wore mourning badges of black crepe on their sleeves as baseball tried getting back to some level of normalcy. With Speaker still in Cleveland and preparing for the funeral Friday, the Indians were skippered by Jack McAllister, with Larry Gardner directing operations on the field. Meanwhile, Lunte was back at shortstop, with Jamieson in center replacing Speaker, and Wambsganss batting second in Chapman's old spot.

The idea of playing baseball appeared a tad unseemly. When Ruth cracked a ball during batting practice that landed far beyond the outfield fence, many of the 18,000 fans began cheering, but stopped suddenly as if such celebration was inappropriate. And when Ruth told a Japanese reporter from a Tokyo newspaper that yes, he'd love to visit the Far East and hit a home run for the "Nipponese," the boys in the press box got quite a chuckle. Still, both teams went about their business for a time "as if they wanted to get through it as soon as possible," wrote William Hanna in the *Herald-Tribune*.

Jack Quinn fanned Jack Graney to start the game, and the Indians seemed to be facing a particularly listless day. But somehow, they scratched a hit here and there to tally a run in the fourth, fifth, and sixth to take a 3–1 lead.

At least the crowd quickly got back into things. In the Yankee first, there appeared to be a brief return to normalcy when Ruth slammed a long fly ball off Jim Bagby that hooked foul at the last moment, but still bounced off the upper deck. And when Gardner instructed Bagby to then walk Ruth, the fans booed long, loud, and cathartically, just like old times.

Ruth didn't manage much that day, sending a long fly ball out to center in the third and grounding out to first in both the sixth and the eighth. The Yanks closed it to 3–2 in the seventh when Lewis cracked a double and scored on Pipp's single to center. Too bad Pipp tried for second on the play—he was nailed by Jamieson, after which Bodie singled. Then Ping was forced by Ruel, and the inning ended when Meusel, limping and with his swollen left leg still bandaged, struck out.

That's where the score remained until the Yankee ninth, when with one gone and the crowd heading to the exits Lewis singled and was replaced on the bases by Fewster, who didn't seem outwardly affected by the Chapman beaning. Up stepped Wally Pipp, who promptly lashed Bagby's first pitch deep into the right-field bleachers for a two-run home run, his ninth of the season. It gave the Yankees a dramatic 4–3 win, gave Rip Collins, who had relieved Jack Quinn in the eighth, a rare win in relief, and added up to another deflating day for the Indians. And if the crowd had any lingering trepidation about celebrating, they didn't show it. They went ballistic, throwing straw hats onto the field and running out on the field to greet Pipp as he rounded the bases—more than making up for the sober emotions of the game's first few innings. The *Times* wrote that Pipp had for a day "usurped Babe Ruth's throne as monarch of the wagon tongue."

On Thursday, Huggins provided further evidence that life at the Polo Grounds had again gotten back to normal when, in the second, with the Yankees already behind 2–0, Connolly tossed him for arguing.

The play that so offended the Yankee manager happened when Steve O'Neill sent a dribbler toward second that Bob Shawkey couldn't field because O'Neill had thrown his bat in the vicinity. Connolly called O'Neill safe, but Huggins claimed interference. When he persisted in arguing, he was sent off.

In the fourth, Babe Ruth made everyone realize that baseball, just baseball, had returned for good when he sent Ray Caldwell's twister far above the right-field roof and onto a nearby ballfield. Ruth's 43rd home run of the season and first in five days sent many in the crowd of 18,000 into a prolonged roar of approval, including one poor man, Theodore Sturm of Bellrose, Long Island, who in celebrating from his box seat behind third base suffered a fatal heart attack.

Even so, the Indians, behind Caldwell, held on for a 3–2 win, putting them another game ahead of the Yanks and a half game beyond the White Sox, who had been rained out at Philadelphia. It gave the Indians their eighth win in 20 games against the Yankees, but they were hardly celebrating; immediately after the game, the Indians, along with Duffy Lewis and Wally Pipp, boarded the Lake Shore Limited for the trip to Cleveland, where on Friday they would attend Chapman's funeral.

The Ray Chapman tragedy left the Indians in need of a proven shortstop. It left the Yankees with decisions as well: Could Mays defy the predictions and pitch again? Could he do so effectively? And how would he and the team be treated in opposing ballparks?

Huggins badly needed an effective Mays. In the previous two months, the pitcher, now at 17–10, had rounded into the Yankees' most dependable starter, supplanting both Shawkey and Quinn, who were increasingly showing signs of wear, tear, and overwork. Another question was what to do about Ward, forever a slick fielder whose bat had deserted him. To resolve that, Huggins and Huston invited Home Run Baker back to resume his old position for the rest of the season. The prospect delighted members of the press corps, who for days peppered their coverage with suggestions that Baker was set to return. But in the end, the old third baseman didn't, choosing to stay at his farm in Maryland (Baker would return in 1921, play 94 games and hit .307, and then retire for good after 1922, having played in two more World Series).

Persistent doubts also remained about Huggins himself, a man who didn't seem to have a friend in the world, particularly since his team had only won two of five games since the western trip. On went the rumors about factions of the Yankees who, as one scribe put it, "were out to get Hug's scalp." Other stories said he'd be replaced for certain when the season ended, and that he alone was responsible for the lack of steady pitching. His only friend in baseball circles seemed to be Joe Vila, who wrote of Huggins in the *Sporting News* that in bringing his team even to third place, he "has accomplished wonders under the most trying of circumstances. . . . [Huggins] has never received the proper encouragement, yet he has plodded along, doing his best and keeping a stiff upper lip."

"Plodded" was the operative word in the Yankees' first two games against the Tigers. On Saturday, August 21, in the opener, Detroit smothered both Collins and Mogridge for 10 runs on 10 hits. The final was 10–3 in favor of the Tigers on a day when the biggest rise came from the lusty boos that greeted Ty Cobb, who the crowd blamed for trying to lead the short-lived Detroit strike against Mays.

Resentment in New York had been building against Cobb for days as a result of the incident, which kicked off when a New York–based United Press International reporter had called Cobb during the week in Boston to get his reaction to the Chapman tragedy. Cobb made no comments blaming anyone, but several New York newspapers reported that he had declared Mays should be barred from baseball, inflaming the feelings of Yankee fans.

That Saturday morning at the Ansonia, Cobb was in bed with a bad cold and a fever when his friend Grantland Rice stopped by to encourage him not to play because he anticipated the reaction would be ugly. Never popular to start with in New York, stemming from a day eight years before when he went into the stands at old Hilltop Park after a heckler who turned out to be disabled, Cobb was determined to play, anxious to deny the angry fans any opportunity to label him a wimp. With that, he went to the Polo Grounds, dressed, and walked onto the field. The nearly 30,000 fans, many of whom had arrived early for the particular purpose of razzing Cobb, threw such abuse at him "as he had rarely heard in 16 stormy seasons in the league," wrote Cobb's biographer, Charles Alexander.

Never one to back away from a challenge and with a dose of the thespian, Cobb walked directly across the field to a spot behind home plate, where he saluted the crowd by doffing his cap and bowing. Then, in a gesture indicating that he had been misinterpreted, he pointed upward to the press box.

Throughout the game, the crowd heckled him. In the seventh, Cobb got a measure of vindication when he singled, stole second, took third on catcher Fred Hofmann's poor throw, and scored on Bobby Veach's single.

But his real revenge came Sunday when the Tigers again thrashed Mogridge and the Yanks in an 11–9 slugfest. Before some 36,000 hostile fans, Cobb flashed his old greatness by hitting safely five times in six at-bats—four singles and a double—and driving in two runs. Despite suffering his worst season since 1906, the cantankerous superstar had saved one of his best days for the kind of nasty atmosphere in which he always seemed to thrive.

Cobb may have been misquoted, a point he continued to make to writers through the weekend, but he remained his old cranky self. On Monday, with Mays back at the Polo Grounds and suiting up for his first start since the fatal beaning, a clubhouse boy approached the pitcher with a note from Cobb.

"If it were within my power," the note read, "I would have inscribed on Ray Chapman's tombstone these words: 'Here lies a victim of arrogance, viciousness and greed.'"

Mays tore up the note and resumed dressing. Then he emerged onto the vast green of the Polo Grounds to a loud ovation from the pregame crowd of about 4,000. Those fans cheered heartily again when Mays went out to the mound just before game time to warm up.

Would the Tigers still carry out their earlier threat and strike? That was still a question as the game's leadoff batter, Tigers second baseman Ralph Young, stepped to the plate. But any doubts about that were quickly settled when Mays reared back and uncorked a strike to the further delight of the crowd, who cheered all over again. Clearly nervous, Mays twice threw curveballs and yelled to the batter "Look out!" when he feared the ball wouldn't break properly.

Cobb would rattle Mays for two hits. So would Donie Bush. In all, the Tigers punched out 10 hits, but Mays kept escaping trouble, thanks to good fortune and some fancy fielding on the part of the Yanks. In seven of the nine innings, the Tigers sent runners to second or third, and Mays struck out not a single batter. But he kept them from scoring, while the Yankees peppered Dutch Leonard and two other unfortunate Detroit pitchers for three runs in the first, single runs in the third and fourth, two in both the fifth and sixth, and another in the eighth. The final was 10–0 Yanks, which coupled with the White Sox being idle and a Cleveland doubleheader split against Boston, moved them to three games in back of the Indians and one back of Chicago.

This was more than another win. This was sweet redemption. Walking off the field after the game, Mays accepted congratulations all around and smiled broadly for the first time that anyone could recall. Under the most trying of circumstances, in which many, including Ban Johnson, had doubted he'd ever even pitch again, Mays had showed them up. For a man used to being the odd one out—the proverbial black hat in the old Western—that was motivation enough.

On Tuesday, August 24, the Yankees lost a golden opportunity in the series' final game against the Tigers to move up on the league leaders. Before 2,000 sailors from the Atlantic Fleet and several hundred orphans from Mt. Laurel School on Staten Island, Bob Shawkey was wild early, giving up a run in the first and three more in the third, with three of the four runners who crossed the plate getting on base via bases on balls. It was more than enough for the Detroits, who hung on for a 5–3 win behind Doc Ayers, who scattered 10 hits, including Ruth's lonely single. It was an opportunity lost, for both the Indians and White Sox lost too.

With the White Sox due in for three games and the St. Louis Browns for three more before the Yankees left for Boston, the time seemed ripe for the Yanks to make a move in the race. On Wednesday, an off-day for the New Yorkers, the Indians lost again—their fifth loss in six games since the Yankee series—and seemed out of sync since losing Ray Chapman. One bright spot for the Indians was the encouraging play of their new regular shortstop, Harry Lunte. After he reached the big leagues in 1919, the Associated Press had accidentally spelled his name as "Bunte," which seemed appropriate given his lowly .195 batting average that season and 15 hits, all singles. But given the chance to start, Lunte was actually starting to hit more than his weight. And he was doing so with warm ovations every time he stepped to the plate—a belated acknowledgment of respect for Chapman.

Considerable minefields awaited the Yankees. Another grueling western swing remained: of the 32 games left, only 11 would be at the Polo Grounds. And though the New Yorkers had taken six of the eight games at home against the White Sox, the Chicagos had quite suddenly jumped back into the race with their patented combination of good starting pitching and dependable batsmen like Joe Jackson and Eddie Collins.

The combination helped the White Sox bludgeon the Yankees in the series' opening game. The Sox bunched hit after hit off George Mogridge and two others—17 hits and 24 total bases in all—to romp, 16–5, and drop the Yankees four games in back of the leaders and three and a half behind the idle Indians. In quickly tallying four runs in the first, the Sox already had a nice lead when Ruth stepped up to the plate in the bottom of the inning. With Pipp on first, the Sultan of Swat clubbed his 44th home run of the year, this one off Dickie Kerr into the lower right-field grandstand. The Yanks tied it briefly in the third, but that was it, as the Sox soon tallied run after run to put the game out of reach.

But the Yankees could be excused for erratic play. With emotions still raw over the Carl Mays incident, the Indians—in Philadelphia to play the A's—took advantage of their off-day to send a petition to other American League clubs requesting they boycott games against the pitcher. With the A.L. owners also in Philadelphia for a meeting, Ban Johnson took advantage of the opportunity to try and ward off any boycott. With official baseball holding its breath to see how opposing teams would react, Speaker played coy.

"I know nothing about the letter," he told reporters after meeting with Johnson. "The club management had nothing whatsoever to do with it, and if one was sent, the players, who naturally feel grieved over the loss of their pal, Ray Chapman, had all to do with it."

Mays seemed damned if he did and damned if he didn't. In Boston, Red Sox players were upset after reading a report that Mays suffered a nervous breakdown, but had still managed to pitch effectively against Detroit. "Razz on that nervous collapse stuff," one player said. "That guy hasn't got any nerves." So what was it that so infuriated the fifth-place Red Sox, five games below .500? Clearly, emotions were still raw that their former teammate had ditched them in 1919 for the Yanks.

The Indians' petition was a bona fide vendetta, and gave rivals the opportunity to get rid of a pitcher they truly loathed—and feared. Word was that the Browns and the Senators were close to boycotting any games with Mays. Notably abstaining from the potential strike were the White Sox, whose manager, Kid Gleason, declared that "every ballplayer should know and should realize that Mays did not intentionally hit Ray Chapman with a pitched ball." Gleason figured Mays would be trying extra hard to avoid hitting any batters, which might give his club an edge.

On Friday, a reporter ambled down to visit Huston in his box seat at the Polo Grounds, asking for a statement on the rumored boycott. "Our only statement," said Huston, pointing to Carl Mays, "is out in the pitcher's box." If everyone else was against Mays, at least the Yankees were behind him. So were the 18,000 Polo Grounds fans, who greeted Mays with another healthy ovation when the pitcher came out to warm up, not letting up until he doffed his cap.

Once again, Mays was shaky early on, giving up a run in the first and two more in the second before settling down. The Yankees meantime had their way with Eddie Cicotte's knuckler, tagging him for a run in the first, another in the third, and two more in the fourth. Too bad Ruth was dropped from the lineup, a victim of a bad wasp sting—or as W. O. McGeehan put it in the *Tribune*, "an infuriated mosquito"—while filming his movie in Haverstraw. Ruth's wrist had become so badly swollen that he decided just before game time to visit his physician immediately, and had to page his driver in the grandstand to get the car. The physician who treated it had to slice a gash three inches long and an inch deep. The sting was costly; in the heat of the pennant race, Ruth would miss six games.

Back at the Polo Grounds, the Yankees and White Sox played a spirited game, trading runs. Things got heated in the second after Ping Bodie struck out and Chicago utility infielder and first-base coach Fred McMullin let fly with choice comments. Taking offense, Bodie invited McMullin to duke it out under the grandstand, but the two were tossed by umpire Bill Evans before they ever got there. "They can call me anything they want to," said a still-seething Ping after the game, "but they got to cut out personalities."

Both teams steamed into extra innings knotted at four. They traded runs in the 10th to make it 5-all. Huggins had lifted Mays, pinch-hitting Sammy Vick, who promptly thrashed a double and later scored the tying run. After Quinn pitched two scoreless innings, the Yanks got busy in the 12th when Ruel opened off Kerr with a single down the third-base line that glanced off Buck Weaver's glove. Quinn sacrificed Ruel to second, and Peckinpaugh, with a steaming liner over Weaver's head, sent him home with the winning run.

About the time that Muddy Ruel crossed the plate, just about all talk of boycott melted away, aided by Yankee support, some quick behind-the-scenes maneuvering by Ban Johnson, and the emphatic insistence on the part of managers and owners like Mack, Gleason, and Browns manager Jimmy Burke that their teams would be ready to play. "The talk about boycotting Mays was preposterous," said Colonel Ruppert, clearly relishing the victory and the ironic support of his cause by Johnson, who detested him. "I am glad that Mr. Johnson has put a stop to it."

Lucky for the Yankees, the boycott talk was short-lived. On Saturday, Ruth reported to the Polo Grounds with his swollen arm in a sling, and spent the day watching the game from a chair leaning against the right-field fence. Displaying his sling to reporters, the Babe grandly announced that "my arm has been suspended for 10 days."

In considerably better spirits was Ping Bodie. With some 300 colleagues from the Tietjen & Lang Dry Dock Company, the Hoboken shipyard where Ping had spent the previous winter as a riveter, on hand to honor him in a pregame ceremony, the Yankee center fielder got considerably more in gifts than the "pair of socks" he had longed for all those months ago. His fellow riveters came armed—presenting their former comrade with a gold watch and a pair of boxing gloves, with a horseshoe stuffed into one glove and a rivet in the other. They even brought along their company's brass band, which kept everybody whistling between innings.

With pennant fever again the rage, the 39,000 who got into the Polo Grounds—representing the latest "greatest crowd ever assembled"—saw Bob Shawkey on his game and taming the big White Sox bats. Shawkey gave up two hits to Joe Jackson, two more to Eddie Collins, and six in all—five of them singles—and shut down the Sox. Against Red Faber, the Yanks broke through in the second, scoring a run when Pratt walked, was sacrificed to second, and scampered home on Ward's single to center. In the end, the lone run was all the Yankees needed. They scratched a few more hits off Faber, and Shawkey did the rest; the final was 3–0 Yanks. The New Yorkers were again in second place—dropping the Indians to third. The American League was again up for grabs.

TEN

"A Tremendous Concept of Anticipation Fulfilled When the Homer Is Made"

The Babe Is Bigger than Baseball

In midsummer, Professor A. Hodges professed to know the secret to Babe Ruth's astounding ability to hit a baseball farther than anyone had ever seen. He told the Cleveland *News-Leader* that the Babe's particular talents were in his ability to connect with the bat's "center of percussion," a point a few inches from the end.

The good professor estimated that Ruth's swing used "24,000 foot-pounds of energy per second, the equivalent of 44 horsepower." Every ballplayer, he said, "is aware when the ball hits this spot on the bat, not only through the absence of jar to the arm, but also through a peculiar satisfaction, which is hard to define."

Oh, so that was it.

The theory underscored that despite the drama of the Ray Chapman–Carl Mays affair, it was hard to ignore the continuing saga of Babe Ruth. With 44 home runs and by continuing to burn the candle at both ends, the Babe was the big story in baseball. Declaring his intention of hitting 50 homers for the year, Ruth kept on swinging for the fences and drawing record-breaking crowds to every ballpark he set foot in.

By midsummer, he wasn't just the biggest story in sports, but with the exception of the presidential campaign, arguably the biggest in America. Quite suddenly, the coverage of other sports seemed trivial—tennis and golf were essentially activities for the smart set, while pro football was in its infancy and the college game was big among the college crowd and alumni, leaving it largely off-limits and uninteresting to the working class. At the other extreme was boxing, not quite respectable enough for the masses.

Grantland Rice argued there were only two other sports figures that were even close to Babe Ruth in popularity in the summer of 1920—and for the next 15 years for that matter. One was heavyweight champion Jack Dempsey, and the other was Man o' War, the racehorse.

Like Ruth, Jack Dempsey grew up poor, but as historian Geoffrey Ward wrote, didn't think "he needed to be nice to be champion," at least on the surface. Translation: Dempsey was damaged goods and wholly unappealing to a country that could use some heroes. Born in a log cabin near Manassa, Colorado, in 1895 and virtually the same age as Ruth, he was hardly a hero young boys could emulate. A rough man in a rough-and-tumble sport, Dempsey was a kind of Mike Tyson of his era—he didn't just want to knock his opponents down, he wanted to annihilate them. Champion since July 4, 1919, when he knocked Jess Willard down seven times, broke his jaw, cracked four ribs, and tore out six teeth, Dempsey fought from a crouch, from any angle, and always furiously.

Dempsey's personal life was just as messy—and controversial. At the time, he was just divorced from his first wife, Maxine, a prostitute. Dempsey would have three more marriages, only one of them happy. Like many prominent athletes of the era, he had been exempted from the draft on grounds that he was the sole support for his family, but after Dempsey won the title, both his first wife and sportswriters howled in protest that he had dodged the draft.

Although Dempsey was exonerated in a trial and he had, in fact, tried twice to enlist, the damage to his reputation was substantial. Later, Dempsey drew big crowds, in part because so many fans considered him a slacker and wanted to see him fail. Dempsey would retain his title until 1926, when he lost to Gene Tunney. In later years, he would serve in the Pacific during World War II and become a beloved figure in New York as the owner of his restaurant, Jack Dempsey's, a Broadway staple.

Man o' War's reign was not nearly as long. Bred by August Belmont II, the racehorse was foaled in 1917, won big in 1919, but by 1920 was nearly finished. Man o' War would retire in January 1921 to a horse farm in Lexington, Kentucky, and live another 26 years—remembered as arguably the greatest racehorse of all time and certainly lionized, but hardly enduring the kind of daily scrutiny received by a ballplayer performing 154 times a year.

Every aspect of Ruth's baseball exploits was being examined, from the length of his bat and how far he stood from the plate to how far his home runs went and where they landed. Indeed, his bat had become so potent that Damon Runyon wondered, in light of the Mays incident, if pitchers were in danger of being struck by a Ruthian line drive. "Ball players say it is a blessing Babe Ruth does not commonly hit the ball through the infield," he wrote on September 9 in the *American*. "He would kill or dangerously injure any man who got in front of one of his powerful punches at short distance.

"Players who know the King of Swat say that he has always had a secret dread of smashing a ball back at a pitcher, or an infielder," Runyon wrote. "It is probably that dread which causes him to pull his punches high, and to right, clearing the infield. No man ever lived who hit a ball as hard as Ruth."

Ruth the public figure was becoming news as well. Photographers discovered his genuine fondness for children, and took to meeting him at hospitals and orphanages, and snapping photos that appeared on the social pages—new territory for ballplayers. For all of Ruth's gruffness at the ballpark, he had an instinct for building good relationships not just with children but with law enforcement officers, which often came in handy when he was picked up for speeding. When Deputy Police Commissioner John Daly sent word to the Yankees in Detroit that he would appreciate one of Ruth's bats to present to the person buying the most tickets for Police Field Day, Ruth sent not just his game-used bat, but a signed ball. The bat and ball promptly went on display in the show window of Weber & Heilbroner, at 1505 Broadway.

The irony of how Ruth could visit a sick child and a brothel on the same day wasn't lost on his teammates. "His excesses only fed his ego," Waite Hoyt once said. "Never in Ruth's baseball career was he tormented by conscience. . . . Among baseball players, Ruth's hardiness in the face of late hours and over-indulgence was more talked about than his home runs."

By the time Hoyt arrived in New York from the Red Sox after the 1920 season, he noticed immediately the changes in Ruth. "In Boston, he had been a surprised young man—hardly able to assimilate the extravagance of success. Now, he was sure of himself. He was developing poise, demanding respect when it was slow to appear voluntarily."

Meanwhile, nerve specialists at a New York hospital chimed in with their explanation of why Ruth was so special. "There arises a tremendous concept of anticipation which is fulfilled when the homer is made," they wrote. "The sympathetic nervous system overstimulates the endocrine substances; the suprarenal gland affects the insoluble glycogen so as to change it to glucose [and] the thyroid gland affects the body's proteid metabolism so as to supply new proteid substances for those which are broken down."

Maybe the nerve specialists were right. Maybe Ruth's proteid metabolism was slowing down a tad, for as the homestand rolled on, Ruth actually started displaying some signs of settling down and not staying out to all hours. Was it a serious talk with Huggins that did it? Hardly. Babe Ruth needed his sleep because he was making a movie.

It was the film *Headin' Home*, for which he had signed in late July, prior to the Yankees' last road trip. As the star, Ruth had to actually curtail his late nights somewhat in order to leave the Ansonia early on several mornings in late August and guide his latest roadster across the Hudson River some 30 miles north to the Rockland County hamlet of Haverstraw. Since there were no bridges or tunnels from Manhattan to New Jersey at the time, Ruth ferried his car across the Hudson and drove up the Palisades Parkway to Haverstraw. There he received makeup and went to work in front of the cameras for several hours before rushing back to Manhattan for the day's game, often with his chalky makeup still on, which never failed to draw gales of laughter from his teammates.

Ruth was the latest baseball star to be lapped up by the booming film industry. Ex-Yankee Hal Chase, his career now in tatters due to one gambling scandal too many, was the first back in 1911, when he appeared in the forgettable film *Hal Chase's Home Run*. Also that year, the Philadelphia A's trio of Chief Bender, Jack Coombs, and Rube Oldring appeared in *The Baseball Bug*. As the decade wore on, other baseball stars such as Frank Chance, Home Run Baker, Ty Cobb, and John McGraw also made appearances. Former Giant star Mike Donlin became somewhat of a film star in his own right, leaving baseball for the bright lights of Hollywood.

Even so, *Headin' Home* was among the last of the silents made in the New York area. Once the center of the movie business, the New York/New Jersey area was fast losing its mantle to Hollywood for several reasons, starting with the sunny California weather, which meant movies could be shot year-round using natural light. Also, the recently formed Motion Picture Patents Company, or "Trust," a partnership between Thomas Edison and his former rival, Biograph, sued just about everybody that dared to use or import non-Edison cameras and projection equipment, forcing filmmakers to look to places like California, Florida, and Cuba. The Trust had an effective method of driving the competition from business: it hired gunmen to shoot holes in their rivals' cameras.

Headin' Home featured subtitles written by Bugs Baer, and told the kind of story you'd expect—how a bashful, young iceman named Babe, played by Ruth, overcomes the odds to become a baseball star. "Babe" lives with his mother and cute little pigtailed kid sister in the fictional town of Haverlock, whittles a bat from a tree limb, and—surprise, surprise—belts a home run five blocks through the stained-glass window of the local church and is on his way. Babe moves away and becomes a legend, but never forgets his idyllic hometown, where he returns, bearing gifts for his family, and marries—another surprise—his hometown sweetheart, the banker's daughter, played by Ruth Taylor. He even pays off the mortgage on the family homestead for dear old mom and little sis, played by Frances Victory.

The film was a long one for those days, running 56 minutes, or six reels, at a time when most movies were about half as long. The producers, Kessel & Baumann, paid Ruth $15,000 in advance and afterwards gave him a check for $35,000, warning him not to deposit it for at least a week so their funds could clear. The Babe didn't mind, and afterwards took great pleasure in pulling the check out of his wallet and showing it to friends, teammates, and anyone else who crossed his path. "I'm a little short," he'd say with a guffaw. "Can you cash this for me?" But months later when Ruth tried to cash the check, the clerk informed the incredulous ballplayer that the company was out of business.

While the film got moderate attention from the New York critics, it was a very big deal in Haverstraw. Extraordinary as it sounds today, most of the movie's baseball scenes were actually filmed in just one morning—Sunday, August 22—when Ruth pulled into town at around 9 A.M. and took part in the first game of a doubleheader. Some 2,000 locals looked on—cramming the roads leading into town and paying 50 cents each to squeeze into every crevice of the local ballpark, also called the Polo Grounds.

"It was perhaps the biggest base ball demonstration that ever took place in Haverstraw," wrote the *Rockland County Times* in one of the bigger understatements of the year. Things had actually kicked off earlier that morning with a parade of fans and ballplayers from the Haverstraw and Nyack teams, accompanied by Professor George Glassing's brass band, which left the U.S. Hotel downtown and marched to the ballpark. There they were met by filmmakers with four cameras—two of which, wrote the local papers, were "great complicated affairs with more wheels, angles and devices than a submarine sounding horoscope on a battleship."

Locals who showed up to see Ruth crack a home run in a real-life game were disappointed, and several complained that they weren't getting their money's worth. This was, well, make-believe, as scenes were filmed over and over again, including one in which Ruth, angry at striking out, slams his bat against home plate, breaking the bat, which the filmmakers had made certain to saw nearly in two. When a man named Lynch, the star of the Haverstraw pitching staff, put some mustard on a few of his pitches, the filmmakers had to remind him to groove them in there and allow Ruth to hit some moon shots.

For the Babe, this was a little like batting practice. He sent one of Lynch's pitches, "seemingly without great muscular effort," the local paper reported, clear over the center-field fence to the top of Constable Peter Reilly's house. Then he sent one even farther into Frank Smith's front yard, and still another ball that landed on the shed in the rear of the Kigler family home, and rolled into the kitchen, where Mrs. Kigler was preparing Sunday dinner.

Then the filmmakers sent Ruth on his way around the bases, and directed a big group of spectators to rush from the stands and greet him at home plate. And just to top off the feeling of make-believe, the filmmakers brought along several actors masquerading as ballplayers, some of whom they actually had to stop to give instant lessons on at least looking like they knew how to hit and pitch. Only with game two—and Ruth gone for the day's game at the big Polo Grounds against the Tigers—did those disgruntled locals get their money's worth, as the Haverstraw nine got to business and pounded the team from nearby Nyack for 25 runs in only five innings.

Just as remarkable as shooting the film's baseball scenes in a single morning was the equally speedy production process. Billed as "a delightful photoplay of youth and happiness," *Headin' Home* opened September 19—less than a month later—to mixed reviews at Madison Square Garden. Not that anyone cared all that much about quality; almost 6,000 people showed up on opening night, and boxing mogul Tex Rickard, who paid $35,000 for the privilege of showcasing the film, made sure that the evening came adorned with all the hoopla he could muster. There was entertainment by Lieutenant J. Tim Brymn and his Black Devil Band of 50, and appearances by many movie stars. A lot of people showed up for the film's run at the Garden, paying 25 or 50 cents for the matinees, or 50 cents, 75 cents, or $1 for the evening shows. Ruth himself showed up later in the week, as did his old friend Jack Dempsey.

The *Tribune* called it "the old story of the prophet who is not recognized in his home town." While critics genuinely enjoyed Ruth's performance— "as an actor, he scored another home run," the *Tribune* added—they threw barbs at the movie itself. "Just how [Ruth] became famous is not shown," sniffed the *Times*, "the story skipping about rather aimlessly, not bothered by continuity and things like that." The *Tribune* concluded that "The story is weak, disjointed and unconvincing." At least the filmmakers had the good sense to throw in a real-life shot of the Babe popping one at the Polo Grounds; everyone liked that scene.

The most interesting aspect of the Sunday, August 29, start of the Yankees' three-game series at the Polo Grounds against the fourth-place Browns could have been the crowd: it was another whopper, as approximately 35,000 fans stormed the ballpark despite a steady rain that fell through-out the day. It could have been in the pitching matchup, an intriguing one that pitted two wily spitballers, Jack Quinn and Urban Shocker.

But it was neither.

The Yanks had jumped out ahead in the fifth, when with two gone Ruel doubled and Quinn lofted a home run, his second of the season, into the right-field stands to make it 2–0. Maybe all the excitement, not to men-tion the straw hats that descended onto the field in celebration, was too much for Quinn, for with one down in the Browns' sixth, Ken Williams tripled to left center, Earl Smith singled him home, and Jack Tobin bunted back to Quinn but beat out the throw. Then Hank Severeid singled, scor-ing Smith and knotting the score at two.

Quinn had lost it quickly, most likely due to the wet ball and a lot of innings that were beginning to take their toll. Out came Huggins, who sig-naled down to the bullpen for . . . Carl Mays. Now here was a situation:

seeing Mays, the large soggy crowd, who had been relatively quiet until then, rose as one, cheering long and loud at the sight of the sinkerballer, once again showing their support. Seething in the dugout were the Browns, who, next to Cleveland and Boston, were the American League team that displayed the most venom for the pitcher.

Mays did his job, but the Yankee infielders didn't. Shocker sent an easy double-play ball to shortstop, but the sure-handed Peckinpaugh fumbled it for error, most likely because of the wetness. Then, with the bases loaded and still only one out, Wally Gerber sent a line drive to left. Duffy Lewis handled it but couldn't hold on, and Tobin, on third, tried to score but was nailed at home on Lewis's peg to Ruel. Joe Gedeon then smacked a single past Ward at third, scoring Severeid to make it 3–2, but when Shocker tried legging it home, he was also cut down by Lewis's bullet throw.

The Yanks tied it at three in the seventh when Pipp singled and Williams and Baby Doll Jacobson collided while chasing Bodie's long fly to left center, allowing the ball to drop in for a double that scored Pipp. After a 30-minute rain delay, play resumed. The game stayed deadlocked into the ninth, when the Browns, cranky already about Umpire Big Bill Dinneen's ball-and-strike calling, tore into Mays. While bench jockeying has always been a part of baseball, the taunts sent out by the St. Louis dugout were particularly vicious and prompted the umpire to tell the Browns to knock it off.

What barbs the St. Louis bench jockeys were yelling is lost to history. But their feelings were clear, and they left a mark, so much so that the *Times* felt compelled to scold the Browns in the next morning's paper. "The conduct of some of the St. Louisans . . . in insulting the hard-working Mays while engaged in pitching provided a touch of slime which adheres to those whose tongues provided it."

If the bench jockeys bothered Mays, he didn't let on. And as happened in other games since the Ray Chapman accident, he had the last laugh. In the Yankee ninth, Lewis opened with a hot smash to third that Smith gloved and dropped. Then he uncorked a hurried and high throw to first, and Lewis was safe. After Bodie sacrificed Lewis to second, up stepped Ward, who was due, having been struck out three times earlier by Shocker. This time, Ward was up to the challenge: he dropped a double inside the right-field foul line to push his average up to the .240 range, send home

Lewis, and take the game 4–3. The Yanks had won it with some drama— closing the gap on the idle White Sox to one and a half games and moving two and a half ahead of Cleveland, which was stopped by Washington. Mays had won another game under excruciating pressure. His record was now 19–11, and he was almost single-handedly keeping the Yankees in the pennant race.

A case in point came three days later on Tuesday, August 31, when after a day off the Yanks were flat in a 3–2 loss in which Browns' pitcher Dixie Davis looked like Walter Johnson in holding the New Yorkers to a paltry five hits. On Wednesday, Huggins, fully aware that Mays had gone only three and two-thirds innings Sunday, handed him the ball for the start.

Again the pressure was on, for while the Yankees were enjoying their off-day and losing Tuesday, the Indians were in the midst of taking three in a row from the Senators in Washington and slinking back into the top spot in the A.L.

This time, Mays was effective from the get-go. He gave the Browns only four hits and a walk, and ran into trouble in only one inning—the seventh—when Sisler, now leading the majors in batting at .396, singled but was stranded at third. It was the farthest any St. Louisian got, as the Yankees won 2–0. Incredibly, the man who Ban Johnson said would never again pitch in the big leagues had won his 20th game, and his third since the Chapman tragedy. The win pushed the Yankees back to a half game behind Cleveland.

With Ruth still out with his infected arm, Carl Mays, and his ability to persevere under brutish pressure both as a starter and in relief, was becoming one of the big stories in baseball. Even when Mays didn't have his best stuff, his teammates seemed to respond—fielding well and scratching away for just enough runs to win, particularly in the latter innings. It was the opposite with Shawkey, for whom the Yanks typically offered little run support.

But Shawkey never gave his teammates much of a chance on Thursday, September 3, in the opener of a five-game series at Fenway Park in Boston. The Red Sox jumped on him for two runs in the first and single runs in the second and the third, and put the game out of reach. "If the Yankees had worn masks and petticoats today they could not have been any more thoroughly-disguised than they were by the kind of baseball they played," the *Times* wrote. Managing only five hits off Elmer Myers, the Yanks lost 6–2.

Badly in need of a win Friday, Huggins relied on a formula that had worked against the Browns. He pitched Quinn seven innings, and with the score knotted at three in the eighth went to Mays, who was proving he could pitch effectively in relief in between starts. Choosing to replace an aging starter late in the season with a closer sounds downright simplistic today, but back then it wasn't, and Huggins was proving himself to be a good 40 years ahead of his time.

Once again, the move worked. Entering the game to a few tentative "boos"—and some scattered applause—Mays again shut down the opponent in the eighth. Then, in the top of the ninth, the Yanks came alive. With two gone, Bodie doubled off the left-field wall, Ward walked, and Meusel doubled them both home. Mays shut his ex-teammates down in the bottom of the ninth, and the Yanks won it 5–3. Cleveland and Chicago both lost on the day, moving the three A.L. leaders into a virtual dead heat, .005 of a percentage point apart. For Mays, it was win number 21—his fourth straight since the Chapman beaning.

Afterwards, several Red Sox players lashed out at the Fenway fans for not being harder on Mays, while others repeated earlier claims that he should be banned because his underhanded delivery was unsafe. One exception was Wally Schang, who had caught Mays when the two were Boston teammates: "I don't mind that underhand ball," he said, "for that it is in fine control, but I know from experience that when Mays pitches overhand the ball is likely to go most anyplace."

Putting some context on the mild reception afforded to Mays was Melville Webb in the *Boston Globe*. "The fans aren't making a hero out of Mays by any means," he wrote. "Their attitude simply is 'On with the dance.'"

In the Saturday, September 4, doubleheader, Ruth returned and supplied enough excitement to keep the newspaper hacks occupied for a month. Somewhere along the line, an enterprising sportswriter had unearthed another otherwise overlooked statistic—organized baseball's all-time, single-season home run record of 45 achieved by one Perry Werden, a member way back in 1895 of Minneapolis of the minor-league Western League. At the time, Werden was winding down a journeyman career spent mostly as a first baseman. In five big-league seasons—he played seven years for six teams—Werden hit 26 home runs, led his league twice in triples, and batted .282. Like big Ned Williamson, the old White Stocking whose big-league record Ruth had obliterated the year before, Werden had the benefit of hitting most of his shots in a quirky home park with a short fence.

But there was nothing cheap about Ruth's work this day. Anxious to see their onetime favorite son, 33,027 filled Fenway Park, the ballpark's largest crowd ever, including several thousand seated in roped-off sections of the outfield. On hand as well were members of the Knights of Columbus, who presented the Babe with a spiffy set of diamond-studded cuff links, which no doubt Ruth accepted with a vow of not losing them.

Ruth gave the Yankees the jolt they needed. In the opener, they jumped on Red Sox starter Sad Sam Jones early, with Peckinpaugh leading off the game by doubling to left, going to third on Pipp's sacrifice, and scoring on Ruth's scorching single off the leg of first baseman Stuffy McInnis—a ball hit so hard that Mike McNally had to replace him at first. Ruth took second on McInnis's errant throw to first, and scored on Pratt's single. Just like that, the Yankees led 2–0.

That was still the score when Ruth stepped to the plate in the third and sent a towering fly ball into the right-field bleachers for home run number 45, a solo shot that increased the lead to 3–0. The Yanks added two more in the fifth with RBIs from Pratt and Bodie to make it 5–0. That was more than enough for Collins and Shawkey in relief. The final: 5–3 Yanks, for the team's 80th win of the year.

Maybe Ruth's home run put the crowd in a good mood. Maybe it was the prospect of the long Labor Day weekend. Or maybe it was Boston's realization that enough really was enough, for as Carl Mays trotted out to start game two, he was heartily cheered.

But right in line with Mays's performances of late, he ran into trouble early before quickly settling down. The Sox jumped out with two runs in the first and another in the fourth, before the Yankees could manage anything off Bullet Joe Bush. Then, with one down in the sixth, Ruth drilled his 46th home run into the right-field stands to start a rally and forever make Perry Werden a statistical footnote. Pratt then walked, Meusel singled, and Bodie doubled to right, scoring Pratt. Meusel then scored on Ward's sacrifice, and the score was suddenly 3-all.

The Yanks thought they had pulled off the sweep by adding another two runs in the ninth to give Mays a 5–3 cushion. All the sinkerballing pitcher had to do was secure three more outs for his 22nd win, which would put the Yanks back into first place. But Wally Schang doubled to left to open the inning, and took third as McInnis was retired. Then Everett Scott doubled to right, scoring Schang. Two batters later, with two gone and the tying run on second and the winning run on first, Harry Hooper rifled a single to center. Off with the crack of the bat was pinch runner Gene Bailey, who slid home into catcher Muddy Ruel fractions of a second ahead of Ping Bodie's throw from center. With the impact of the collision, the ball squirted from Ruel's mitt toward the screen behind home plate, scoring Joe Bush all the way from first with the winning run. The Sox had pulled it out 6–5 with three runs in the bottom of the ninth, keeping the Yanks out of first place on a day when the Indians beat the Tigers and the White Sox split with the Browns. Watching the winning run score from the mound was Carl Mays, who should have been backing up the play from behind home, where he could easily have nailed Bush.

Mays's oversight brought the Yankee road trip to a somber end and underscored the importance of their last western swing of the season, set to kick off five days later in Cleveland. In between was a rare Sunday off-day and a welcome three-game series at the Polo Grounds against the lowly A's—a Labor Day doubleheader followed by a Tuesday single game. With the pennant race heading into its last four weeks, every play and every pitch and at-bat were becoming critical, and the baseball world seemed finally to be getting over the distraction of the Ray Chapman–Carl Mays affair. But quicker than a Walter Johnson fastball, baseball's distractions returned—this time with a scandal that threatened the core of the game.

ELEVEN

"Burn My Bridges and Jump Off the Ruins"

The Black Sox Shake Baseball's Core

The scandal broke at the same time that Ruth was pounding out his 45th and 46th home runs at Fenway Park. Kicking it off were reports that William L. Veeck Sr., president of the Cubs, had received several telegrams and telephone calls on the afternoon of Tuesday, August 31, informing him that gamblers had swamped betting parlors with $50,000—all bet on a Phillies victory that afternoon against the Cubs. The heavy action swung the odds from 2-1 in favor of the Cubs to 6-5 for the Phillies, and prompted Veeck to suspect that the day's scheduled starting pitcher, Claude Hendrix, had been bribed to throw that day's game. Veeck ordered Cubs manager Fred Mitchell to hold out Hendrix and instead start Grover Cleveland Alexander, the team's ace, on three days' rest. Veeck offered Alexander a $500 bonus if he won, but despite his best efforts, the Phillies won anyway, 3–0, providing newspapers with a lot to report, while bringing up other lingering suspicions of devious behavior.

Veeck had reason to believe that some of his players were on the take. In June, former Cubs second baseman Lee Magee sued for the remaining salary he claimed Veeck owed him, and pledged to "take quite a few noted people with me." Back in March, Magee, along with notorious game fixer and former Yankee Hal Chase and another former Cub turned Giant Heinie Zimmerman, had been quietly pushed out of baseball for crooked play, a move that prompted Magee to come clean on the details behind his teaming with Chase to deliberately lose games while with the Reds.

211

Baseball officials traced a $500 check Magee had written to place a bet on a game with gambler John Costello, clearly establishing his guilt. His suit for back pay went nowhere, nor did his threat to name names, or as he put it, "burn my bridges and then jump off the ruins." Magee hadn't made a dime from his shenanigans, claiming that Chase double-crossed him after secretly taking the money placed on the opponents and putting it on Cincinnati.

The cases of Magee and Hendrix were the baseball establishment's wake-up call. Putting an exclamation mark on the events was Chase's inability to be honest. Banned by the major leagues, Chase drifted back to his native California, where he joined the Pacific Coast League but lasted only until August after trying to bribe a Salt Lake City player. How sad that the gifted Chase, who played for the Yankees for nearly nine years and another six with the White Sox, Reds, Buffalo Feds, and Giants, was so corrupt—had this slick fielder, talented batsman, and fan favorite nicknamed "Prince Hal" been honest, he'd have a plaque in Cooperstown.

Following the Cubs-Phillies game, Veeck felt strongly enough about what he had heard that he asked the Chicago chapter of the Baseball Writers Association to help him in launching an investigation. With rumors still festering that the 1919 World Series was dropped on purpose by the White Sox, the writers sensed yet another cover-up and asked prominent Chicago businessman Fred Loomis for help. At his suggestion, the writers crafted a letter, published under Loomis's signature on the front page of the sports section of the *Chicago Tribune*, calling for a full-scale investigation of both the August 31 Cubs-Phillies game and the 1919 Series. "Those who possess evidence of any gambling in the World Series," the letter stated, "must come forward so that justice will be done."

A storm of public anger that such a thing could happen followed. Sensing an opportunity to get some publicity—and facing reelection—Illinois State Attorney Maclay Hoyne conferred with Judge Charles MacDonald of the state criminal court. Wasting little time, Judge MacDonald convened a Cook County grand jury on September 7 to look into the allegations.

For starters, they found that Hendrix, the Chicago pitcher, had on the day of his scheduled start against the Phillies sent a telegram to Kansas City gambler Frog Thompson, placing a bet against the Cubs. That was enough for Veeck to release him from the team after the season, and although Hendrix was never officially expelled from the game, the 10-year veteran was essentially blacklisted and never again played organized baseball.

Suspicion fell on three other Cub ballplayers—first baseman Fred Merkle, pitcher Paul Carter, and infielder Buck Herzog, all veterans. No conclusive evidence was ever mounted against the three, but Carter and Herzog, a 13-year veteran, were also released after the season and never played in the majors for another minute. Merkle, a 16-year veteran best remembered for his baserunning blunder back in 1908 that cost the Giants a big game and arguably the pennant, also left the bigs after the season, returning five years later as a player-coach with the Yankees.

Moving on to more general areas of baseball corruption, the grand jury heard from its first key witness, Giants pitcher Rube Benton, who claimed that back in September 1919 Herzog and Chase had offered him $800 to throw a game to the Cubs. Benton also claimed that Giants manager John McGraw knew about the offer, but had taken no action.

Turning to the World Series, former Cubs owner Charles Weegham testified that his friend, Chicago gambler Monte Tennes, had told him back in August 1919 that seven members of the White Sox were set to throw the World Series. Weegham claimed that Tennes's story seemed too fantastic to be true, so he never reported the allegations. He was right about one thing: that a bunch of ballplayers could carry off the swindle of America's greatest sporting event was extraordinary.

Against this backdrop, it was a relief to focus on baseball. The American League leaders played on, bunched more tightly than ever. With the Yankees idle Sunday, September 5, the White Sox downed St. Louis 4–1 and the Indians beat Detroit 4–3, putting the three teams into a virtual deadlock. Although the schedule makers had put the Yankees at a severe disadvantage—only 7 of their remaining 22 games would be at home—at least their next 3 games were against the pitiful A's.

Dead last and 41 games under .500, the A's were awful—so awful that Connie Mack couldn't stomach making the trip. "No wonder [he] doesn't come over from Philadelphia to see his lads play ball," the *Times* cracked. "As he watches them make errors, those green elephants on their uniforms probably turn pink right before his eyes."

For a time at least, it appeared that Mack may have goofed. Before 10,000 in the morning game of the Labor Day twin bill, Dave Keefe, who like Mordecai Brown, the old Cubs pitcher, had only three fingers on his pitching hand and was nicknamed "Three Finger," gave Ruth fits, striking him out in the first, the third, and again in the fifth. But in the end it didn't matter, for the Yanks were blessed, as the *Times* put it, with "a violent attack of good pitching," thanks to Herb Thormahlen, who didn't allow a hit until Chick Galloway's scratch single in the sixth, and only five in all. The Yanks took the game 4–1.

Shawkey took over the afternoon game when 30,000 ignored the threat of rain to pile into the Polo Grounds. As in the opener, the A's threw in a rookie pitcher who Ruth found a challenge—a 6'6" stringbean of a right-hander, the suitably nicknamed Bryan "Slim" Harriss, who yielded a laser of a double off the right-field wall to the Babe in the first before discovering the secret of keeping him from chalking up extra-base hits: bases on balls. Ruth walked the rest of the day, and Shawkey shut down the A's on three measly singles as the Yanks coasted 5–0. Too bad for them that both the White Sox and Indians swept their doubleheaders; the standings remained bunched at the top with Cleveland at 81–49, leading the 81–51 White Sox and the 82–52 Yankees by a slim half game.

On Tuesday, the Yanks closed out their brief homestand with another easy victory over the A's—this one a 2–0 four-hitter by Mays, his 22nd win of the season. The win, combined with the Tigers' and Dutch Leonard's 5–0 shutout of the White Sox, moved the New Yorkers up to second place, a half game out. With the team packing to push off after the game for the west, there was one lingering piece of business connected with the Ray Chapman affair. Even with the fans looking on Mays with some sympathy, Huston announced that the Yankees had decided that the pitcher would not go with them to Cleveland. "We are not taking Mays to Cleveland, not because we think there is danger of any trouble, but out of respect to the feelings of the people there," he said. "We don't want to offend them. It is largely a matter of sentiment."

For Huston, it was a hard decision. On one hand, it avoided the potential of any troubles in Cleveland, where anger against Mays had triggered several to write threatening letters to the pitcher, but on the other hand it kept the Yankees from using the services of their best pitcher. After all, wrote Mike Sowell in *The Pitch That Killed*, Huston had developed a particular fondness for Mays, admiring his toughness and "the way he stood up to his critics and continued to perform in the face of incredible hardships." Besides, Huston thought, baseball needed to get back to the business of, well, baseball.

The Indians faced their own challenges. While Harry Lunte would continue to bat his weight—the early version of the "Mendoza line," so named a half-century later for the Pittsburgh shortstop who never hit much above .200—the 27-year-old rookie was continuing to prove himself more than an adequate replacement for Ray Chapman, drawing raves with his range and accurate arm. "I've seen Lajoie, Wagner and all the great infielders, but never have I seen a better pair of hands than Lunte's," said Speaker, no question caught up in the moment. On Sunday, Lunte drew three standing ovations from the home fans for his glove work in the Indians' 4–3 win against Detroit. But on Monday, in the second game against the Tigers, Lunte rounded first base after singling to left and felt a pain in his left thigh. Helped from the field, Lunte had pulled a muscle. His season and moment in the spotlight were suddenly finished, and the Indians again went looking for a new shortstop.

Three days later, the Yanks suffered an injury of their own. En route to Cleveland, the team stopped for an exhibition game against the Pirates in Pittsburgh. As incredible as it seems today that team owners would stop to play a meaningless game in the middle of a pennant race, that was the custom in those days. Before 25,000 at Forbes Field, Bodie tripled in the second, and sliding home a minute later to score on a wild pitch, he twisted his right foot on the rubber of the plate. First diagnosed with a sprained leg, Bodie had in reality fractured his ankle. The .290 hitter was finished for the season—replaced by Ruth, with Duffy Lewis and Meusel platooning in right.

Cleveland's solution to their ongoing problem at shortstop was to plug in utility infielder Joe Evans, an even weaker hitter than Lunte, for now, and send for 21-year-old Southern Leaguer Joe Sewell. Speaker knew about Sewell, who was short at 5'6", but in 92 games at New Orleans had batted a respectable .289. "Let's gamble on anything now," the Indians' manager said in calling up the untested Sewell, just four months removed from the University of Alabama.

On Thursday, September 9, Sewell watched his first big-league game from the end of the bench. Keeping him out on purpose was Speaker, who wanted the youngster to get his bearings before entering a game. That the opposition happened to be the New York Yankees seemed ironic if the unfortunate rumors of the last few days were to be believed—on Wednesday afternoon, a story spread that several Yankees including Ruth, Pratt, Meusel, and Lewis had been killed or badly injured in a car accident on the way to Cleveland. The report, received via "flash" at the Wall Street brokerage house of W. E. Hutton and Co., was spread by telegrams sent from gamblers in Pittsburgh, Cincinnati, Chicago, and Cleveland, and suddenly shifted the odds heavily against the Yanks, underscoring gambling's hold on baseball.

Huston moved deftly to trim the rumors. "[It's a] sure thing gamblers started these vicious stories," he said on reaching Cleveland. "Unfortunately, this is something baseball authorities have no way of stopping. I want to say, however, that there has not been a suspicion of anything wrong [with the upcoming series], no matter what one may think about betting on baseball."

Maybe the nasty rumors were why the game-one crowd of 18,000 at League Park treated their visitors with surprising deference, applause, and sportsmanship. They watched as the New Yorkers jumped on Stanley Coveleski for two in the first, before the Indians pounded Jack Quinn almost at will, scoring in four of the first five innings. Quinn and his spitter had a lot of trouble finding the plate; he walked eight in only four and two-thirds innings, after which Cleveland held a 6–3 lead.

At least Ruth was enjoying himself. Joining the Yankees throughout their western swing at the Babe's invitation was the band from the St. Mary's Industrial School in Baltimore, in town to serenade its most esteemed graduate and raise funds for the school, where several buildings had been destroyed by fire the winter before. What a moment it was in the third when Ruth sent one of Coveleski's spitballs high over the fence in right field for his 47th home run of the season. "The band almost wrecked their instruments in making a demonstration over the event," the *Times* wrote. The rest of the crowd liked it too—reserving their loudest ovation of the day for the big blast. Unfortunately for the listless Yanks, it was the day's high spot. Quinn, Collins, Mogridge, and Bob McGraw all were rocked for more damage. By the time the unusually long 2-hour, 31-minute game—a good 40 minutes beyond the usual 1:50 games back then—was done, the Indians had pounded out 14 hits in a 10–4 win to move one and a half games up on the Yanks and a half game ahead of Chicago.

How fortunate that the St. Mary's Industrial School Band, dressed in handsome sailor uniforms and hats, and dwarfed by the big brass instruments they had to lug around, showed up early on Friday. For one reason, an immense crowd descended on League Park, spilling out of the stands and onto the field in both left and right, requiring ground rules limiting any ball hit into the sea of people in the outfield to a double. For another reason, the Yankees and their man Ruth peppered the Indians' Ray Caldwell from the get-go.

After only one out in the first, Caldwell walked Pipp. Then he got two quick strikes on Ruth before the Babe connected, sending the ball over the right-field fence for home run number 48, driving home Pipp. Caldwell made it to the fourth, by which time Shawkey and the Yankees had built a 6–0 lead. Shawkey took over the rest of the way, limiting the Indians to six hits and one lonely run. The 6–1 final was Bob's 16th win, and sixth in seven tries against Cleveland.

Thanks to the early rout, the St. Mary's Industrial School Band was in a celebratory mood, belting out one jazzy tune after another. Overlooked in all the hoopla was the debut in the fifth of the pint-sized Sewell, who was warmly greeted by the big crowd but fouled out to Ward near third base. It was hardly a memorable start, but Sewell would quickly catch on and for the next 11 years be a Cleveland mainstay at shortstop, earning a plaque in Cooperstown.

Somehow, even more people—31,000—found space in League Park for the conclusion of the three-game series on Saturday. They had reason to be optimistic about their Indians, for on the mound was their ace, Jim Bagby, already with 26 wins. With Carl Mays back home in New York, the Yankees countered with the erratic left-hander Herb Thormahlen, who at least had looked good his last time out in the Labor Day shellacking of the A's.

Everyone did their part. The Yankees banged out 15 hits, including six doubles—two of them hard ground-rule smashes into the crowd that again lined the fences. The Indians, meanwhile, mustered little offense off

Thormahlen, who gave up only seven hits, walked just one, and should have had a shutout, except for two throwing errors in the ninth by Pipp that let in a couple of runs. The 6–2 final made the pennant race microscopically close—the biggest difference being that the Yankees had played five games more than Cleveland—requiring the statisticians to break down the percentages separating the A.L.'s top three teams into five digits:

A.L. STANDINGS (SUNDAY, SEPTEMBER 12)

	Won	Lost	Percentage	Games Behind
Cleveland	82	51	.61654	—
New York	85	53	.61594	½
Chicago	84	53	.61314	½

You would think that the Yankees, having taken two of three in Cleveland and heading to Detroit to play three games against the hapless Tigers, would relish the moment. But the fact is they were a deeply divided team, beset with dissension. The most recent incident had developed over Ruth's famous wasp bite. Even with the Babe back in the lineup and hitting tremendous blasts everywhere he went, there was simmering anger over his film exploits and how his movie-making injury had kept him out of the lineup, probably costing the Yankees some wins.

Meanwhile, several Yankees continued to openly grouse at Huggins's authority, a situation aggravated by almost constant criticism in the press against the Yankee manager every time his team didn't come through. Never one to back down, Huggins shot back at his players to play alertly, perform the fundamentals, and run out every ground ball. He hated slackers, and reserved particular criticism for Meusel, who despite loads of talent tended to loaf. The situation reached a climax in Detroit, where Sammy Vick, upset that Huggins was riding him to play more aggressively, took a swing at the manager in view of the other players. Thinking his baseball career was quite suddenly finished, Vick was amazed the next day when Huggins walked up to him and said, "I'm glad to see you have some spirit in you after all."

It took some doing, but the Yankees made good in Detroit. Rejoining his teammates there, Carl Mays sauntered out to the Navin Field mound to start game one on Sunday, September 12, before 30,000 fans who filled every crevice of the park and gave him a stupendous razzing. But that soon turned to cheers when Mays had trouble getting anyone out: Ralph Young doubled, Cobb singled, Bobby Veach and Harry Heilmann doubled, Chick Shorten singled, and just like that, the score was 3–0 Tigers. Off went Mays to genuine applause, so much so that he tipped his hat, and in came Collins, who gave up a single to Babe Pinelli that brought the damage to 4–0. Only a double play stopped the bleeding.

But these were the sixth-place Tigers, and they had little pitching. The Yanks stormed back with one in the second and five in the third, all off Bill Dauss. Pipp walloped a two-run homer into the right-field bleachers, followed by singles from Pratt and Meusel, and a three-run homer to right by Duffy Lewis. The Yankees tacked on four more in the sixth, and by the time they were finished with Dauss and three other Tigers pitchers, they had pounded 14 hits, including five doubles. Collins went the rest of the way for his 12th win and the Yanks had taken a wild one, 13–6, to keep pace with the Indians, who were 5–2 winners over the A's.

Embarrassed by his dismal showing on Sunday, Mays retreated to his hotel room after the game and wondered what had gone wrong. He'd simply had a bad day, but he felt fresh, having lasted only one-third of an inning. Mays sought Huggins out that evening and asked for a shot the next day. Huggins agreed.

This time, there were only 10,000 fans at Navin Field to greet Mays, this time with applause. When he gave up a walk and singles by Donie Bush and Veach for a run in the first, it appeared that it might be another long day. But the sinkerballer soon settled down, and the game became an old-fashioned pitchers' duel, with the Yanks managing just a lone run through the first five innings off Howard Ehmke.

That changed in the sixth, when, with the Yankees behind 2–1, two down, and Wally Pipp on first base, Ruth stepped to the plate and ran the count to 3–2. Ehmke fired his next pitch low on the outside corner, and Ruth smoked the ball, sending it high and far into the right-field bleachers. It was a microcosm of the way Ruth could change the complexion of a game in a heartbeat: his 49th home run put the Yankees up 3–2 and sent the crowd into a conniption. As Ruth touched home plate and jogged back to the dugout, parents hoisted their small children onto the field to shake hands with the great slugger.

Mays held on, thanks to some snappy fielding on the part of his team-mates, who compiled three double plays. The 4–2 final—Mays's 23rd win—was further redemption for the beleaguered Yankee pitcher. At least the Yanks kept pace with the Indians, who, thanks to the spirited play and bat of their new shortstop, Joe Sewell, again clipped the A's, this time, 3–2.

So the Yankees hung in. So did the band from St. Mary's Industrial School, which had become a kind of good-luck symbol for the Yankees, much to the appreciation of Ruth, who had contributed $100 to their cause. In the final game against the Tigers on Tuesday, Ruth hit no home runs, much to the disappointment of 12,000 fans who implored him to hit number 50, but did manage to score two runs to tie another record—the A.L. record of 147 runs scored, set back in 1912 by Ty Cobb. Despite his home run on Monday, Ruth was having a frustrating go of it against the Tigers' pitchers, who walked him eight times in the three games. "I can't sock them if they don't let me reach the ball," the Babe said.

Other Yankees were doing their share. They teed off again against the overmatched Bill Dauss, amassing 16 hits, including four from Pratt, three from pitcher Shawkey, and two each from Pipp, Ward, and Hannah, who was playing for the injured Ruel. It wasn't much of a contest, and ahead 7–2 after the third, Shawkey coasted the rest of the way for his 18th win. Even Vick contributed as a fifth-inning replacement for Meusel, who ruptured his often-injured left leg. Sammy had a double.

Combined with the A's 8–0 drubbing of Cleveland, and Washington's 7–0 win at Chicago, the win put the Yankees back in first place. With the Brooklyn Robins about to sew up the National League flag, wonderful thoughts of an all–New York series danced in the heads of gamblers and Yankee owners everywhere. "Cap Huston's friends are already telegraphing him for tickets," opined the *Times*, only half joking.

Baseball players are a superstitious lot, and on arriving at the Cooper Carlton Hotel in Chicago on Wednesday evening, September 15, after playing an exhibition game that day in Toledo, the first thing Yankee players noticed was Cap Huston's friend Billy Fleischman holding court in the lobby. It was a bad omen.

So who was Billy Fleischman, and why was he so unwelcome? Officially, he was William Fleischman, the team's assistant to the president, a figurehead title that meant little. In reality, Fleischman was another of Cap

Huston's cronies, "a nice old fellow," as Ruth said, who by his presence alone seemed to send the Yanks into a team-wide tailspin.

"He loved to see us play and couldn't stay away," Ruth wrote. " 'Holy cow,' I said, 'there's that guy Fleischman again to put the whammy on us!' "

The Babe was right. After five straight wins, the Yanks lost it and dropped all three games of the series to the White Sox. They were devastating losses and essentially ended the team's pennant chances at a time when every at-bat and every pitch took on exaggerated importance. Sensing a slump coming, Huggins tried everything, summoning both Quinn and Thormahlen before game one to warm up, with the idea of picking the most effective one to start.

Huggins watched both men and pondered his choice. He chose Quinn, who early in the season had been a workhorse, but who had been knocked out early in his previous two starts—the sign of a tired arm. Huggins was hoping this time around he'd be rested and ready for the Sox.

He wasn't. Not only was Quinn clocked early—he gave up four runs in the second before being lifted for Mogridge—but the Yankees tried and failed time after time to deliver in the clutch. They had their chances—Dickie Kerr walked six and twice loaded the bases—but the team could manage little in a discouraging 8–3 loss. "The Yankees should be kept after school and spanked for losing," wrote the *Times*.

If this had been Hollywood, the Yanks would have busted out in the sixth inning. With the score knotted at two, and with two on and two out, Ruth stepped to the plate, looking for his 50th home run, which would have put the Yanks ahead 5–4. Twice he swung and missed, and twice Kerr threw balls. Then, with the count 2–2 and the 25,000 fans at a fever pitch, Kerr threw and Ruth watched it go by for strike three. The mighty Babe had been caught looking, the ultimate embarrassment for a slugger.

Any chance the Yanks had to mount a comeback evaporated in the seventh when the White Sox tallied three more, two of the runs coming on a routine Happy Felsch bouncer to short that went through Peckinpaugh's legs for an error. Too bad for the St. Mary's Industrial School Band: they were there all right, but never got a chance to do much celebrating.

The loss, combined with Cleveland's 1–0 win over Washington, hurled the Indians back into first, with the Yankees and White Sox a fraction behind. Things went from bad to worse on Friday, September 17, when in game two, the Sox again jumped on Yankee pitching early—this time

Thormahlen, who with two gone in the first gave up a triple to Eddie Collins, thanks to Meusel's lollygagging after the ball. Collins then scored when the throw got by Truck Hannah. Up next, Joe Jackson rifled another triple to almost the exact same spot in right, and scored when the next batter, Felsch, sent yet another triple into the outfield.

The White Sox had run a track around the bases in the first inning, yet there was Thormahlen going back to the mound a few minutes later to start the second. And the first batter, shortstop Swede Risberg, did what? He hit another triple. In the stands, Huston groaned. Out walked Huggins to the mound to retrieve his ineffective left-hander, replacing him with Mays.

Risberg then scored to make it 3–0, hardly an insurmountable lead especially for the Yankees. But Red Faber was on his game, and limited the New Yorkers to two runs in the third and another two in the ninth by the time the game was out of reach. And although the 30,000 Comiskey Park faithful implored the Babe to clock number 50, he had another lost day, going hitless in three at-bats. The 6–4 final was a devastating loss, putting further distance between the second-place Yankees and the Indians, 9–3 winners against Washington.

In the clubhouse after the game, Huggins put his best spin on the loss, but only made things worse for himself, when, chatting to Huston, he said, "I still think we can finish second, Cap." Huston, still smoldering that Huggins had been hired in the first place, exploded. "Who the hell wants to finish second?" he stormed, before walking away.

The next morning in the dining room at the Cooper Carlton, Huston boiled over again in frustration, this time by banging his fist on the table and complaining in a voice loud enough for everyone to hear. "This race is not over!" he shrieked. "Remember what Commodore Perry said at Lake Erie? 'Don't give up the ship until your trunks hit the water!' "

If the race wasn't over that Saturday morning, it was by late afternoon. Egging on their Sox with cowbells and horns, 43,000 fans filled every crevice of Comiskey Park. It was the latest largest-ever crowd to see a ballgame, and they had a White Sox pennant on their minds. It hardly mattered that Eddie Cicotte was merely mediocre in giving up nine runs on 11 hits, including just a single to Ruth. The Sox put the game out of reach early with three in the first, pounding Bob Shawkey, who was lifted after one and a third innings, and three other Yankee pitchers for 21 hits and 15 runs.

In the sixth, after the White Sox had scored their 15th run, Huggins threw in the towel and sent in the scrubs. Although the Yankees still had a mathematical chance at the pennant, the sloppy, spiritless 15–9 loss dumped the Yankees into third place with a sudden thud—all but eliminating them now at 4 games back with only 10 to play. So just like that, the Yanks were done, and the A.L. race was down to two teams, the Indians and White Sox, now just a game back. "With Chicago ablaze with enthusiasm for the fighting, climbing White Sox, the spiritless endeavors of the Yanks during this series have been sad," the *Times* wrote. "At the big moment of their career, when its greatest opportunity was within its clutches, the team fell down." For the Yankees, everyone was responsible, from pitchers to batters, including the Babe, who did not score a single run during the series and seemed stuck on homer number 49—hit five days before. Only one question remained for the Yankees: how many more home runs could Babe Ruth hit?

That the White Sox players managed to stay focused was remarkable, considering the events rapidly unfolding some two miles north of Comiskey Park at the Cook County grand jury. As September wore on, the evidence was building to implicate several Sox players in what was turning into the most fantastic sports swindle of the era—the great World Series fix of 1919.

For the public, weary of the rumors, the charges, counter-charges, and allegations with no proof, the testimony was starting to sound like babble. Keep in mind the climate of the era, one rife with stories of not just baseball gambling, but of the Republican Party buying Warren Harding's election in the race for the White House, and of almost continual political corruption, with occasional outbursts of violence. In fact, on September 15, as the Sox prepared to meet the Yankees, the Chicago Democratic Party went to the polls amidst the usual amount of shootings, robberies, and one attempt to steal a ballot box. One result of the primary was that State Attorney Hoyne was voted out of office, after which he went home, packed his suitcases, and departed with his wife for a leisurely vacation in New York—a last boondoggle while still on the state payroll.

Following the events closely and moving rather nimbly himself was Ban Johnson. Frustrated that the grand jury appeared stalled, the blustery American League president tried taking things into his own hands by traveling to New York, where he visited Arnold Rothstein, the man thought to be the mastermind of the 1919 Series fix. Rothstein, the aristocrat of the New York gambling world, dressed sharply, carried tremendous wads of cash in his pockets, and probably owned more policemen than anyone anywhere. He told Johnson he'd heard about the fix, but wasn't involved. It was a little hard to believe.

Johnson wasn't done—he was motivated by a powerful hatred of Charles Comiskey, and the defeat of Hoyne, who Johnson didn't view as a man with the backbone to follow through on his pledge to clean up baseball. Back in Chicago, Johnson marched into the office of Chief Justice Charles MacDonald of the Cook County Criminal Courts Division and announced he had 30 names of baseball people with gambling contacts. He leaned on MacDonald to push the investigation and not let it go. After all, Johnson intimated, there had been talk of starting a new baseball commission, and the judge himself might be just the man to lead the organization.

The prod was all MacDonald needed. On Monday, September 21, Assistant State Attorney Hartley Replogle announced that subpoenas had gone out to baseball players, officials, hangers-on, and gamblers, seeking their testimony. Among the first to testify was Comiskey, who claimed that he'd heard rumors of the fix, but that Johnson had done nothing to investigate. The fact is that Comiskey had more than compelling evidence that many of his best players had deliberately lost the Series, thanks to his own internal investigation of the matter, but had kept it under wraps in the interests of keeping his powerful team intact. Comiskey had even refused a meeting with Joe Jackson when the slugger came to see him, ready to confess his guilt.

Comiskey's charge was all Johnson needed to lash back and break the scandal wide open. "I have evidence," the A.L. president boomed, "and much of it is now before the Grand Jury, that certain notorious gamblers are threatening to expose the 1919 World Series as a fixed event unless the Chicago White Sox players drop out of the current race intentionally to let the Indians win. These gamblers have made heavy bets on the Cleveland team."

Johnson was so steamed that he seemed uncertain who to blame for the scandal. He admitted to hearing rumors that the White Sox wouldn't dare win this year's pennant because the gamblers to whom they were connected were backing the Indians. Other rumors had George M. Cohan losing

$80,000 in the 1919 Series. "I had no doubt the 1919 World Series was crooked," said State Attorney Hoyne, "and that at least one Chicago player was crooked."

Meanwhile, a parade of baseball people marched to the Cook County grand jury to report a complicated and extensive web of gambling-related baseball wrongdoing. John McGraw explained the sordid tale of Hal Chase and Heinie Zimmerman, admitting that he'd "never been more deceived by a player than by Chase," who had still inexplicably remained on the Giants' roster for most of the 1919 season.

On September 24, as the White Sox played the Indians, Giants pitcher Rube Benton testified that he'd been offered $800 by Buck Herzog and Chase to throw a game to the Cubs the previous September. Benton said further that it was Chase who had tipped him that the 1919 Series was fixed, and that Chase had won more than $40,000 betting on the Reds—a charge that the notoriously corrupt Chase vehemently denied to the deathbed. Benton also said that gamblers had told him the Series was a whitewash, and that some of the players involved—Chick Gandil, Happy Felsch, Lefty Williams, and Eddie Cicotte—had been paid more than $100,000 to fix the result. Benton, who admitted he had made $3,800 himself betting on the Reds in the Series, recommended that the grand jury talk to Cicotte.

Then, on September 27, the whole story of the team that became known as the "Black Sox" broke in the *Philadelphia North American*. The story was a bombshell, an interview with gambler Bill Maharg, who explained in detail how he and former journeyman big leaguer turned gambler "Sleepy Bill" Burns had orchestrated much of the fix by paying the players to lose deliberately in the first, second, and eighth game of the nine-game Series. Maharg, which was "Graham," his real name, spelled backwards, had a particular motivation for revealing the plot: he and Burns had in turn been double-crossed out of any earnings on the fix by Abe Attell, a onetime featherweight champion and now a frontman for Arnold Rothstein.

Cicotte's testimony two days later concurred with Maharg's version. The veteran knuckleballer testified in detail of how he and seven team-mates had lost the Series on purpose, and how easy it had been. In addition to Gandil, Felsch, and Williams, he said Joe Jackson, Fred McMullin, Swede Risberg, and Buck Weaver were also involved. The whole plot had come together a year before in New York at the Ansonia, of all places, where White Sox conspirators had gathered in Chick Gandil's room to organize. "Just a slight hesitation on the player's part will let a man get to base or make a run," said Cicotte, who had been rocked in games one and four. "I did it by not putting a thing on the ball. You could have read the trademark on it the way I lobbed it over the plate."

As the White Sox's ace, Cicotte was the key man in the fix, and helped bring in the others. For his chicanery, Cicotte had been paid $10,000—cash in advance—which he found under his pillow the night before the White Sox left for Cincinnati to begin the Series. He sewed the wad of cash into his jacket.

"I've lived a thousand years in the last 12 months," Cicotte told the grand jury. "I would not have done that thing for a million dollars. Now, I've lost everything—job, reputation, everything. My friends all bet on the Sox. I knew it, but I couldn't tell them. I had to double-cross them. I'm through with baseball."

Others were too. "Up to this time, baseball has been accepted by the public as the one clean sport above reproach," one fan, summarizing the feelings of many, wrote in the *Chicago Tribune*. "The game must be cleaned up and it must be cleaned up fast. . . . It is immaterial how this is to be done, whether by the newspaper men or by the owners of the ball clubs, or by a committee of citizens, but no matter who does it, it must be done if baseball is going to survive."

More Sox conspirators came forward, acknowledging their guilt. But not Weaver, who claimed to have known about the fix, but who hit .368 in the Series, and said he'd played hard and not revealed the plot out of friendship. Almost overlooked was the current pennant race, which oddly, the White Sox, while playing well for the moment, seemed almost unwilling to lead.

The unevenness underscored the tenor of the year for Chicago, which seemed to play well in spurts, but never really got into sync. Were the White Sox on the take in 1920? While there is no concrete evidence to prove it, the answer is almost certainly "Yes." Years later, Eddie Collins said his suspicions were sealed on September 11 against Boston, when Jackson and Felsch let a routine fly ball drop between them that many "thought should have been caught"—followed by a perfect peg by Dickie Kerr to force a runner at third that popped out of Weaver's glove.

"We knew something was wrong," said Collins of the game, which the Red Sox won 9–7, "but we couldn't put our fingers on it." When the inning ended, Kerr flung his glove across the diamond in frustration, and back in the dugout glared at Weaver and Risberg, saying, "If you'd told me you wanted to lose this game, I could have done it a lot easier." There was a near-riot in the dugout, which ended only when manager Kid Gleason broke it up.

A footnote to the event came late in the season when writer Fred Lieb in New York received an urgent telegram from Bill Veeck Sr., requesting his immediate presence in Chicago. "DROP EVERYTHING," the telegram said. "TAKE NIGHT TRAIN TO CHICAGO. WILL MEET YOU IN THE STATION. IMPORTANT." Thinking he was about to be offered a job as assistant to the new baseball commissioner, Lieb hopped on the train, but on arriving in Chicago was surprised to discover the reason for his trip: Veeck and Will Hays, the chairman of the Republican National Committee, wanted him to nail down Babe Ruth's endorsement of Warren Harding for president.

If Lieb could pull it off and persuade Ruth to be photographed with Harding at the candidate's home in Marion, Ohio, there was $4,000 in it for the Babe and $1,000 for Lieb. So it went in the 1920 presidential election, when celebrity endorsements were a big deal; Ty Cobb, for instance, had already come out for Democratic candidate James Cox. Broaching the subject with Ruth, the Babe replied that "I'm a Democrat, but I'll go to Warren for the money."

But as the pennant race tightened, neither Huggins nor Huston allowed Ruth to be taken out of the lineup for the trip to Marion. Ruth remained interested, and asked Lieb to see if he could secure a part of the payout as an advance to bind the agreement. That didn't work, but the date was finally set for Thursday, September 30, the day after the close of the season. But after the Black Sox scandal broke and the integrity of baseball was getting bombarded daily in the press, Veeck dropped the subject. Ruth never did make it to see Harding in Marion.

TWELVE

"Almost as Many Home Runs as Heinz Has Pickles"

A Titanic Blast When Baseball Needed It Most

Traveling with the Yankees as the team closed out their last western swing, Ruth's old mentor Brother Matthias joked that back at St. Mary's whenever the Babe didn't hit a home run, he'd have to spank him. Ruth grinned when he heard that. So did reporters. "It looks as if he ought to take him over his knees again," the *Times* wrote.

Playing out the string in St. Louis against the Browns, the Yanks lost again on Sunday, September 19, 6–1, but took the last two games against the fourth-place Browns, 4–3 behind Mays, who notched victory number 24, and 8–3 with Shawkey on the mound for the team's 90th win. Throughout the series, Ruth hammered singles, doubles, and even a triple all over Sportsman's Park—breaking Cobb's record for most runs scored in a season, but seemingly incapable of hitting home run number 50.

Back home on Friday, September 24, for the start of the last home series of the season—a doubleheader followed by two single games against the Senators—Ruth got down to business, just as the White Sox had finally managed to move into first place, courtesy of a 10–3 thrashing of the Indians at League Park. In most cases, a late-season twin bill between two non-contending teams would draw scant interest. Not so at the Polo Grounds, where 25,000 fans, including members of the Giants and Brooklyn Dodgers, taking in the games on their off-day, showed up hoping to see and later brag that they'd seen history in the making.

On a day when headlines blared more sordid details of the White Sox fix, Ruth didn't disappoint. Unfortunately for him, the Yankees were already behind, thanks to Mays giving up three hits and two runs in the first, when the slugger came to bat in the inning's bottom half against Senator rookie right-hander Jose Acosta.

Advantage Ruth. Acosta, a 31-year-old, 5'6" wisp of a Havana native, had been in the majors less than two months. Everyone knew full well how the Babe hammered rookies. With two down and the bases clear, Ruth worked the count full, not swinging at a single pitch, before drilling Acosta's next delivery on an arc toward right field. Could it be? Absolutely! It was number 50, and the crowd erupted in a crescendo of noise.

"The crowd went quite mad," Damon Runyon wrote in the *American*. "They had witnessed something no other people had ever seen before. Perhaps no one now living will ever see such a thing again. . . . Babe Ruth is the greatest showman of these times."

Ruth rounded the bases in his now-familiar pigeon-toed gait with his head turned slightly down, and grinned broadly as he crossed the plate, shaking hands with Del Pratt, the next batter, and, as he made his way back to the dugout, doffing his cap toward the stands. The ball was thrown back to Ruth, who had gotten into the habit of saving as many of his home run balls as possible, often giving an autographed ball to the fan or clubhouse attendant who brought the home run ball forward. And once again, hats were tossed on the field as telegraphs rattled off the big news around the country and the newspapermen again banged out their latest superlatives.

"Baseball has never before developed a figure of such tremendously picturesque proportions as this home-run king of the Yankees," the *Times* wrote. "With no weapon but a primitive club, he has manipulated it in a manner which would make the famed clubbers of the Stone Age look like experts in battledore and shuttlecock. Ruth has hit almost as many home runs as Heinz has pickles."

The Babe had reached another Herculean mark just as the news of the Black Sox was getting really bad, giving baseball fans and America a break from the grim headlines of baseball dishonesty. Cynics said Ruth's mark was a mere distraction. But real fans knew that number 50 was another mark of greatness in an extraordinary season of single-minded batting devastation that was helping to save baseball at its darkest time.

Along with home runs came other records. Ruth would lead the league in 1920 not just in homers, but in runs, runs batted in, bases on balls, on-base percentage, and slugging percentage. "These are man-sized records, the heavyweight records of baseball," wrote Donald Honig of Ruth's records that season. "And here was the one man sweeping them all in, all at once, with nothing gradual about it. It was as if in 1920 he had landed in New York from another planet, product of a bigger, stronger more monstrous species than we knew about."

You would think that Jose Acosta would be honored to have gone into the record books as the pitcher to give up number 50. Instead, he was still fuming that he had meant to jam Ruth, but hung the ball out over the plate instead. But Acosta, urged on by a gathering of New York–area Cubans, bore down and stopped the Yanks on a measly four hits en route to a 3–1 win. Ruth would donate the bat he'd used to hit number 50 to the Near East Fund to auction for funds to benefit starving Armenians in Turkey.

In game two, Ruth added an exclamation mark to his special day. In a virtual copy of number 50, the Babe stepped to bat with two down in the first inning and walloped a pitch from Jim Shaw into the right-field stands for number 51, the 100th home run of his career. Later, he singled in the fourth and the sixth and doubled in the ninth for a perfect four-for-four performance. The day's only negative: in the sixth, Ruth was thrown out trying to steal home in an effort to break the 1–1 tie. No worry—Thormahlen, who entered the game after Rip Collins turned an ankle in the third, continued his September comeback by holding the Washingtons down the rest of the way. That allowed the Yankees to win it with some drama in the ninth, after Ruth had doubled and scored on Pratt's single to left center. The final was 2–1.

The *American* came closest to putting the day in context. "There were thousands of young boys in the crowd," Runyon reported in his game summary. "They had been taken by their fathers, who wanted them to see Babe Ruth. When these boys are old men with white whiskers, they will still be telling how they saw Babe Ruth hit his fifty-first home run."

Next to Runyon's story was the newspaper's "Ruthermometer," a drawing of a thermometer with numbers indicating Ruth's home run count and a grinning mug shot of the man of the moment himself. And in a two-column article near the Ruthermometer was the latest in a series of disturbing stories that detailed the evolving Black Sox scandal. The contrast of Ruth's news against the scandal in Chicago was stark—it was good versus bad, the bright, new future of the game against the sinister elements that, without this new phenomenon, threatened to destroy baseball. Yes, Ruth's timing was extraordinary.

It would be fitting to report that Ruth ended his season at the Polo Grounds in a further blaze of glory with another multiple home run day. But with attention of fickle New York baseball fans focused more on the Brooklyn Dodgers, about to play their first World Series in four years, it's remarkable that 25,000 fans showed up Saturday and another 30,000 on Sunday to see the Yanks close out the home season. Just about everybody was there, reported the newspapermen, to see the Babe hit at least one more. Oh, there were home runs all right—on Saturday, Aaron Ward hit one, as did Washington pitcher Harry Courtney, who also nailed down the 5–2 win for the Senators. On Sunday, there were two more by Ward, but none from Ruth. Quinn took the 9–5 win, his 18th of the season. Ward's sudden slugging prowess gave him 11 homers for the season; the home runs, along with a .256 final batting average, were good numbers for the rookie.

There was a final piece of business for the Yankees—three games at Shibe Park in Philadelphia against the lowly A's, always a good bet for inflating their opponent's batting stats. On Monday, Ruth did just that, teeing off for two more tremendous home runs, both to right field off Ed Rommel—number 52 in the first with Wally Pipp aboard, and number 53 in the sixth, a solo shot. The homers accounted for all the Yankee runs, which were plenty for Carl Mays, who notched win number 26—number 7 for the month of September. Mays gave up seven lonely hits, and backed up by three Yankee double plays won it 3–0.

A Tuesday rainout brought the Yankees' season down to its last day, a doubleheader on Wednesday, September 29, that served as a microcosm for their season. In trampling the A's in both games—7–3 in the first to give Collins his 14th win, and 9–4 in the second to earn another 20-win season for Bob Shawkey—the Yankees hammered 22 hits, 11 in each game, ending the season with a record of 95 wins and 59 defeats. Their performance that day showed what kind of team they could have been, had they played with greater consistency in what was still the franchise's best season of its 17 years. Doing his part, Ruth sent his 54th and last home run of the season over the right-field wall in the last inning of game one off his Labor Day adversary Slim Harriss.

And just like that, the New York Yankees ended their 1920 season, in third place, but arguably the most significant third-place team in baseball history.

By then, Shoeless Joe Jackson had joined Eddie Cicotte in detailing the World Series fix of the year before. Later in the week, Charles Comiskey suspended the eight players implicated, and though the Sox were somehow still clinging onto the Indians, only a half game in back of the lead, their makeshift lineup didn't measure up. On the other hand, the Indians continued to find strength from unlikely places—namely Joe Sewell, whose sparkling fielding combined with a Chapmanesque .329 batting average in 22 games. Throw in the fine performance of an eccentric 24-year-old left-hander named Duster Mails, self-named "the Great," who went 7–0 with a 1.85 ERA. Cleveland hung on, winning the pennant by two games over Chicago and three over the Yanks.

The Great Mails even won a World Series classic, a three-hit 1–0 shutout in game six over Brooklyn. The next day, October 12, Stanley Coveleski shut out the Dodgers again, 3–0, to take the best-of-nine series five games to two, and give a grateful Cleveland its first Series title. Coveleski, 3–0 in the Series, was the pitching star. Speaker hit .320, and in a strange and memorable game five, Elmer Smith hit the first World Series grand slam in baseball history. Then, with the Dodgers threatening in the fifth, Bill Wambsganss speared a line shot by Clarence Mitchell for one out, stepped on second to double up Pete Kilduff for the second out, and tagged base runner Otto Miller for a true rarity—the first and still the only unassisted triple play in World Series history.

Many ballplayers had spectacular seasons in 1920. Speaker ended the regular season batting .388, second to Sisler's .407, with Jackson third at .382. The Indians benefited from superior starting pitching, notably by Jim Bagby, 31–12, Coveleski, 24–14, and Ray Caldwell, 20–10. So did the White Sox, who had four 20-game winners—Faber, Cicotte, Williams, and Kerr. How ironic then that for all the Yankee pitching inconsistency, the team still led the American League in ERA at 3.31 and shutouts with 16, thanks largely to their pair of 20-game winners, Mays and Shawkey. Bob even took the league's individual ERA title at 2.45, .004 ahead of Coveleski.

Other Yankees had solid seasons, most notably Meusel, who despite injuries and occasional indifference batted .328 with 11 home runs and 83 RBIs. Pratt batted .314, Bodie .295, Pipp .280, and Peckinpaugh .270. And the season's find? Aaron Ward, with his quick hands, surprising power with 11 home runs, and respectable .256 batting average.

But the real story of 1920 was Babe Ruth, who dominated the season as no other athlete in baseball or in any other sport ever had. His statistics were unthinkable, unimaginable, unfathomable, and downright scary: despite missing 12 games, Ruth's 54 home runs alone were more than twice that of his nearest competitor, George Sisler, who hit 19; the National League home run leader was Fred "Cy" Williams of the Philadelphia Phillies with 15. Ruth also hit more than any other team, with the sole exception of the last-place N.L. Phillies.

When Ruth touched home plate after his final home run of the season, he had surpassed the 1919 Yankee team total by 9, and pushed the 1920 Yankee team total to 115. Almost half of those belonged to the Babe, marking a modern-day record, second only to the inflated figure generated by Ned Williamson of the 1884 Chicago White Stockings. Ruth's 137 RBIs also led both leagues, as did his 158 runs and unreal .847 slugging average— an unbroken record until some nifty power hitting 81 years later by Barry Bonds. About the only batting categories in which Ruth failed to finish atop the American League were total bases—he was second to Sisler—and batting average, where his .376 was fourth. The Babe even led the Yankees in stolen bases with 14.

In later years, Ruth would top most of his feats in 1920, including his stolen base mark. But even Barry Bonds couldn't top his home-field slugging percentage, which baseball historians John Thorn and Pete Palmer estimate was an unworldly .985 in 1920 at the Polo Grounds. Nor could Bonds top Ruth's home run percentage of 1 every 11.8 at-bats.

Baseball statisticians have also discovered some other startling things about 1920. Thanks in part to Ruth, American League batters scored almost 1,000 runs more than the Nationals that year, and had 523 more hits. Meanwhile, both leagues batted at an extraordinary clip—finishing above .300 were 42 batters in the A.L. and 20 in the N.L. Two American

League teams—the Indians and the Browns—even finished above .300, the first twentieth-century big-league teams to do so. Within a year or two, everyone had discovered the big Ruthian bats—three seasons later, 36-year-old Cy Williams would nearly triple his 1920 home run output.

Another number was just as important to Colonels Ruppert and Huston. It was 1,289,422—the number of spectators who passed through the turnstiles at the Polo Grounds to see Ruth and the Yankees play in 1920. The figure was an all-time single-season record, and represented a sizable chunk of the more than 9 million fans who paid their way into big-league ballparks in 1920—showing that despite the enveloping Black Sox scandal, baseball had reaffirmed itself as the king of sports. The overall figure broke by a comfortable 1.75 million the old major-league mark set back in 1909.

Those clicking turnstiles were music to the Yankee owners. Word has it that when the season ended, they had basically earned back their investment from buying the team in 1915. The attendance figure marked the first time the Yanks had outdrawn the Giants in a single season—by a whopping 360,000—and the first time any big-league team ever exceeded 1 million. It was more than twice the number that the Yanks had drawn in 1919, their previous high mark, and a number so astounding that it had revived a rash of stories about construction of a new Yankee ballpark, this time perhaps along Broadway between 136th and 138th Streets.

Just as critical for baseball were the staggering crowds that squeezed all year into visiting ballparks to see the Yanks play. More than 9.12 million people attended major-league ballgames in 1920—a 60 percent rise from the year before. Baseball, in spite of its increasingly seamy reputation, was—thanks to a slugger and his ability to play the game a whole new way—a bigger success than ever.

"Cox or Harding? Harding or Cox?" one writer asked. "You tell us, populi; you've got the vox."

Indeed, they did, and in November, America voted Warren G. Harding and his running mate, Calvin Coolidge, the governor of Massachusetts, into the White House by 7 million votes and a whopping Electoral College margin of 404 to 127. Clearly, neither Woodrow Wilson's coattails nor the eloquence of Democratic vice-presidential candidate Franklin Roosevelt were enough to stem the Republican landslide. Nor was the first-time vote of women or Socialist Eugene Debs, who emerged from prison to capture more than 900,000 votes for president. "America's present need is not heroics but healing," Harding said, "not nostrums but normalcy; not revolution but restoration; not surgery but serenity."

That sounded reasonable, but Harding soon proved to be one of history's most lackluster presidents—a man more interested in boozy rounds of poker with his cronies and visiting his mistress for sex than governing. In a sense, he fit the times in calling for a government that let big business stay big and kept out of foreign affairs. A Democratic leader called Harding's speeches "an army of pompous phrases in search of an idea." Their very murkiness seemed effective, and Harding never really made clear what he thought of the League of Nations. Despite his popularity, Harding's friends soon got the best of him, and word began leaking that some of them were using their offical positions for their own enrichment. Alarmed, Harding seemed lost: "My friends," he said, "they're the ones that keep me walking the floors nights."

Looking worn and fearing the political damage of the growing scandal, Harding journeyed west in the summer of 1923, but never got the chance to find out what people thought: reaching San Francisco, he died of a heart attack. Calvin Coolidge succeeded him as president.

The reality is that for all the excitement Babe Ruth generated, which arguably saved the game at its darkest hour, the 1920 Yankees were a one-dimensional team, not good enough to win the American League. "Without his wonderful batting and influence, the Hugmen would have been easily outdistanced by the Speakers and the Gleasons," Joe Vila wrote in the *Sporting News*. "Ruth has proved to be the biggest paying investment in the history of baseball and he deserves all the popularity that he now enjoys."

Also weighing in was W. A. Phelon in *Baseball Magazine*: "Corollary and climax of it all: Babe Ruth. The Busting Babe has become a baseball idol such as the game's history cannot know how. He's the Whole Works, the Main Squeeze, and the Big Attraction. In other words, it has been settled, for all time to come, that the American public is nuttier over the Home Run than the Clever Fielding or the Hitless Pitching. Viva el Home Run and two times viva Babe Ruth, exponent of the Home Run, and overshadowing star."

Not everyone celebrated the heroics of Babe Ruth. Cranky holdovers continued to reserve their praise for the dead-ball game or "inside baseball," like Ty Cobb, John McGraw, and sportswriter Ring Lardner. Irking Lardner more than anything was Ruth's extraordinary ability to reach down and deliver almost when he wanted to, or so it seemed. "I have always been a fellow who liked to see efficiency rewarded," Lardner wrote. "If a pitcher pitched a swell game, I wanted to see him win it. So it kind of sickens me to watch a typical pastime of today in which a good pitcher, after an hour and fifty minutes of deserved mastery of his opponents, can suddenly be made to look like a bum by four or five great sluggers who couldn't have held a job as bat boy on the Niles High School scrubs."

Two incidents fueled Lardner's bleak mood. One was the Black Sox scandal, which revealed the depths of corruption in the game he adored. The other was his conviction that the owners juiced the ball on purpose when they saw how excited people became at watching home runs.

While Lardner, Cobb, and McGraw brooded, the rest of America glorified Babe Ruth's domination. This was a new way to play an old game—and it created a level of enthusiasm that carried the game at what could have been a destructive time. Even so, the Black Sox scandal dragged on into 1921, when on August 5, the eight White Sox players, though still suspended, were found not guilty of criminal conspiracy. It was said that some of the jurors felt that the players had thrown games, but that it was not necessarily a criminal offense. In the end, it didn't much matter, for the man the owners had hired the previous November to lead them as baseball's first commissioner—Federal Judge Kenesaw Mountain Landis, an imposing man with an imposing name—threw down a devastating ruling: each conspirator was banned from baseball for life, destroying with a single thunderbolt the future of the White Sox. With its heart ripped out and soul gone, Comiskey's once-formidable Sox tumbled to seventh in 1921, and wouldn't reach the World Series again until the Eisenhower administration—in 1959, nearly 40 years later.

The son of a Civil War Union surgeon who had lost a leg to a Confederate cannonball, Landis was named for the Georgia battlefield where his father had served. Landis was in fact a wiry man, but he had a chiseled face, a gravelly voice that made every sentence sound important, and a stern look that reflected a titanic ego—what writer Robert Smith called "a pathological urge to flaunt his power." Appointed to the bench in 1905 by President Theodore Roosevelt, Landis was hard to categorize as a

judge—he disliked big business, organized crime, and particularly Social-
ists and union organizers, who he called "filthy, slimy rats." He made his
name in targeting big-time businessmen like John D. Rockefeller, who he
had browbeaten on the stand in 1916 in a case that led to a $29 million
antitrust judgment against Standard Oil. When the sentence was reversed
by a higher court, Landis was unimpressed: "To hell with the law," he
sneered, "I know what's right."

There is little doubt that most of the accused Black Sox players were
guilty of deliberately losing the World Series. The lone exception was Buck
Weaver, who went to his grave insisting that he had played his best—he
hit .383 in the Series and fielded flawlessly—although he admitted that he
had known about the fix. Weaver enlisted the support of the Chicago
District of the Masonic Brotherhood, and 20,000 Masons signed a docu-
ment requesting that Landis drop the ban against him. The commissioner
never wavered, and neither Weaver nor any of the other implicated Sox ever
again played big-league baseball.

By banning the players, Landis had demonstrated that his "powers," as
he put it, "are to be absolute." The other major victim of baseball's new
one-man fiefdom would be Ban Johnson, an egomaniac himself who
endured as American League president but found it difficult to cede his
once-iron authority to Landis. When, in 1921, Johnson suggested that the
final draft of the redrawn National Agreement should give the new commissioner the power to merely "recommend" punitive damage against players or others who acted against the game's best interest, Landis took offense
at the concept and threatened to quit unless he was given complete control. The owners sided with Landis, and Johnson's star fell fast. He and
Landis feuded on other matters, and the two became enemies. The final
straw came in 1927, when Johnson and Landis clashed about the case of
whether Ty Cobb and Tris Speaker were guilty of fixing a game. Johnson
banned them, but Landis overruled him, restoring both players, a move
engineered to get rid of the A.L. president once and for all. It worked:
Johnson resigned, and three years later was dead from diabetes. It was a
hard fall and an unhappy ending. The *Sporting News* called his demise "a
knifing that will be as historic as that which handled Caesar."

Thank goodness then for Babe Ruth. "The Judge ran the curtain down on
a sleazy scene," wrote Fred Lieb of the betting scandals. "Babe Ruth,
already sticking his head out from the wings, would in the next scene make

sports fans forget almost overnight what had just happened." Late in 1921, the commissioner and the Babe would have the first of their several public spats, when Landis refused Ruth permission to make a barnstorming tour. Ruth went anyway, saying the games had already been set up and advertised, and paid dearly. Landis suspended him for the first 40 days of the 1922 season.

Ruth's impact on the public was readily apparent. "Because of him, a new type of fan was appearing at the Polo Grounds," wrote Frank Graham in his Yankee history. "This was the fan who didn't know where first base was but had heard of Babe Ruth and wanted to see him hit a home run. When the Babe hit one, the fan went back the next day to see him hit another. Pretty soon he was a regular, and knew not only where first base was but second base as well."

The birth of radio—baseball games were first broadcast by Pittsburgh station KDKA in 1921—fed the Babe's legend. So did newspapers, as they turned more and more reporters onto the baseball beat. By the mid-1920s, the sports pages looked more like the social pages, with coverage of ballplayers on a par with movie stars and socialites for the attention of Americans.

On the ballfield, other teams began catching on to the advantages of the long ball. In 1921, big-league sluggers sent a whopping 307 more home runs out of parks than they had in 1920—108 more in the A.L. and 199 more in the N.L. Although the Indians were again good in 1921, the Yanks were even better, taking their first A.L. flag but losing to the Giants in an eight-game World Series.

Ruth was even more extraordinary in 1921, powering 59 home runs and batting .378. But the big difference for the Yanks was another shrewd couple of dealings with the Red Sox after the 1920 season. First, Ruppert and Huston bagged Boston manager Ed Barrow as the new business manager of the Yankees to replace the late Harry Sparrow. Barrow went to work quickly, and on December 15 engineered a blockbuster deal that sent Pratt, the erratic Thormahlen, the light-hitting Muddy Ruel, and the bad-tempered Sammy Vick to his old team in return for pitchers Waite Hoyt and Harry Harper, catcher Wally Schang, and infielder Mike McNally.

Hoyt, a 31-year-old Brooklyn native, was key. The winner of only 10 big-league games when he was bought by the Yankees, the right-hander blossomed in New York, winning 19 games in each of the next two years and becoming a big part of the powerful Yankee teams of the 1920s. Along the way, Hoyt became a pal of Ruth's, but after being traded to the Tigers in 1930 was the victim of the Babe's famous inability to remember a name: "Good-bye, Walter," said Ruth in soberly bidding his old friend farewell.

The Yanks made other changes immediately after 1920. Ward moved to second base to replace Pratt. Serving as all-round super sub was Chick Fewster, who flashed his great range in the field and even hit .280. At third, finally, was Home Run Baker, who decided to leave his Maryland farm after all for another shot at the big time. It worked, and the 35-year-old Baker hit .294 in 1921 and .250 in the World Series. He retired after 1922 with a lifetime .307 batting average and a ticket to Cooperstown.

Hoyt went 19–13 in 1921 to match another strong year from Mays (27–9) and more consistency from Shawkey (18–13) and Collins (11–5). Two years later, Herb Pennock joined the Yanks from the Red Sox, and he and Hoyt became Yankee mainstays through the dynasty years of the 1920s. Both would earn plaques in Cooperstown.

Headed to the Hall of Fame as well was Miller Huggins, although that was still hard to fathom after the 1920 season. It would be a tempestuous ride the entire way, as the manager and his players continued to squabble, sometimes in public but mostly in private. Because of his players' rowdy behavior at spring training back in Jacksonville, Huggins moved 1921 spring training to Shreveport, Louisiana, but the revelry started up all over again, which was extensively reported in the newspapers, causing criticism that the Yankee manager just didn't seem to have any control over his charges.

If the harping wasn't about that, it was about Huggins's use of his pitching staff, and his constant struggle in motivating a highly skilled team. Huggins just put his head down, bore it all, and soldiered on. Never amused by the jokes about his size, he cajoled and urged his charges on to the World Series in 1921, 1922, 1923, 1926, 1927, and 1928. The Yankees were world champions in three of those years—1923, 1927, and 1928.

It required all the talents of a determined, hard man to motivate these Yankees. There to publicize Huggins's every wrong move was the pack of sportswriters, one of the prices of playing in New York. Huggins got a bit of a break in 1923, when his nemesis Huston sold his share of the ballclub, leaving Ruppert in charge. But there was still a club to manage, and for all the talent the Yankees showed on the field, they were an increasingly rowdy bunch, often unwilling to respond to authority figures.

Babe Ruth was the chief instigator. He and others caroused all night, flouted curfews, and fought. In 1922 alone, Ruth and Pipp, and later Meusel and Schang, fought on the bench. By 1925, with Ruth back in the lineup after missing several months with a bad case of gonorrhea and other ailments, but continuing to flaunt the rules, Huggins benched and fined his star. Ruth reacted with rage and hot words, but Huggins stood his ground. Although the team fell to seventh place in 1925, Huggins had them back in the World Series in 1926.

There were several reasons why. Critical to the Yankees' success was the endless time and care Huggins took with younger players in whom he recognized talent. Lou Gehrig, fresh off the Columbia University campus, was one. He joined the Yankees in 1923, and by 1925 had supplanted Wally Pipp as the regular first baseman. Tony Lazzeri was another, as were Leo Durocher, Hoyt, and Pennock. All became Hall of Famers.

The turmoil took a fearful toll: as the years wore on, Huggins, frail to start with, suffered from an increasingly painful bout of neuritis, a condition aggravated by the worries piled on him by his tempestuous players. At times, Huggins's right leg shook in nervous spasms, and he went through periods of insomnia and a loss of appetite.

On September 20, 1929, with the Yankees in a distant second place behind the A's, Huggins appeared at Yankee Stadium sporting an oversized red blotch under his left eye.

"I must have picked up some kind of infection," he told trainer Charlie O'Leary. "I first noticed it last night. I'll have a doctor look at it after the game."

"It looks like a boil to me," O'Leary said. "You're all run down, Hug. That's what's the matter. Why don't you go home and take it easy this afternoon and then see a doctor and have that thing taken care of?"

So Huggins did, leaving the team's managerial duties that day to coach Art Fletcher and gathering his strength in the clubhouse before leaving. Just before going home—despite feeling awful—he still managed to have a conversation with a slumping Waite Hoyt.

"How old are you, Waite?" Huggins asked.

"I was 30 the other day—three days ago."

Nodding slowly, Huggins looked at his pitcher. "I'm going to tell you something, Waite," he said, "and I never want you to forget it. In baseball especially, you can't do after 30 what you've done before. Every year from now on, if you live soft in the winter, as you have been doing, you'll find it harder to get in condition in the spring. You and Pennock are finished for the year. I've already told him. I'll see you in the spring. And keep in shape this winter."

That was the last conversation Huggins had with one of his players. Dr. Edward King, the team's consulting doctor, checked Huggins into St. Vincent's Hospital, where the Yankee manager was diagnosed with erysipelas, a form of blood poisoning triggered by an infection, a serious illness in those preantibiotic days. Within a week, the Yankee manager was suddenly, shockingly dead at 50.

All of baseball mourned. The day after Huggins died, major-league games were called off in tribute. His body was taken to the Little Church Around the Corner on East 29th Street, where some 2,000 people filed by his coffin. Said a distraught Ruth, who served as a pallbearer: "It is one of the keenest losses I have ever felt. I cannot realize yet that we won't have him with us again on the bench."

Buried in Cincinnati, Miller Huggins is recalled today as among the game's shrewdest judges of talent. "It is doubtful that there ever was a better judge of playing material, either in the rough or with a sparkling finish," the *Times'* John Kieran wrote. "He rarely went wrong. It's difficult to recall more than a scattered few players who amounted to much in the big leagues after Huggins had traded or released them."

THIRTEEN

"I Ain't Gonna Be Leaving for a While Yet"

The Making of the Myth

Not quite three years after Babe Ruth's heroics of 1920, Jacob Ruppert opened Yankee Stadium in the Bronx. On April 23, 1923, more than 74,000 jammed the new immense ballpark to see Babe Ruth, as if on cue, smack the stadium's first home run in a 4–1 win over the Red Sox. "The [ballpark's] upper tier of the stand juts out over the field like a hanging cliff," wrote Damon Runyon in the *American*. "Only a veteran dweller of tenth and eleventh floors of apartment houses can sit up there without feeling a bit squeamish. It would be a long fall from the top seat to the ground. A man would have time to think over a lot of things."

Yankee Stadium would become the country's temple to baseball, and the Yankees the sport's greatest team of the 1920s, and eventually the greatest in history. But in a game that prizes youth, most of the 1920 Yanks, the ones who kicked off the team's era of glory, had faded away by decade's end. Joining Ruth as the only other 1920 Yankee still playing in the big leagues in 1929 was Bob Meusel, but he too would be gone from New York by 1930 before playing another year with the Reds and retiring. Moody and withdrawn until the end, Meusel batted .309 lifetime in 11 big-league seasons, playing in six World Series, all with New York. "His attitude is just plain indifference," a frustrated Huggins once said of Meusel, who he thought was good but could have been better. In 1977, the 81-year-old Meusel died in Downey, California, predictably leaving no last words.

Continuing to make noise was Ping Bodie, even after he was traded in 1921 to—who else?—the Red Sox. When Yankee officials turned down his request for a half share of the 1921 World Series bonus, he refused to report to Boston, went home to California, and never again played in the big leagues. Instead, Bodie spent the next seven seasons with Vernon and San Francisco in the Pacific Coast League, Des Moines in the Western League, and San Antonio in the Texas League. Then he retired for good and took his baseball stories of "crashing the old apple" to Hollywood, where he worked as an electrician on movie sets for 32 years, becoming a friend of stars such as Carole Lombard and Charles Boyer. Bodie, who watched with pride as other West Coast Italian-Americans like the DiMaggio brothers and Frank Crosetti reached the big leagues, died in 1961 at the age of 74.

Duffy Lewis never really recovered from his 1920 knee injury and latched on with the Senators in 1921 before retiring with a .284 lifetime batting average. Forever lionized in Boston, where he'd spent 8 of his 11 big-league seasons, Lewis became the longtime traveling secretary for the Braves, later accompanying the team in its 1953 move to Milwaukee. Many who never saw him play remembered him more as a baseball official with his trademark brim fedora, snazzy diamond stickpin, and sporty fancy vests.

Lewis insisted that the Braves travel first class and became known as a big tipper. "Pay another buck and go first class," was his motto, and door-men, bellhops, and cab drivers in cities throughout the National League looked forward to visits by Lewis and the Braves. In 1935, while with the Braves in Pittsburgh, Lewis saw Ruth's last three major-league home runs—making him the only man who'd witnessed the Babe's first big-league home run, in 1915, and his last.

Lewis finally retired in 1961 to New Hampshire, where he spent a lot of time at Rockingham Racetrack. In Lewis's later years, both Tris Speaker and Harry Hooper, his old Red Sox outfield teammates and Hall of Famers, did their best to get Lewis into Cooperstown as well. Lewis still hasn't made it to Cooperstown; he died in 1979 at 91.

Other 1920 Yankees also enjoyed productive careers. In 1921, the Yankees traded Roger Peckinpaugh to the Red Sox, who a month later sent him to the Senators, where he became the centerpiece of Washington's 1924 and 1925 World Series teams. The Senators took the Series in 1924, but lost to the Pirates the following year in a seven-game series in which Peckinpaugh committed a record eight errors, which rankled him right to the end.

After 1927, Peckinpaugh, who had managed the Yankees briefly back in 1914, retired with a .259 lifetime average and became a bona fide big-league manager with the Indians, who he managed until midseason of 1933.

Rehired by Cleveland in 1941, Peckinpaugh moved into the front office as general manager and vice president the following season to make room for Lou Boudreau, another youthful manager who was all of 24. Peckinpaugh stuck around until 1946, when Bill Veeck Jr. bought the team and brought in his own staff. He then retired to Cleveland and died in 1977 at the age of 86.

Bob Shawkey and his trademark red undershirt retired as well after 1927, with 196 big-league wins. He then became a Yankee coach, and in 1930, after Huggins's death, the team's manager. He lasted only a year, dismissed after a third-place finish and replaced with Joe McCarthy. So Shawkey became a minor-league manager, first with Jersey City and later with Scranton, Newark, Watertown (New York), and Tallahassee. Then came stints as a pitching coach with the Pirates and the Tigers. From 1952 to 1956, Shawkey was Dartmouth College's baseball coach. Bob, who threw out the first ball at renovated Yankee Stadium to open the 1976 season, died in 1981 at 90.

Jack Quinn didn't stay a Yankee long after 1920—he, too, was traded to the Red Sox, in 1922—but every time he seemed washed up, he'd come back and pitch some more, becoming a remarkable testament to durability. Quinn won 38 games in three years in Boston, and then at the age of 41, was bought by Connie Mack, then in the midst of another rebuilding era with the A's. Quinn pitched five-plus seasons for the A's, and in 1930 became the oldest player, at age 46, to play in a World Series. But Quinn still wasn't finished, and with Brooklyn in 1931 and 1932 he ranked among the National League's best relievers. He pitched briefly with the Reds in 1933, being released shortly after his 49th birthday. Although several players have made token appearances after age 50, Quinn is still the big-league's oldest regular roster player, the oldest to hit a home run (at age 45), and the oldest to win a game (at 48).

The remarkable Jack Quinn spent 23 years in the big leagues, winning 242 games. In 1934, he pitched a few games for Hollywood of the Pacific Coast League, but then returned to Pennsylvania, where he managed Johnstown of the Mid-Atlantic League in 1935. Quinn then retired and spent the remainder of his life in or near his native Pottstown, Pennsylvania, where he died in 1946 at the age of 61.

Nobody else from the 1920 Yankees lasted nearly as long. Wally Pipp soldiered on at first base, but was replaced by Lou Gehrig in 1925 when Pipp's skull was fractured by a beaning. He never did return to the regular lineup. Traded in 1926 to the Reds, Pipp played three more years, then retired in 1928 after 15 big-league seasons with a .281 lifetime batting average and 90 home runs. Unfortunately, the story of Pipp's 1925 fracture would take on apocryphal proportions, particularly since Gehrig would go on to play 2,130 straight games. In time, Pipp's fracture became a headache for which Huggins recommended he take two aspirin, and to be "pipped" or to pull a "Wally Pipp" became a common baseball phrase for an injured player whose replacement goes on to have a big day. After baseball, the real Wally Pipp went home to Michigan and sold auto parts; he died in 1965 at the age of 71.

Aaron Ward remained as the regular Yankee second baseman for six seasons. He was replaced by Tony Lazzeri after 1926 and traded to the White Sox. Ward remained a steady fielder, and by the time his 12-year big-league career was over, his lifetime batting average had risen to .268. Distinguishing Ward were clutch World Series performances—in three Series he batted .286 and hit three home runs. In 1923, after the Yankees beat the Giants for the team's first Series title, Colonel Ruppert delivered a speech praising several ballplayers including Ruth, Meusel, Pennock, and "Wardie," as he called him, along with "little Hug, the fine manager of this fine team." Delivered with Ruppert's strong German accent, the speech became a favorite for New York baseball writers to imitate.

After leaving the big leagues in 1928, Ward played in the minors until 1933 and managed New Iberia, Louisiana, of the Evangeline League in 1946. He died in a New Orleans veterans' hospital in 1961 at the age of 64.

Ward's career was a case of promise fulfilled. But Chick Fewster's, despite his battling back from the terrible spring-training beaning in 1920, was not. It wasn't that Fewster was bat-shy after his return—he refused to wear a special padded batting helmet the Yankees made for him—"but something had gone out of his play," the *Sporting News* wrote. "The great prospect of the 1920 training season became just an ordinary player."

Fewster's proudest moment came at spring training in 1921 in Shreveport, when he faced the man who had beaned him the year before, Jeff Pfeffer, and hammered a triple. In the 1921 World Series he played the last three games in left field, replacing Ruth, out with a wrenched knee, and homered in game six. Then, in 1922, Fewster was traded to the Red Sox, and then went the next year to Cleveland. By early 1926, Fewster was a true journeyman, released to Kansas City and then to a series of minor-league teams before making one more brief big-league stop, in Brooklyn, and retiring in 1929. In 11 big-league seasons, almost all spent as a slick-fielding utility player, Fewster batted .258.

After the big leagues, Fewster operated a private baseball stadium and coached amateur players in Brooklyn. In World War II, he joined the Merchant Marine and ran Allied supplies for the invasion of Africa—a risky venture that included the sinking of his ship in the Persian Gulf. Honorably discharged, Fewster died unexpectedly back in his native Baltimore in 1945. The onetime Yankee phenom was six months shy of his 50th birthday.

Del Pratt continued to excel after he was traded to the Red Sox, for whom he batted .324 in 1921 and .301 in 1922. That winter, Pratt went to Detroit, played two more solid seasons with the Tigers, and retired in 1924 after 13 big-league seasons with a .292 lifetime batting average. Then Pratt went home to Texas and became a Texas League stalwart—first as player-manager with Waco and then as manager with Galveston and Fort Worth. He retired from baseball after 1934 and remained in Texas, where, in 1977, he died at 89.

Also returning to Texas was Rip Collins. Traded as well to Boston after 1921 because Huggins was finally fed up with his carousing, Collins went 14–11 with the Red Sox in 1922, and then spent five years in Detroit—winning 14 games in 1924—before spending three years with the Browns, where he wound up his 11-year big-league career in 1931. Collins's 108–82 career record was good, but he never attained the promise that he had as a Yankee rookie back in 1920, due perhaps to his lack of interest in baseball. Once described as a pitcher "with a million dollars worth of talent and 25 cents worth of enthusiasm," Collins pined not for the bright lights of Broadway, but for Texas.

Collins managed to have a fine time anyway. A couple of years before his big-league career ended, a reporter told him, "You look a lot older than 32," to which Collins drawled, "You can't buck liquor and Broadway without getting marked up."

His career done, Collins worked as a law enforcement officer, first with the Texas Rangers and later as sheriff of Travis County. He died in 1968 at the age of 72.

One gets the impression that Rip Collins moved on after his baseball career with ease, never looking back on what might have been. But not the irascible Carl Mays, who went to his deathbed, predictably, in turmoil, forever indignant about how his baseball career had turned out.

Carl Mays was even better in 1921 than he was in 1920, winning 27 games and opening the 1921 Series against the Giants brilliantly by pitching a five-hit shutout and racking up a 3–0 victory. Waite Hoyt followed with another shutout, this one also 3–0, and after two games the Yanks had a 2–0 lead in the best-of-nine Series.

Things started out splendidly for the Yanks in game three as well, when they jumped on Fred Toney for four runs in the third. But the tide quickly turned in the bottom of the inning when the Giants pounded Bob Shawkey for four runs themselves to tie the game. Then, in the seventh, the Giants scored eight more runs on the way to a 13–5 rout.

So it was up to Mays in game four to keep the Giants from evening the Series. Pitching against the spitballer Phil Douglas, Mays seemed to be in a groove, pitching hitless ball through five innings, and then giving up only a couple of singles in the sixth and seventh. But in the eighth, with the Yankees ahead 1–0 on a Babe Ruth home run, Mays lost it in a hurry, giving up four hits and committing fielding blunders that a Little Leaguer wouldn't make.

First up for the Giants was Irish Meusel, Bob's big brother, acquired earlier in the year from the Phillies. He smacked a triple off the wall. Johnny Rawlings, the next batter, sent Meusel home with a single, and Frank Snyder followed with a sacrifice bunt that Mays tried fielding, but he fell before he could make a play. Douglas sacrificed both runners up, and with runners on second and third with only one gone, George Burns doubled to left, driving them both home. Mays took care of the next two batters, but within the space of a few minutes the tide had turned and the Giants were ahead, 3–1.

The final was 4–2, and the Series was suddenly tied after the Yanks had been so close to breaking it open. Mays had pitched well, giving up nine hits and no walks. No one thought much about it, except for Huggins, who was furious at Mays for blatantly disregarding his command to throw Meusel a fastball and instead delivering a slow curve that the batter hit for the triple.

That night, Fred Lieb, having filed his game story earlier in the day, was back at the Commodore Hotel when he was approached by a man named

George Perry. Perry was helping visiting writers, in town to cover the Series, with their accommodations. With him was a well-known Broadway actor with quite a story to tell Lieb.

The actor told him that Mays had tanked that day's game, stating that at the start of the eighth, Mays's wife, sitting in the grandstand, had flashed a signal to her husband by wiping her face with a white handkerchief. According to the actor, Mays had been offered a big sum of cash to intentionally lose any close game, and that the handkerchief signal was a gesture to show that she had received the money. Then Mays surrendered the four quick runs, and lost the game.

Like the sordid tale of the 1919 White Sox, still fresh in the minds of America, it seemed too fantastic to believe. But Lieb felt obligated to report the story anyhow, and tracked down Colonel Huston, sleeping off a bender at the Hotel Martinique. Well after midnight, back at the Commodore, and with Commissioner Landis also present, the actor repeated his story for both men.

Both Huston and Landis listened intently. Landis said he would use detectives to make a full investigation of the charge, and pleaded with Lieb to write nothing about the suspicions. Lieb never did, nor did he think to ask Landis what he thought after Mays lost the seventh game of the Series, 2–1, when Frank Snyder of the Giants drove in the winning run with a two-out double in the seventh. Landis's sole comment about the investigation came after the Giants had won the Series in eight games, which was that the detective agency had been unable to find anything to implicate Mays.

The story died, and it would have been forever forgotten if not for a chance encounter in 1927 when Lieb and his wife, Mary Ann, accompanied several baseball officials and other writers during an off-season gathering at Dover Hall near Brunswick, Georgia. Before a roaring fire and having imbibed a goodly amount of rum and Coke, Huston, sitting with Wilbert Robinson, felt compelled to let Lieb in on a dirty little secret.

"Freddy," the Colonel started, "I am going to tell you the damnedest story a baseball owner has ever told a reporter."

Sitting nearby was Robinson, himself having consumed a great deal of alcohol, but suddenly rapt with attention about the story Huston was about to share.

"No, no, Colonel," Robinson said. "Don't tell him, don't tell him!"

Huston, by now nearly passed out from the free-flowing booze, did anyway. "I wanted to tell you that some of our pitchers threw World Series games on us in both 1921 and 1922."

"You mean the Mays matter of the 1921 World Series?" Lieb asked.

"Yes," Huston said, "but there were others—other times, other pitchers." And with that, the Colonel drifted off into a drunken slumber.

Once again, Lieb didn't follow up in print. The next morning, he left for New York and once home, looked up Mays's record in the 1921 Series. In three games, Mays had pitched 26 innings and given up 20 hits, but in only two of those innings the Giants had scored four runs on seven hits.

Years later, the alleged incident came up again in a conversation with Miller Huggins about the sorry financial straits of certain former players at a time when there was no union or pension plan. Huggins, who had a soft spot for most of his former players, couldn't help but show his utter contempt for Mays.

"Any ballplayer that played for me on either the Cardinals or the Yankees could come to me if he were in need and I would give him a helping hand," Huggins said. "I make only two exceptions—Carl Mays and Joe Bush. If they were in the gutter, I'd kick them."

Lieb was stunned. "How could such a kindly gentleman carry such a deep hatred?" he thought to himself. But before Lieb could ask, the conversation had veered to other things and other players.

But Lieb was certain that Huggins's overt hostility had been triggered by Mays's refusal back in the 1921 Series of his command to throw the fastball to Meusel. Similar incidents had happened in the 1922 Series with Bush, who Huggins believed had also ignored his directives and intentionally lost games. In the first and fifth games, Bush had carried a lead into the eighth inning, but in both games gave up three runs that inning and lost.

After 1921, Mays was never the same as a Yankee. In 1922, the New Yorkers outlasted St. Louis to win the pennant by one game, but Mays dropped to a mediocre 13–14. He fell even further in 1923, finishing with a 5–2 record and an uncharacteristic 6.20 ERA in only 81 innings—despite drawing the largest salary of any pitcher on the staff.

By then, Huggins was using Mays so sparingly that the pitcher was baffled, taking his questions to the writers. "What's wrong with me?" he asked. "Why doesn't Huggins pitch me?"

Huggins was determined to let Mays suffer. "Why should I use him?" he said one day in 1923. "I'm winning an easy pennant without him." After weeks of sitting Mays on the bench, Huggins finally gave him the start in Cleveland on June 17. Rusty from being so inactive, Mays was shelled, but Huggins left him in, refusing to change pitchers. Mays hung in there, but gave up 20 hits and four walks, and hit a batter. The final was 13–0 Indians, and Mays was forced to endure all nine innings.

"He pitched me maybe two innings here, one inning a week later," Mays said of Huggins after the shellacking. "So even though I have a sound arm, I am in no shape to pitch a nine-inning game. A strong-armed pitcher like me needs to work every fourth or fifth game to have his stuff."

Huggins just shrugged when asked why he kept Mays in the entire game. "He told me he needed lots of work, so I gave it to him," he said. Still, the game was humiliating for Mays, painful even for his teammates to watch. Said shortstop Everett Scott, another Red Sox player turned Yankee, to Mays after the game: "In all my years in baseball, I've never seen anything so rotten."

It got worse. Another day, while dressing for a game against Boston, a frustrated Mays called out to Huggins in front of the writers, "Hey, Hug? Why won't you let me pitch?"

Huggins looked over at Mays and feigned surprised. "Why, Carl, are you still with the club?"

After the season, the Yankees placed Mays on waivers, but no club picked him up, leaving the New Yorkers to ship him to Cincinnati. Arriving at the club's office to negotiate his contract, Mays was presented with a remarkable letter from Huggins to Reds president Garry Herrmann.

"Dear Garry," the note opened, "Just a note to tell you that in selling Mays to you I may be selling the best pitcher I've got. But I don't want him pitching for me and I don't want him pitching against me. He is a very hard man to handle and I suggest that you begin by cutting his salary in half."

Herrmann didn't halve his salary, but he cut it. But before leaving, Mays gave his new employer a pledge: "If you give me 30 starts, I'll win 20 games."

In 1924, Mays got his 30 starts—37 in fact—and came through, finishing with a 20–9 record and earning for himself a $1,500 bonus. After a sore arm idled him for most of 1925, Mays had another good season in 1926, winning 19 games and keeping the Reds in the race into September until he was knocked out with a shin injury. Without Mays, the Reds finished second.

That was Mays's last season in the sun. By 1927, he was 35 years old, and had become another injury-plagued veteran just trying to hang on. He did for another three seasons, barely—and after spending 1929 with John McGraw and the Giants, Mays retired. In 15 big-league seasons he had won 209 games and lost 126, a .623 winning percentage, and compiled an ERA of 2.92—impressive numbers, and better than several Hall of Fame pitchers.

After leaving baseball as a player, Mays suffered a series of unfortunate tragedies. Back in Oregon, he lost his savings of $175,000 in the 1929 stock market crash, forcing him to return to the game for two seasons as a minor-league pitching coach. Then, in 1934, his wife, Freddie, only 36, died from complications of an eye infection, leaving Mays on his own to raise the couple's two children.

Just as he'd done in baseball, Mays fought back. Remarried shortly after Freddie's death to a schoolteacher, he ran a fishing camp, scouted for several big-league clubs, and managed a baseball camp. "I try to teach them everything," Mays said of the youngsters he enjoyed teaching, "but the big thing I do is teach them safety in baseball."

But Mays remained bitter about the treatment he received from baseball. Every year, he watched pitchers without the numbers he had compiled enter the Hall of Fame. Among those who did were his Yankee teammates Waite Hoyt and Herb Pennock, both of whom won more games than Mays, but weren't close in winning percentage or ERA.

As the years wore on, Mays grew increasingly bitter that he was never voted into the shrine at Cooperstown. Convinced that he had never lived down the Ray Chapman incident, he said late in life that "I won over 200 big-league games, but no one remembers that. When they think of me, I'm the guy who killed Chapman with a fastball."

Fred Lieb, who spent many years as a member of the Hall of Fame's Veterans Committee, insisted otherwise. "Carl Mays' name has frequently come before the committee, but no one has ever brought up the Chapman tragedy as a reason why Carl should not be in the Cooperstown shrine," he wrote in his memoirs. "Rather, the question mark has often been his performance in the Series of 1921."

In 1971, Rube Marquard, the winner of 201 games, with a .532 winning percentage and an ERA of 3.08, was voted into the Hall of Fame. When a writer telephoned Mays for his reaction, the 79-year-old former pitcher conceded that "Rube Marquard was a great pitcher and I'm glad he made it, but my record is so far superior to his that it makes me wonder. I guess the answer is they just don't like me."

By then, Mays was spending winters in San Diego, where he worked with the pitchers at Hoover High School. On March 19, 1971, Mays watched one of the Hoover games from his pickup truck, felt tired from a bout with continuing chest pains, and checked into a hospital. Two weeks later, Carl Mays was dead. After he died, the newspaper obituaries in their opening paragraphs recalled him as the "Yankee pitcher who threw the fastball that hit and killed Cleveland batter Ray Chapman in 1920." Carl Mays never did live down his one deadly pitch.

Then there was Babe Ruth. If 1920 was the year he became a legend, the 1920s was the decade he became an immortal. With an incredulous America looking on, Ruth continued living life large and at a pace that would flatten everyone else.

This is what he did in the 1920s:

- He led the American League in home runs eight of ten years.
- He played in six World Series.
- He drew a salary that rose rapidly from $52,000 to $70,000 to $80,000.
- He and his heroics provided the budget to build Yankee Stadium, packed it for years afterwards with adoring fans, and hit the first home run in the stadium's history.
- He continued to remake what had been a scientific, low-scoring game into a virtual extension of his own slugging style.

Ruth remained his ever-engaging self, despite his expanding waistline. Lining up with his teammates one sweltering day in Washington to be formally introduced to President Calvin Coolidge, Ruth waited his turn.

"How do you do, Mr. President," Hoyt said.

"Good day, sir," said Pennock.

"Mr. Ruth," the president said, shaking hands with Ruth.

"Hot as hell, ain't it, Prez?" Mr. Ruth said.

One day, while the Yankees were in Philadelphia, Pennock was asked to attend a formal party in nearby Wilmington, Delaware, and asked Ruth,

Joe Dugan, and Meusel to attend. The players were game, and so was Huggins, provided they get back in time for a good night's rest before the next day's game at Shibe Park.

At the party, Ruth was a big hit. Yes, he told the guests, baseball had come easily to him, but he had to work hard to perfect his skills. And his swing? Well, he always admired the way Joe Jackson had swung the bat, so he copied it. As for the Yankees, he said they had a good shot to repeat as champions, provided he could stay healthy and keep swinging for the fences.

The baseball talk flowed freely with the alcohol, and after a couple of hours, Ruth set his roving eye on one of the women, a maid.

"Babe," said the boxing promoter who had arranged for the visit of the players, "you've got to get out of here."

"Not without that broad," Ruth said.

"Come on," the promoter reasoned, "I'll get you broads in Philly better than her."

"You sure?" Ruth said.

The boxing promoter kept his word, and took Ruth to a whorehouse. Hours and hours later as the sun rose over Philadelphia, the promoter, thinking about the Yankee game later that afternoon, reckoned that Ruth should return to the team's hotel.

Sitting in a lounge chair with a woman on each knee and an open bottle of champagne upside down on his head, Ruth thought it over. "I ain't gonna be leaving for a while yet," he said.

That afternoon at Shibe Park, Ruth pronounced himself ready to take on the A's.

"I feel good," said Ruth, who had probably not slept.

"You don't look so good," said Fred Merkle, a longtime Giant finishing his career with the Yankees.

"I'll hit one," said Ruth.

"Bet?" Merkle said.

"A hundred," said Ruth.

"Wait a minute," said Merkle. "This is an easy ballpark."

"All right," said Ruth. "I'll give you two-to-one odds."

In his first at-bat, Ruth cracked one into the left-field stands and won the bet. Next time up, he tripled to right. Later he tripled again, driving a ball over Al Simmons's head in center. And in his fourth at-bat, he homered again, finishing the day four-for-four.

In 1927, Ruth and the Yankees had a season for the ages. Ruth belted 60 homers, his personal record, which was more than every other team in the American League, and he hit .356 to help the Yankees win the pennant by 19 games. Gehrig had quite a run himself, hitting 47 home runs and batting .373. Then, at batting practice before game one of the World Series against the Pirates at Forbes Field, the Yankees launched home run after home run in an awesome display, unnerving the upstart Pirates, who the Yankees promptly swept in four games.

By then, the game had spawned a generation of home run hitters—Gehrig, Jimmie Foxx, and Hack Wilson among them—but the mighty Ruth was still king. Ruth's 1927 output came in a year when the whole American League hit 439 home runs, meaning he alone accounted for nearly 14 percent of the league's total. When Roger Maris hit 61 home runs in 1961, the A.L. hit 1,534, leaving Maris's share at less than 4 percent.

"There is no other real way to compare one generation with another, but in fairness to Ruth it must be said that no player in history ever dominated his competition to such an astounding degree," wrote Lee Allen, a Ruth biographer. "Ruth hit home runs when no one, with the exception of Gehrig, hit them in quantity."

The Babe's 1929 marriage to Claire Hodgson—made possible after the estranged Helen died in a Massachusetts fire—calmed Ruth down a tad. The couple adopted Claire's daughter from a previous marriage, giving the Babe two daughters, and the family moved to Hodgson's 11-room, seventh-floor apartment, down the hall from her mother, at 345 West 88th Street in New York. (In 1942, the Ruths moved to another 11-room apartment, this one at 110 Riverside Drive at 83rd Street.) Claire accompanied him on road trips, and also took considerable interest in Ruth's finances, working with a wily agent turned money manager named Christy Walsh to tame her husband's cavalier spending. She and Walsh, who had set up a trust fund for the family, gave Ruth a budget, and wrote him $50 checks whenever he needed cash. The system worked, cutting down on Ruthian habits like tipping $100 for a 35-cent ham sandwich and granting him financial security for life.

He remained the Babe, a bit pudgier, a tad slower than the titan of 1920, but still a carouser when he could get away with it. And the public still craved to know exactly how he managed to do what he did. One day in 1930 while waiting to step into the batting cage before a game in St. Louis, Ruth got to talking with Browns manager Bill Killefer.

"Your face is getting fatter and fatter," Killefer said.

"Yeah?" said Ruth, sending a stream of tobacco juice toward the ground. "Well, I don't hit with my face."

"Is the wife on the trip with you?"

"Sure."

"Having a hard time dodging the old phone calls?" Killefer asked, with a smile.

"Oh, go to hell."

"What books are you reading?" asked a nearby reporter, joining the conversation.

"Books?" Ruth asked. "Reading isn't good for a ballplayer. Not good for his eyes. If my eyes went bad even a little bit, I couldn't hit home runs. So I gave up reading."

"You must do some reading," the reporter said. "Who are your favorite authors?"

"My favorite Arthurs? Nehf and Fletcher."

"Not Arthurs. Authors, writers."

"Oh, writers," said Ruth. "My favorite writer is Christy Walsh."

"What is the psychology of home runs?"

"Say, are you kidding me?"

"No, of course not. I just want an explanation of why you get so many home runs."

Ruth spat again. "Just swinging," he said.

"Have you ever had an idol, someone you thought more of than anyone else?"

"Sure he has," said teammate Tony Lazzeri, standing nearby. "Babe Ruth."

"Go to hell," Ruth said. "Excuse [me], it's my turn to hit."

By 1934, Ruth's salary had dropped to $35,000 and the skills of the 39-year-old ballplayer were eroding. That year, the Babe was merely mortal—swatting 22 home runs, including his 700th, and batting .288. After the season, the Yankees released him, and Ruth went back to Boston, this time as a utility outfielder and assistant manager with the lowly Braves. But the titles didn't mean much, because Ruth was there to hit home runs, but by the end of May had hit only six and was batting .181. So he retired.

His last three home runs were, well, Ruthian. He hit them on May 25, 1935, at Pittsburgh's Forbes Field, the last one a solo shot in the seventh inning off the Pirates' Guy Bush. Ruth sent the ball clear over the ballpark's massive right-field grandstand in "a prodigious clout," as reported by the Associated Press. Home run number 714 was the first ball ever hit over that roof, and was said at the time to be the longest drive ever hit at Forbes. Of his 714 home runs, Ruth hit 347 at home, 367 on the road, and 499 off righties, and 215 off left-handers.

That last blast sent Ruth trotting around the bases with his patented short, pigeon-toed trot for the last time as the crowd of 10,000 roared like thunder—although, as writer Lawrence Ritter put it, "many older fans seemed to be crying as much as cheering."

Some four decades later, Guy Bush recalled the moment like it had just happened. "He'd gotten to where he could hardly hobble along," he said of Ruth. "When he rounded third base, I looked over there at him and he kind of looked at me. I tipped my cap, as if to say, 'I've seen everything now, Babe.' He looked at me and kind of saluted and smiled. We got in that gesture of good friendship. And that's the last home run he ever hit."

For Babe Ruth, the end came four days later. On May 26, 1935, he struck out three times and went hitless. On the 27th, he pinch-hit and walked. Nor did he get a hit on the 28th or the 29th. And on May 30, Babe Ruth, still the greatest player to ever lace up a pair of spikes and America's greatest sportsman ever, grounded out in the first, benched himself, and called it a career.

Ruth was hoping to stay in the game as a manager. But no team would take a chance on a man who, as Ruppert had bluntly told him, "can't take care of himself." One of the reasons Ruth had signed on with the Braves was that the managerial job held by Bill McKechnie was said to be Ruth's for the asking in 1936. But the job offer evaporated, and no big-league managerial offer ever came.

Ruppert suggested that Ruth manage the International League's Newark Bears, a Yankee farm team, as an apprenticeship. Ruth refused, pointing to star players who had never managed a day in the minors before landing a position in the bigs, among them Ty Cobb, Mickey Cochrane, Joe Cronin, Rogers Hornsby, Christy Mathewson, Tris Speaker, and Bill Terry. Ruth was upset: "I gave 22 years of my life to big-league baseball," he told the Baseball Writers' dinner at the Waldorf-Astoria in New York, "and I'm ready to give 25 more." Nearly 1,000 baseball officials heard his plea, but still, nobody budged.

Claire encouraged him to take the Newark job, but Ruth refused. Instead, he hung around the apartment, waiting for the managerial call that never came, and carved out a new life crowded with golf, bowling, hunting, hosting a radio program, and making appearances too numerous to name. He continued to visit kids in hospitals and orphanages, and in the evenings generally stayed home, playing cards and listening to the radio. His favorite shows were "The Lone Ranger" and "Gangbusters."

In February 1936, Ruth was named one of five charter members elected to the new Baseball Hall of Fame. Of the 226 ballots cast, Cobb was named on 222, Ruth on 215, Honus Wagner on 215, Mathewson on 205, and Walter Johnson on 189. Three years later, Ruth joined most of those charter members—all but Mathewson, who had died in 1925—for the opening ceremonies in Cooperstown, New York, along with Eddie Collins, Napoleon Lajoie, George Sisler, and Tris Speaker, who had also since been elected.

In 1938, Ruth signed on for a stint with the Brooklyn Dodgers as a coach and gate attraction. But that would be his last job in baseball, because by then he and his family, thanks to Walsh's conservative investments, had prospered enough so that he could retire for good.

In the fall of 1946, Ruth began to suffer periodic pains over his left eye, and his voice cracked. When the pain became intense, he entered French Hospital on West 13th Street for a checkup. The doctors diagnosed throat cancer, but never told Ruth about it. As the Babe would tell Connie Mack: "The termites got me."

Ruth left French Hospital three months later, and had become so weak that he needed help to reach his car. His health declined steadily, and on July 26, 1948, Ruth checked into Memorial Hospital on East 68th Street in Manhattan. At 8:01 P.M., August 16, 1948, Babe Ruth's restless, crowded, stranger-than-fiction life ended. He was 53.

Three days later at Ruth's funeral, a taxi driver echoed the feelings of the 100,000 or so who lined the rainy streets of Manhattan and the Bronx to watch Babe Ruth's funeral procession: "Even the skies wept for the Babe." Added Arthur Daily in the *Times*: "The Babe would have gloried in it; the final tribute would have left him shining-eyed and choked up because he always had the soft-hearted sentimentality of a small boy."

Those sentiments matched the outpouring of grief at the passing of America's greatest sportsman. There were front-page stories in every newspaper in America, and 77,000 people filed past his coffin as he was lying in state at Yankee Stadium. A mass at St. Patrick's Cathedral conducted by Cardinal Spellman followed, and when the service ended, Ruth's mahogany casket was carried out of the cathedral just as the rain, which had fallen steadily through the morning, suddenly stopped.

The mourners, many of them middle-aged teammates of Ruth, took several minutes to pile into automobiles for the 30-mile trip north to Gate of Heaven cemetery in the Westchester County hamlet of Hawthorne, where the Babe would be buried. The rain held off, only to begin again once the procession was on its way. Some 250 policemen directed them up 5th Avenue from 51st Street to 120th Street, on to Madison Avenue and 138th Street, and across the Madison Avenue Bridge into the Bronx. From there, the cavalcade of 25 cars traveled north up the Grand Concourse, past Yankee Stadium, scene of so many of Ruth's great moments, and into Westchester County.

The rain continued. Lining the roads were thousands of fans, many having removed their hats out of respect. Others watched from rooftops and windows. When the procession reached the cemetery at 1:43 P.M., it was met by another crowd—this one a tightly packed bunch of 6,000, who had waited since early morning.

The 86-year-old Mack was a pallbearer. So were two of Ruth's longtime Yankee teammates, Joe Dugan and Waite Hoyt. As the weather cleared and the sun came out, Dugan turned to Hoyt and said, "I'd give a hundred bucks for an ice-cold beer."

"So would the Babe," whispered Hoyt.

As many as could crowded around the canopied plot in front of the receiving tomb, where the coffin, with "George Herman Ruth" on its silver nameplate, was placed for the brief committal service. Ruth wasn't actually buried until October 26, 1948.

The grave, in the cemetery's hill section, is within 200 feet of the grave of Mayor Jimmy Walker, an old friend, who once told him, "Never let those poor kids down." Babe Ruth, the man who had saved baseball in its darkest hour, never did.

APPENDIX

Statistics

1920 American League (league leaders in bold)

FINAL STANDINGS

	W	L	PCT	GB	Runs	2B	3B	HR	BA
Cleveland	98	56	.636		**857**	**300**	95	35	.303
Chicago	96	58	.623	2	794	267	92	37	.294
New York	95	59	.617	3	839	268	71	**115**	.280
St. Louis	76	77	.497	21.5	797	279	83	50	**.308**
Boston	72	81	.471	25.5	651	216	71	22	.269
Washington	68	84	.447	29	723	233	81	36	.291
Detroit	61	93	.396	37	651	228	72	30	.270
Philadelphia	48	106	.312	50	555	219	49	44	.252

THE YANKEES

Position	Player	AB	BA	HR	RBI
1B	W. Pipp	610	.280	11	76
2B	D. Pratt	574	.314	4	97
SS	R. Peckinpaugh	534	.270	8	54
3B	A. Ward	496	.256	11	54
RF	B. Ruth	458	.376	**54**	137
CF	P. Bodie	471	.295	7	79
LF	D. Lewis	365	.271	4	61
C	M. Ruel	261	.268	1	15
OF	B. Meusel	460	.328	11	83
C	T. Hannah	259	.247	2	25

Pitchers	G	IP	W	L	ERA
C. Mays	45	312	26	11	3.06
B. Shawkey	38	268	20	13	**2.45**
J. Quinn	41	253	18	10	3.20
R. Collins	36	187	14	8	3.17
H. Thormahlen	29	143	9	6	4.14
G. Mogridge	26	125	5	9	4.31

INDIVIDUAL LEAGUE LEADERS
Batting and Base Running

Batting Average

G. Sisler (St. Louis)	.407
T. Speaker (Cleveland)	.388
J. Jackson (Chicago)	.382
B. Ruth (New York)	.376
E. Collins (Chicago)	.369

Slugging Average

B. Ruth (New York)	.847
G. Sisler (St. Louis)	.632
J. Jackson (Chicago)	.589
T. Speaker (Cleveland)	.562
H. Felsch (Chicago)	.540

Home Runs

B. Ruth (New York)	54
G. Sisler (St. Louis)	19
T. Walker (Philadelphia)	17
H. Felsch (Chicago)	14
J. Jackson (Chicago)	12
E. Smith (Cleveland)	12

Total Bases

G. Sisler (St. Louis)	399
B. Ruth (New York)	388
J. Jackson (Chicago)	336
T. Speaker (Cleveland)	310
B. Jacobson (St. Louis)	305

Runs Batted In

B. Ruth (New York)	137
B. Jacobson (St. Louis)	122
G. Sisler (St. Louis)	122
J. Jackson (Chicago)	121
L. Gardner (Cleveland)	118

Hits

G. Sisler (St. Louis)	257
E. Collins (Chicago)	222
J. Jackson (Chicago)	218

Runs Scored

B. Ruth (New York)	158
T. Speaker (Cleveland)	97
H. Hooper (Boston)	88

Doubles

T. Speaker (Cleveland)	50
G. Sisler (St. Louis)	49
J. Jackson (Chicago)	42

Triples

J. Jackson (Chicago)	20
G. Sisler (St. Louis)	18
H. Hooper (Boston)	17

Bases on Balls

B. Ruth (New York)	148
T. Speaker (Cleveland)	97
H. Hooper (Boston)	88

Home Run Percentage

B. Ruth (New York)	11.8
G. Sisler (St. Louis)	3.0
T. Walker (Philadelphia)	2.9

Pitching

Winning Percentage

J. Bagby (Cleveland)	.721
C. Mays (New York)	.703
D. Kerr (Chicago)	.700
E. Cicotte (Chicago)	.677
U. Shocker (St. Louis)	.667
R. Caldwell (Cleveland)	.667

Won-Lost Record

J. Bagby (Cleveland)	31–12
C. Mays (New York)	26–11
S. Coveleski (Cleveland)	24–14
R. Faber (Chicago)	23–13
L. Williams (Chicago)	22–14

Earned Run Average

B. Shawkey (New York)	2.45
S. Coveleski (Cleveland)	2.49
U. Shocker (St. Louis)	2.71
J. Bagby (Cleveland)	2.89
R. Faber (Chicago)	2.99

Strikeouts	
S. Coveleski (Cleveland)	133
L. Williams (Chicago)	128
B. Shawkey (New York)	126
R. Faber (Chicago)	108
U. Shocker (St. Louis)	107

Complete Games	
J. Bagby (Cleveland)	30
E. Cicotte (Chicago)	28
R. Faber (Chicago)	28
C. Mays (New York)	26
S. Coveleski (Cleveland)	26
L. Williams (Chicago)	26

George Herman "Babe" Ruth

Born: February 6, 1895, in Baltimore
Died: August 16, 1948, in New York City
Bats: Left
Throws: Left
Height and weight: 6'2" and 215 pounds
Big-league debut: June 11, 1914

BABE RUTH'S CAREER STATISTICS

Batting

Year	Age	Team	G	AB	H	2B	3B	HR	R	RBI	SB	BB	SO	BA	OBP	SLG	FP	G/POS
1914	19	Boston	5	10	2	1	0	0	1	2	0	0	4	.200	.200	.300	1.000	p-4
1915	20	Boston	42	92	29	10	1	4	16	21	0	9	23	.315	.376	.576	.976	p-4
1916	21	Boston	67	136	37	5	3	3	18	15	0	10	23	.272	.322	.419	.973	p-44
1917	22	Boston	52	123	40	6	3	2	14	12	0	12	18	.325	.385	.472	.984	p-41
1918	23	Boston	95	317	95	26	11	11	50	66	6	57	58	.300	.410	.555	.949	outfield-59/p-20/1B-13
1919	24	Boston	130	432	139	34	12	29	103	114	7	101	58	.322	.456	.657	.996	outfield-111/p-17/1B-5
1920	25	New York	142	458	172	36	9	54	158	137	14	148	80	.376	.530	.847	.936	outfield-141/1B-2/p-1
1921	26	New York	152	540	204	44	16	59	177	171	17	144	81	.378	.512	.846	.966	outfield-152/1B-2/p-2
1922	27	New York	110	406	128	24	8	35	94	99	2	84	80	.315	.434	.672	.964	outfield-110/1B-1
1923	28	New York	152	522	205	45	13	41	151	131	17	170	93	.393	.545	.764	.973	outfield-148/1B-4
1924	29	New York	153	529	200	39	7	46	143	121	9	142	81	.378	.513	.739	.962	outfield-152
1925	30	New York	98	359	104	12	2	25	61	66	2	59	68	.290	.393	.543	.974	outfield-98

1926	31	New York	152	495	184	30	5	**47**	139	146	11	**144**	76	.372	**.516**	**.737**	**.979**	outfield-149/1B-2
1927	32	New York	151	540	192	29	8	**60**	**158**	164	7	**138**	89	.356	**.487**	**.772**	.963	outfield-151
1928	33	New York	154	536	173	29	8	**54**	**163**	**142**	4	**135**	87	.323	.461	**.709**	.975	outfield-154
1929	34	New York	135	499	172	26	6	**46**	121	154	5	72	60	.345	.430	**.697**	**.984**	outfield-133
1930	35	New York	145	518	186	28	9	**49**	150	153	10	**136**	61	.359	**.493**	**.732**	.965	outfield-144/p-1
1931	36	New York	145	534	199	31	3	**46**	149	163	5	**128**	51	.373	**.495**	**.700**	.972	outfield-142/1B-1
1932	37	New York	133	457	156	13	5	41	156	137	2	**130**	62	.341	**.489**	.661	.961	outfield-128/1B-1
1933	38	New York	137	459	138	21	3	34	97	103	4	**114**	90	.301	.442	.582	.970	outfield-132/1B-1/p-1
1934	39	New York	125	365	105	17	4	22	78	84	1	103	63	.288	.447	.537	.962	outfield-111
1935	40	Boston (NL)	28	72	13	0	0	6	13	12	0	20	24	.181	.359	.431	.952	outfield-26
Total: 22 years			2,503	8,399	2,873	506	136	714	2,174	2,213	123	2,056	1,330	.342	.474	.690	.968	outfield-2,241/p-163/1B-32

Pitching

Year	Age	Team	W–L	PCT	G	CG	IP	H	BB	SO	ERA
1914	19	Boston	2–1	.667	4	1	23.0	21	7	3	3.91
1915	20	Boston	18–8	.692	32	16	217.2	166	85	112	2.44
1916	21	Boston	23–12	.657	44	23	323.2	230	118	170	1.75
1917	22	Boston	24–13	.649	41	35	326.1	244	108	128	2.01
1918	23	Boston	13–7	.650	20	18	166.1	125	49	40	2.22
1919	24	Boston	9–5	.643	17	12	133.1	148	58	30	2.97
1920	25	New York	1–0	1.000	1	0	4.0	3	2	0	4.50
1921	26	New York	2–0	1.000	2	0	9.0	14	9	2	9.00
1930	35	New York	1–0	1.000	1	1	9.0	11	2	3	3.00
1933	38	New York	1–0	1.000	1	1	9.0	12	3	0	5.00
Total: 10 years			94–46	.671	163	107	1,221.1	974	441	488	2.28

BABE RUTH'S WORLD SERIES STATISTICS
Pitching

Year	Team	W–L	PCT	G	CG	IP	H	BB	SO	ERA
1916	Boston	1–0	1.000	1	1	14	6	3	4	0.64
1918	Boston	2–0	1.000	2	1	17	13	7	4	1.06
Total:	2 years	3–0	1.000	3	2	31	19	10	8	0.87

Batting

Year	Team	G	AB	H	2B	3B	HR	R	RBI
1915	Boston	1	1	0	0	0	0	0	0
1916	Boston	1	5	0	0	0	0	0	1
1918	Boston	3	5	1	0	1	0	0	2
1921	New York	6	15	5	0	0	1	3	4
1922	New York	5	17	2	1	0	0	1	1
1923	New York	6	19	7	1	1	3	8	3
1926	New York	7	20	6	0	0	4	6	5
1927	New York	4	16	6	0	0	2	4	7
1928	New York	4	15	10	3	0	3	9	4
1932	New York	4	16	5	0	0	2	6	6
Total:	10 years	41	129	42	5	2	15	37	33

Key to Abbreviations

Batting

    G: games
    AB: at-bats
    H: hits
    2B: doubles
    3B: triples
    HR: home runs
    R: runs scored
    RBI: runs batted in

SB: stolen bases
BB: bases on balls
SO: strikeouts
BA: batting average
OBP: on-base percentage
SLG: slugging percentage*
FP: fielding percentage

Pitching

W-L: won-lost record
PCT: winning percentage
G: games
CG: complete games
IP: innings pitched
H: hits allowed
SO: strikeouts
ERA: earned run average

---

*Slugging percentage is total bases divided by times at bat. Ruth's lifetime .690 is the highest of all time, followed by Ted Williams's .634 and Lou Gehrig's .632.

Bibliography

Books

Alexander, Charles C., *Our Game* (Henry Holt and Company, 1991).

Alexander, Charles C., *Ty Cobb* (Oxford University Press, 1984).

Allen, Lee, *Babe Ruth: His Story in Baseball* (G.P. Putnam's Sons, 1966).

Appel, Marty, *Slide, Kelly, Slide: The Wild Life and Times of Mike "King" Kelly, Baseball's First Superstar* (The Scarecrow Press, Inc., 1999).

Asinof, Eliot, *Eight Men Out* (Ace Books, 1963).

Creamer, Robert W., *Babe: The Legend Comes to Life* (Simon & Schuster, 1974).

Ellis, Edward Robb, *The Epic of New York City* (Old Town Books, 1966).

Falkner, David, *The Short Season: The Hard Work and High Times of Baseball in the Spring* (Times Books, 1986).

Fischler, Stan, *Uptown, Downtown: A Trip Through Time on New York's Subways* (Hawthorn/Dutton, 1976).

Frazier, Nancy, *William Randolph Hearst: The American Dream* (Silver Burdett Press, 1989).

Gallen, David (editor), *The Baseball Chronicles* (Galahad Books, 1991).

Gilbert, Thomas, *Dead Ball: Major League Baseball Before Babe Ruth* (Franklin Watts, 1996).

Gilbert, Thomas, *The Soaring Twenties: Babe Ruth & The Home Run Decade* (Franklin Watts, 1996).

Ginsburg, Daniel E., *The Fix Is In: A History of Baseball Gambling and Game Fixing Scandals* (McFarland & Company, Inc., 1995).

Graham, Frank, *The New York Yankees: An Informal History* (G.P. Putnam's Sons, 1951). First published in 1943.

Gropman, Donald, *Say It Ain't So, Joe: The True Story of Shoeless Joe Jackson* (Carol Publishing Group, 1992).

Gutman, Dan, *Baseball Babylon: From the Black Sox to Pete Rose, the Real Stories Behind the Scandals That Rocked the Game* (Penguin Books, 1992).

Holway, John B., *The Baseball Astrologer and Other Weird Tales* (Total Sports/Sports Illustrated, 2000).

Honig, Donald, *Baseball America: The Heroes of the Game and the Times of Their Glory* (Barnes & Noble, Inc., 1997). Originally published by Scribner, 1985.

Kahn, Roger, *A Flame of Pure Fire: Jack Dempsey and the Roaring '20s* (Harcourt Brace & Company, 1999).

Kahn, Roger, *How the Weather Was* (Harper & Row, 1973).

Keene, Kerry, Raymond Sinibaldi, and David Hickey, *The Babe in Red Stockings: An In-Depth Chronicle of Babe Ruth with the Boston Red Sox, 1914–1919* (Sagamore Publishing, 1997).

Lane, F. C., *Batting* (The Society for American Baseball Research, 2001). Originally published in 1925 as a *Baseball Magazine* subscription premium.

Lieb, Fred, *Baseball as I Have Known It* (Bison Books, The University of Nebraska Press, 1996). Originally published by G.P. Putnam's Sons, 1977.

McCabe, Neil, and Constance McCabe, *Baseball's Golden Age: The Photographs of Charles M. Conlin* (Harry M. Abrams, Inc., 1993).

McDonald, Brian, *My Father's Gun: One Family, Three Badges, One Hundred Years in the NYPD* (Dutton, 1999).

Mote, James, *Everything Baseball* (Prentice Hall Press, 1989).

Murdock, Eugene C., *Ban Johnson: Czar of Baseball* (Greenwood Press, 1982).

Mushabac, Jane, and Angela Wigan, *A Short and Remarkable History of New York City* (Fordham University Press, 1999).

Nasaw, David, *The Chief: The Life of William Randolph Hearst* (Houghton Mifflin Company, 2000).

Okkonen, Marc, *The Federal League of 1914–1915: Baseball's Third Major League* (Society for American Baseball Research, 1989).

Okrent, Daniel, and Steve Wulf, *Baseball Anecdotes* (Harper & Row Publishers, Inc., 1989).

Pietrusza, David, *Judge and Jury: The Life and Times of Judge Kenesaw Mountain Landis* (Diamond Communications, Inc., 1998).

Plimpton, George (editor), *Home Run: The Best Writing About Baseball's Most Exciting Moment* (Harcourt, Inc., 2001).

Ritter, Lawrence S., *Lost Ballparks: A Celebration of Baseball's Legendary Fields* (Viking Studio Books, 1992).

Ritter, Lawrence S., and Mark Rucker, *The Babe: A Life in Pictures* (Ticknor & Fields, 1988).

Ritter, Lawrence S., *The Glory of Their Times: The Story of the Early Days of Baseball Told by the Men Who Played It* (The MacMillan Company, 1966).

Robinson, Ray, *Iron Horse: Lou Gehrig in His Time* (W.W. Norton & Company, Inc., 1990).

Ruth, Babe, with Bob Considine, *Babe Ruth: My Story* (Dutton Publishing, 1948).

Scheinin, Richard, *Field of Screams: The Dark Underside of America's National Pastime* (W.W. Norton & Company, Inc., 1994).

Smith, H. Allen, and Ira L. Smith, *Low and Inside: A Book of Baseball Anecdotes, Oddities and Curiosities* (Breakaway Books, 2000). First published in 1948.

Sobol, Ken, *Babe Ruth and the American Dream* (Random House, 1974).

Solomon, Burt, *Where They Ain't: The Fabled Life and Untimely Death of the Original Baltimore Orioles, the Team That Gave Birth to Modern Baseball* (The Free Press, 1999).

Sowell, Mike, *The Pitch That Killed: Carl Mays, Ray Chapman, and the Pennant Race of 1920* (Macmillan Publishing Company, 1989).

Spatz, Lyle, *New York Yankee Openers: An Opening Day History of Baseball's Most Famous Team, 1903–1996* (McFarland & Company, Inc., 1997).

Stump, Al, *Cobb: A Biography* (Algonquin Books of Chapel Hill, 1994).

Thorn, John, Pete Palmer, Michael Gershman, and David Pietrusza, *Total Baseball, Fifth Edition: The Official Encyclopedia of Major League Baseball* (Viking, 1997).

Wagenheim, Kal, *Babe Ruth: His Life and Legend* (Praeger Publications, Inc., 1974).

Ward, Geoffrey C., and Ken Burns, *Baseball: An Illustrated History* (Alfred A. Knopf, 1994).

The Baseball Encyclopedia: The Complete and Official Record of Major League Baseball (The MacMillan Company, 1969).

The New York Times: The Century in Times Square (The New York Times, 1999).

Papers

Beston, Greg, *The Story of Hal Chase: How Baseball Officials Allowed Corruption to Exist in the Game from 1905–1919* (History thesis, Princeton University, 1997).

Index

Sothoron, Allen, 86, 157
South Atlantic League, 76
Southern Association, 160
Southern Michigan League, 155
Southside Park, 25, 44, 54, 56, 62
Sowell, Mike, 85, 189, 215
Spanish-American War, 135, 137
Sparrow, Harry, 46, 67, 77, 139, 239
Speaker, Tris, 10, 16, 37, 53, 82, 83, 85, 116,
117, 118, 156, 164, 166, 178, 179, 182, 184,
215–16, 233, 244, 257, 258
Black Sox scandal and, 238
Chapman's injury and death, 183, 185, 187,
188, 190, 196
floral display presented to, 176
traded to Indians, 2, 4
in World Series, 233
Spellman, Cardinal, 259
Spink, J. G. Taylor, 51
Spitballs, 99–100
Sporting News, 6, 7, 11, 29, 30, 50, 51, 55,
56, 63, 73, 79, 98, 100, 141, 142, 150, 160,
161, 169, 173, 175, 184, 187–88, 193, 236,
238, 246
Sports Illustrated, 155
Sportsman's Park, 23, 123, 169, 170, 229
Sportswriting and sportswriters, 26–30, 115,
187–88, 239
Standard Oil, 238
Stengel, Casey, 129
Stevens, Harry, 19, 71, 72, 138
Stokes, William Earl Dodge, 145
Stoneham, Charles, 133, 134
Stricklett, Elmer, 99
Strunk, Amos, 5
Stump, Al, 129
Stumpf, Bill, 114
Sturm, Theodore, 192
Suffolk Athletic Club, 10, 11
Sullivan, Billy, 85
Sun, 29

Taft, William Howard, 127
Taylor, Luther, 22–23
Taylor, Ruth, 203
Tennes, Monte, 213
Tenney, Ross, 116, 117
Terry, Bill, 257
Texas League, 244, 247

Thomas, Chet, 117
Thompson, Frog, 212
Thormahlen, Herb, 28–29, 36, 56, 74, 104,
120, 123, 140, 142, 143, 144, 153, 157, 158,
162, 163, 173, 214, 217, 218, 221, 222, 231,
239
Thorn, John, 234
Tietjen & Lang Dry Dock Company, 198
Tigers. *See* Detroit Tigers
Titcomb, Cannonball, 25
Tobin, Jack, 86, 124, 157, 205, 206
Toney, Fred, 248
Toscanini, Arturo, 145
Trachtenberg, Leo, 52
Tri-State League, 94
Trick pitches, 99–100
Tunney, Gene, 200
Tyson, Mike, 200

Uhle, George, 120
United News, 108
United Press International, 108, 193
Universal Negro Improvement
Association, 92

Vangilder, Elam, 170
Vanity Fair, 27
Veach, Bobby, 153, 194, 219
Veeck, William, Jr., 245
Veeck, William, Sr., 211, 212, 227
Vick, Sammy, 33, 45, 53, 62, 73, 106, 122,
197, 218, 220, 239
Victory, Frances, 203
Vila, Joe, 29–30, 55, 56, 63, 73, 79, 98, 142,
150, 160, 161, 169, 173, 175–76, 184,
187–88, 193, 236
Villa, Pancho, 42
Virginia League, 76

W.E. Hutton and Co., 216
Wagenheim, Kal, 3, 28, 153
Wagner, Honus, 10–11, 19, 36, 258
Walker, Jimmy, 259
Walker, Tilly, 8
Walsh, Christy, 255, 256, 258
Walsh, Ed, 99, 100
Walters, Roxy, 37
Wambsganss, Bill "Wamby," 83, 165, 178,
179, 182, 190, 233